'This book represents a particular lens for analysts and therapists, dissecting a case study's life experience to better understand how trauma has shaped his behaviour, both violent and sexual. His passage through the Criminal Justice System is as compassion-free as his therapist is trauma-informed. This was a pleasure to read; Glyn Hudson-Allez has critiqued many assumptions that we have traditionally regarded as undisputed, evidenced her thoughts with neuroscience research and thereby making us think again. The brutalisation of this young man is laid bare for all to see; you will need to read to the end to be able to address your own thoughts as to what or who caused the greatest damage. It leaves me with the question, "will we ever learn?"'

Antounette Phillipedes, *Chair, StopSO*

'This is a brilliant read for practitioners who work with people who have sexually offended in society. The book is completely underpinned by neuroscience and what is understood about how traumatic childhood experiences damage people. Many damaged children become damaged adults if not given the right trauma-informed support at the right time. This is what I see 100% of the time in my own working practice working with men, women and children. Glyn Hudson-Allez has brilliantly linked the theories into what they look like in practice with the character in the book.'

Terri Van Leeson, *PhD, Consultant Forensic Psychologist*

'This unique book is essential reading for any practitioner who works with clients who offend, or are at risk of offending, online. It provides engaging insight from a case throughout and comprehensive explanations into some of the psychological mechanisms underlying this type of offending.'

Clare Allely, *Professor of Forensic Psychology, University of Salford*

'A multi-layered book, based on a lifetime of delivering therapy to the most marginalised. Whilst not losing focus on child protection and welfare, the text offers a revealing insight into the part trauma and neurobiology play in internet offending, particularly for males who are neurodivergent. This is a progressive, humane and necessary book, informed by a desire for balance and justice for all.'

Andrew Smith, *PhD, Risk Assessor/Forensic Therapist and Expert Witness*

T0384977

A Trauma-Informed Understanding of Online Offending

This book examines the contemporary one-size-fits-all model of treatment for sexual offenders and challenges the confrontational approach to working with this group.

In recent years, the incidence of people (predominantly men) getting arrested for inappropriate online usage has increased exponentially. This book attempts to understand why this is the case, and what can be done to help these individuals and, in turn, reduce the risk of them re-offending. A stand-alone follow-up text from Hudson-Allez's popular *Infant Losses, Adult Searches*, this book carries forward the compelling case study of Gordon from the previous text. Throughout his journey from arrest to rehabilitation, the chapters provide insight into the addictive nature over compulsively viewing pornography throughout adolescence, and the relationship between internet offending and dysfunctional attachments and neurodiversity. Our current understandings of childhood trauma, transgenerational transmission, and diagnoses of autism spectrum disorder and ADHD are all investigated in relation to cases of online offenders, and practical therapeutic models are presented.

This book is relevant to psychologists, psychotherapists, counsellors and therapists working with forensic clients, and probation officers, social workers and police officers working within child-protection agencies.

Dr Glyn Hudson-Allez is a BPS Chartered Psychologist and a Registered Member and Supervisor of the College of Sexual and Relationship Therapists. She has worked as a therapist for nearly 40 years, 8 of which were in primary health care, latterly specialised in working with people who have diverse or potentially deviant sexual behaviour, using her unique therapeutic style of integrating attachment theory and neuroscientific research. She has published four books: *Time Limited Therapy in a General Practice Setting* (1997, Sage); *Sex & Sexuality: Questions and Answers for Counsellors and Psychotherapists* (2005, Whurr); *Infant Losses, Adult Searches: A Neural and Developmental Perspective on Psychopathology and Sexual Offending* (2011, Karnac) now in its second edition, and her edited book, *Sexual Diversity and Sexual Offending: Research, Assessment and Clinical Treatment in Psychosexual Therapy* (2014, Karnac). In 2020, Glyn became a Trustee of the charity Specialist Treatment Organisation for the Perpetrators and Survivors of Sexual Offending (StopSO), and is currently Vice Chair. Glyn has two professional fellowships: The Association of Counsellors & Psychotherapists in Primary Care (CPC), and The College for Sexual and Relationship Therapists (COSRT).

A Trauma-Informed Understanding of Online Offending

Adult Losses from Adolescent Searches

Glyn Hudson-Allez

Routledge
Taylor & Francis Group

LONDON AND NEW YORK

Designed cover image: © Getty Images

First published 2024
by Routledge
4 Park Square, Milton Park, Abingdon, Oxon OX14 4RN

and by Routledge
605 Third Avenue, New York, NY 10158

Routledge is an imprint of the Taylor & Francis Group, an informa business

British Library Cataloguing-in-Publication Data
A catalogue record for this book is available from the British Library

Library of Congress Cataloging-in-Publication Data
Names: Hudson-Allez, Glyn, author.
Title: A trauma-informed understanding of online offending : adult losses from
adolescent searches / Glyn Hudson-Allez.
Description: Abingdon, Oxon ; New York, NY : Routledge, 2024. |
Identifiers: LCCN 2023021410 (print) | LCCN 2023021411 (ebook) |
ISBN 9781032362359 (hardback) | ISBN 9781032361826 (paperback) |
ISBN 9781003330899 (ebook)
Subjects: LCSH: Sex offenders--Rehabilitation. | Online sexual
predators--Rehabilitation. | Sex offenders--Mental health. | Online sexual
predators--Mental health. | Sex offenders--Mental health services. |
Online sexual predators--Mental health services.
Classification: LCC RC560.S47 H833 2024 (print) | LCC RC560.S47 (ebook) |
DDC 616.85/830651–dc23/eng/20230724
LC record available at https://lccn.loc.gov/2023021410
LC ebook record available at https://lccn.loc.gov/2023021411

ISBN: 978-1-032-36235-9 (hbk)
ISBN: 978-1-032-36182-6 (pbk)
ISBN: 978-1-003-33089-9 (ebk)

DOI: 10.4324/9781003330899

Typeset in Times New Roman
by Taylor & Francis Books

This book is dedicated to all the StopSO therapists throughout the United Kingdom, who work to support people with a trauma history that leads to their inappropriate harmful sexual behaviour. And to the StopSO Trustees, both past and present, who freely give their time and energy in the pursuance of a charity designed to make a difference in protecting children. Through their dedicated work, even though what they hear might pollute their dreams, they are persistently and rigorously working to make a safer and kinder society. And finally, a special mention for my dear friend, Ruth Hallam Jones, whose insight and vision gave the impetus to make this organisation happen.

Contents

Figures

Acknowledgements

Writing a book can be a lonely enterprise, and it can be very easy to get wrapped up in oneself and carried away with ideas. I want to thank the following colleagues for listening endlessly to my rants and raves about the UK Criminal Justice System for online offenders, which I so dearly would love to change: Clare Allely, Dana Braithwaite, Tricia Evans, Barry Gower, Trudy Hannington, Nigel Hatton, Sue Malone, Sue Maxwell, Antounette Phillipedes, Ian Richards, Andrew Smith, Tom Taylor and Terri Van Leeson.

Thank you to Grace McDonnell of Routledge for being willing to take a risk with this book. And finally thank you to Ian Banks for his pedantic rumination over some of my diagrams.

Preface

When I was working in primary care in the mid- to late 1990s as a counselling psychologist, I found that my GP colleagues were sending patients to me with sexual problems that I felt I could not adequately address as a counsellor. So, I went off and trained as a psychosexual therapist, and consequently felt better equipped to deal with the ubiquitous sexual issues that people brought into the consulting room. What I hadn't anticipated was that, once qualified as a psychologist and sex therapist, people with diverse and potentially criminal sexual behaviour would find their way to my door as well. Off I went again to train in applied forensic psychology, to have a greater understanding of the psychological and criminological side of their presenting issues. Sadly, a change in government meant a change in the working conditions of primary care, so I went into full-time private practice. However, a short interview on BBC radio at that time led to an influx of potential clients seeking me out to talk about their potential, or actual, criminal sexual behaviour. This led me to realise the error of the contemporary myth that all people who commit sexual offences are deviant, manipulative and have no interest in changing their behaviour. They certainly did want help; they were coming to see me from all over the country. When I queried why they would make such long journeys for therapeutic sessions, the response was always the same: 'counsellors hear what I have to say and then say they can't work with me'; 'who else is willing to listen to this stuff?'; 'the statutory services are not interested in helping or supporting me unless I have been prosecuted for an offence'; 'who else is going to help you stop crossing the line and committing the first offence?'. Clearly, here there is a child protection issue that was simply not being addressed in a preventative way.

Things have moved on somewhat in the following 30 years, but still have a long way to go. There are now organisations that do offer help and support for people who may potentially or actually commit a sexual offence. The Lucy Faithful Foundation is a UK-wide charity established to prevent child abuse by offering courses to adults and young people demonstrating harmful sexual behaviour. In addition, they have established a confidential helpline called Stop It Now! for people to use when they feel concerned about their sexual thoughts or behaviour. Other organisations have also been established: Circles of Support offers community support for people going through the criminal justice system, and Safer Lives offers support for people during their investigation into sexual offences, to name but two.

In late 2010, I took a break from clinical practice. The following year, a group of experienced psychosexual therapists came together to debate their deepening concern that people exhibiting harmful sexual behaviour who had no place to go to find therapeutic support without fear of rejection or vilification. This group comprised Ruth Hallam Jones, Trudy Hannington, Dana Braithwaite and Juliet Grayson, with police input from Nigel Hatton. They knew that the UK needed a register of therapists who were willing and trained to work therapeutically with people who committed harmful sexual behaviours. From these inspired individuals came the foundation of the charitable organisation now known as StopSO UK (The Specialist Treatment Organisation for the Perpetrators and Victims of Sexual Offending). StopSO now has a large register of experienced and forensically trained therapists to support individuals fearful of committing an offence, and helping in their rehabilitation after it. They also help with the collateral damage of these offences: their victims and their families. StopSO's mission statement is to try and prevent the first crime against a child. When I returned to clinical practice, I was honoured to be offered a position of StopSO therapist, supervisor, trainer and trustee.

The Covid pandemic of 2019 created the prefect storm for online sexual offences. With individuals trapped in their homes with only the Internet as access to the outside world, there became a tsunami of online sexual offences as (predominantly) men viewed indecent images of children online while viewing pornography, and had indecent conversations with children online via social media. It was considered that over a thousand individuals a month were being arrested (getting 'the knock') for online sexual offences over a two-year period, and thousands more were considered to have evaded the attention of the police. Although the number is considered to have dropped to about 750 a month, it is still a massive number. Vast policing resources were diverted to try and capture and arrest every one, leading to logjams in the High Tech Crime Units investigating each individual's (sometimes many) devices – phones, tablets, laptops, games consoles, etc. – capable of accessing the Internet, followed by delays in the Crown Prosecution Service's overview of potential charges, and then delays getting each individual through the courts. In some policing areas, it was taking 3–4 years for an individual's journey through the Criminal Justice System, leading to the stress, anxiety and depression of long-term uncertainty and high suicidality. Did this mean that there was a huge number of covert paedophiles living in our midst? Did this mean that these arrests were making our children safer within our society? The answer to both questions is negative. A minority of these individuals would have groomed and arranged to meet a child or a teenager with evil intent. But the majority are viewers of imagery, trapped in an addictive process of Internet browsing and sexual arousal, changing the way

they feel from their own hidden traumas of childhood. That is not to under-
mine the enormity of the trauma victimisation of the children within these
images, but this book is written to try and put this *Zeitgeist* into perspective, to
try and understand from where this omnipresent problem stems, as the paradox
is that the punitive (and essentially unsuccessful) response to it is creating
attachment injuries, trauma and psychological damage to the families and
children of the offenders.

Chapter I

The knock

Implications and subsequent losses

Case study

The door opened, and she saw a tall, thin young man in his thirties, with unkempt dark red hair, light-coloured stubble on his face, and a scowl etched in his brow, as his eyes darted around the unfamiliar room. He was dressed in a light grey track suit, with grease marks on the arms and around the cuffs, and old battered trainers on his feet.

'Come in, Gordon,' she said pleasantly. 'Take a seat.'

Deciding on a chair nearest the door, Gordon slumped down in his seat so far that his bottom was perched on the chair's edge. He thrust his hands into his tracksuit trouser pockets so that his hands couched his genitals.

She took a seat to one side of him, so they were not looking directly at each other. 'As we said on the phone, your referral to StopSO[1] has been passed on to me, so that you can undertake some therapy to help you move forward with your life. Is that what you would like to happen?'

'Well I'm here, aren't I?' he snapped, as he thought to himself 'what's this old bat like!'.

'Tell me why you are here.'

Gordon's right knee started bouncing up and down as his heel played a rhythm on the carpeted floor. His cheeks flushed red and he averted his gaze from her. 'I've been arrested, and my brief recommended I call Stop It Now!,[2] and have some counselling with StopSO.'

'Arrested? What was that for?' she asked mildly.

'Cos I was looking at porn on the Net.'

'Well, watching pornography isn't illegal, Gordon. Did your viewing take you into looking at inappropriate images of children?'

Gordon shuffled uncomfortably in his seat, his cheeks burning as he muttered 'Yeah'. He still couldn't look at her.

'OK. So, you have been arrested for making indecent images of children, then?'

Gordon sat abruptly up in his seat. 'I didn't make any pictures,' he protested. 'I didn't take any photos! I only looked at what was there, in PornHub[3].' He stared hard at her to reinforce his point.

DOI: 10.4324/9781003330899-1

'Yes, I am sure that is the case, Gordon,' she said gently. 'But if the police find evidence on your devices – your phone or your computer – they will charge you with making images, on the grounds that you have created a new image on your computer cache. Making images commands a higher sentence than viewing or possessing, you see.'

'Well I never meant to. I was just down after losing Rach. And I lost my job. So I was just at home on the computer and kept looking and looking.' The foot started bouncing again.

'Rach?'

'Rachel. My wife. We don't live together anymore. She and my boy live in one of those women's houses. They won't let me see them.' His neck sunk into his shoulders, and his fists clenched.

'Do you mean a refuge? Is she living in a woman's refuge?'

Gordon's anger bubbled up. 'Yeah!' he spat and jumped up out of his seat. 'If they would just let me talk to her and get her to see it was all a mistake, then everything would be alright. I tried searching for her to say sorry, but they just accused me of stalking her and threatened to get the police again. It's not fair! She is my wife and he is my boy, and they have taken them away from me!' Tears of frustration start in his eyes as he leans over her.

She reached out and touched his arm gently. He flinched from her touch as if he had been hit. 'I can see you are very upset about all this Gordon. Why don't you sit down, take a breath, and then start from the beginning?'

Online sexual offending: the focus of this book

An online sexual offender is not a heterogeneous group. There are many individual features of this group who are labelled as a sexual offender and/or a paedophile, the majority of whom may never come into physical contact with a child. It is also true that not all people who do assault children are paedophiles. Paedophilia, in my view, is a sexual orientation toward children that may or may not lead to child sexual abuse, and is not open to change. Many choose to manage their desires in appropriate ways and may refer to themselves as minor-attracted persons (MAPs) (Levenson, Grady & Morin, 2019), or virtuous paedophiles. In an online survey, 85% of MAPs felt they had developed their preferential attraction to boys or girls younger than themselves around the age of 12, with 66% realising while they were still minors themselves (B4U-ACT, 2020); this is the age of post-puberty, where the sexual template and sexual script come online, to be discussed in more detail in Chapter 3.

Child sexual abuse, alternatively, involves sexual contact with a child, which may or may not be due to paedophilia (Camilleri & Quinsey, 2008). The paedophilic sexual attraction to children would be toward a pre- or early post-pubescent child, usually considered to be under 13 years. For infants and toddlers, the sexual preference is called nepiophilia, and for sexual preference toward children between the ages of 14–17 it would be considered hebephilia. The psychological and social process involved in these three distinctions are fundamentally different. This distinction, however, does not apply to the UK Criminal Justice System, who defines all children as a person under the age of 18 years.

The use of the term online offender and internet offender will be used interchangeably throughout this book. These offenses are as follows, and mostly apply to men as women are in the vast minority, although this is not an exhaustive list:

- Those who have looked at extreme pornography online including grossly offensive and violent rape scenarios, necrophilia, bestiality or snuff (real scenes of death).
- Those who have behaved in extremely violent situations towards other adults or animals and sent the recording to others online.
- Those who have looked at child sexual abuse material (CSAM).
- Those who have looked at CSAM in sexually harmful situations.
- Those who have collected CSAM in digital catalogues.
- Those who have sent pre-existing CSAM to other people online, perhaps to be the payment, or subscription, to allow access to a particular online group.
- Those who trade in CSAM online.
- Those who have sent photographs or videos of themselves in sexual situations to child recipients (e.g. 'dick-pics').
- Those who have previously taken images of children in sexual or indecent situations to send to others online.
- Those who have had sexual conversations with children.
- Those who have had sexual conversations with children, usually through social media, with the aim of receiving indecent images.
- Those who have sexual conversations with children with the aim of meeting them (grooming) for sexual encounters.
- Those who have sexual conversations with adults through social media under the false belief that they are children.
- Those who make arrangements online with adults to view images of children in sexual situations in real time, often directing how the abuse should take place.
- Those involved in child-sex tourism to alternative jurisdictions.
- Those who search for adults using dating sites like Match, BeNaughty, Gaystryst, Craigslist, to meet people with the intention to sexually assault them.

The predominant focus of the book is looking at the ubiquitous offences of possessing and distributing CSAM and chatting with children (or whom they presumed to be a child) on social media. It is not about a classic life-long self-confessed paedophilic orientation toward children leading to predatory contact offences.

Child sexual abuse material

Under Section 1 of the Protection of Children Act 1978 and Section 160 of the UK Criminal Justice Act 1988, it is illegal to take, make or distribute indecent images of children under the age of 18 years. This includes actual pictures and also 'pseudo' pictures where digital technology and computer graphics have been used to create such images. The charge of 'making' images applies to any attachment received in an email, an image downloaded from the internet, storing an image in a directory on a computer, accessing a pornographic website in which indecent images appeared by way of automatic pop-ups, or viewed live-streaming as the computer stores the viewing history. Making indecent images tends to be the most commonly used charge rather than possession, the former commanding a maximum sentence of 10 years' imprisonment, whereas the latter commands a maximum sentence of 5 years' imprisonment. As mentioned, extreme pornography, for example of extreme violence or of bestiality, is also illegal, as is its dissemination.

The law requires that there must be a deliberate and intentional act, done with the knowledge that the image is, or is likely to be, an indecent photograph or pseudo-photograph of a child. However, there have been many cases where a prosecution has occurred, the evidence being in the history of the computer, without the intention of the viewer being established; possession, even if the image has been deleted, is considered sufficient evidence. Assumptions that judges make about the thought processes of the offender during the offence can lead to variations on the length of sentence they will receive. Another confusion that occurs in the prosecution of these offences and the concept of intent is the assumption is made that the viewer knows the age of the person in the indecent image. In a society where well-developed young people are made to look older than they are, and older people are made to look younger than they are, for example, in school uniforms (Mahoney, 2009), the notion of intent gets further blurred.

Online offender typologies

Beech et al. (2008) proposed a four-group typology:

- Individuals who access pornographic images impulsively out of curiosity. This group includes those who never exhibited sexual problems until they began using the internet (Delmonico & Griffin, 2008).
- Individuals who access or share pornography due to their pre-existing sexual interest in children.
- Individuals who use the internet as part of a pattern of offline contact offending, including those who use it to procure victims for their own sexual interest, or to disseminate images that they produce, often as a subscription to dark web paedophilic groups.

- Individuals who download pornographic images for nonsexual reasons, like financial gain. It is unclear whether this group has any paedophilic interest or whether they view CSAM more than the general population (Quayle, 2004).

Tener, Wolak and Finkelhor (2015) also proposed a four-dimension typology based on offense characteristics, in a continuum of criminal expertise, ranging from high to low:

- *Experts*: sophisticated offenders who systematically use the internet to procure multiple victims. These experts may work alone or collaborate with a group, and they use elaborate grooming techniques. They are not emotionally involved with their victims.
- *Cynical:* usually know their victims, which is usually only one. They are aware they are committing a crime, although their pornography usage is less extensive than that of the expert. Meeting up to have sex is the goal, so there is no real emotional investment.
- *Attention-focused:* meet their victims online with a view of obtaining a real relationship. The offender and the victim mutually enjoy the relationship without a real understanding of the criminality of the behaviour. Pornography is rarely used in these circumstances.
- *Sex-focused:* the lowest level of criminal expertise. Commences with viewing or seeking sexual interaction with adults, so no grooming or manipulation is involved. They may inadvertently meet a child online posing as an adult, and may continue the sexual encounter even though the victim's age is revealed.

This typology was based on a very small sample of 75 forensic cases, so it has its limitations as to the range of sexual offences committed online. What is missing from this typology are all of the viewers and collectors of CSAM, who have absolutely no intention of meeting up with or harming a child, which is the predominant focus of this book, and links with the curious group in the typology of Beech et al. (2008).

Online grooming

Sexual predatory individuals may access internet sites that children and young people visit in order to search for potential victims by location or interest. Children and young people may often reveal personal information online, such as where they live or go to school, or their family name, which is used by groomers to manipulate behaviours and build relationships with their victims. Information may be published through a number of different online platforms which are accessible to others, including social networking sites, multi-player gaming portals and other web-based forums. Section 36 of the UK Criminal

Justice and Courts Act 2015 amends section 15 of the Sexual Offences Act 2003 (the offence of meeting a child following sexual grooming etc.) so that the number of initial occasions on which the defendant must meet or communicate with the child in question in order to commit the offence is reduced from two to one. There tends to be three methods used to access children: overseas Pay-per-View live streaming of abuse, for example by children in the Philippines; chat rooms like Snapchat,[4] Tumblr[5] and Kik;[6] or produced by the children themselves, either to share with their peers, or as a result of manipulation or blackmail do so. It is thought that 50% of CSAM on the web have been self-produced.

The Paedophile Online Investigation Team (POLIT)

These specialist teams have been established throughout police forces to tackle the huge increase in demand to seek out individuals who view and/or distribute indecent images of children online, or who engage in conversations with others either about children, or with (who they perceive to be) children. These officers proactively seek out potential offenders either from referral from social media agencies, like Facebook, Kik, Tumblr or Snapchat, or from their own undercover police activities.

The Knock

'The knock' is the colloquialism for when the police arrive at an individual's (most commonly a man's) door after it has been discovered that he has been viewing indecent images of children (CSAM) online, or has been engaged in online sexual conversations either with, or about, a child under the age of 18 years. It was considered that in 2021, following the UK country-wide lockdown due to Covid-19 in 2020, 1,000 men a month were being arrested, or receiving the knock. More recent estimates as the country opened up again place it at 750 men per month (S. Bailey, personal communication, 2022). It is thought that the International Child Sexual Exploitation (ICSE) database exceeds 17 million unique images, which is added to by 500,000 every two months (Grant, 2021a). One fallacy is that these images only occur in the dark web, but this applies to less than 1% of offenders, the remainder actually view from freely accessible sites, like YouTube[7] and PornHub.

Sometimes the knock occurs very early in the morning, say 6 a.m., where half a dozen or so police officers surge into the suspect's house or flat to arrest him and to make an immediate search of the premises. All devices capable of accessing the internet will be seized for forensic analysis, including the devices of the man's partner and children. The man will be taken into police custody while the search is conducted, usually overnight. A duty solicitor will be appointed to give preliminary advice, and then the alleged offender is released in the morning on bail, with conditions regarding where he is allowed to go, and to whom he is allowed to speak. These restrictions will include not going back to the home where any children are residing and sometimes not having any communication with the children's mother. At the same time, the man's place of employment may be visited, and his work computers seized, thus informing not only his employer, but all his work colleagues by default. Other police forces, however, are much more circumspect in the knock, which occurs in a much quieter way with a couple of plain-clothes detectives at a more respectable time of the day, which does not advertise it to the neighbours. Indeed, some forces make no arrests at this time, simply seizing the devices for forensic examination.

Sometimes a prohibition that investigating police officers place on an alleged offender is that they must stop using the internet altogether. As all devices have been seized, that is clearly not going to be hardship in the first instance. But to live without the internet in contemporary society is a definite handicap. Banks have closed because the assumption is that people prefer to conduct their financial affairs online. People shop, buy goods and services, and look for work using online facilities. Even government agencies, like applications for Universal Credit, prefer online communication. Communicating with your phone and internet provider without your phone or your laptop available becomes a nightmare. Remember, it is not just the alleged offender's devices that have been removed, but the whole household.

The individual is then placed in a situation of limbo for many months, and in some police force areas, a couple of years. Bail will be ceased as it is a waste of everyone's time to keep calling the person back on a monthly basis, so the person may be 'released under investigation'. This has no time limits and no conditions like bail, although alleged offenders are recommended to follow the same conditions as their former bail conditions. This places the alleged offender (and his family) into a position of impasse, for a period under current estimates for up to 3 years and sometimes more. The reason for this delay is currently three backlogs in the Criminal Justice System: delays in getting all the devices for each alleged offender forensically examined; delays for the case to be determined by the Crown Prosecution Service (or Procurator Fiscal in Scotland) as an appropriate case to go to court following a cost-benefit analysis; and then delays in the Magistrates and any subsequent Crown Court proceedings.

The knock, *per se*, is traumatising to the alleged offender (Gunter et al., 2011), inducing fear and anxiety over an extended period of time, and can lead to post-traumatic stress disorder as a result of their own action (Gray et al., 2003), especially if the victim was a family member (Papanastassiou et al., 2004). Uncertainty is one of the most stressful situations anyway, but for a man who has lost his relationship, his children, his home, his job, his financial certainty, his friendships, and his self-esteem, even before he has been convicted, it becomes unbearable. As is the post-traumatic stress that the person experiences, not only from the knock, but when they are faced with their own offending when the knock shakes them out of their addictive trance. Suicidal ideation is common, as is depression, anxiety, obsessive compulsive disorder, and a sense of hopelessness and helplessness. This long-lasting uncertainty can lead to 'allostatic overload', which is the cumulative burden of chronic stress following the life event of the knock, where the challenges of the stress exceed the person's ability to cope with it. McEwen & Wingfield, (2003) highlighted that allostatic overload is a vicious cycle of altered brain architecture and systemic pathophysiology, which further damages the capability of the subject to cope with uncertainty, leading them into a high risk of depression, cognitive impairment, myocardial infarction, stroke and suicidal ideation. Many of these alleged offenders feel suicidal for an extended period of time, with peaks and troughs when the case moves to its next phase through the Criminal Justice System. And for the therapist, the client's suicidal ideation and behaviours can only be accurately predicted as a successful suicidal attempt little more than by chance (Ribero et al., 2016).

StopSO therapists report that the proportion of clients they see as a consequence of inappropriate internet viewing or communicating with minors is much higher from the neurodivergent population than would have been found by chance. I must emphasise here that I am not implying that neurodivergence is a causal factor leading to offending, but that offending can occur as a consequence of their neurodivergent preferences, for example trying to learn about sex or communicating with like-minded individuals via the computer rather than social interaction. I will be discussing this phenomenon later in Chapter 4, but in the context of receiving the knock, these clients can rapidly deteriorate into autistic burnout, leading to self-injury, suicidal ideation and suicidal attempts (Raymaker et al., 2020). The life stress of the knock, with a lack of cognitive understanding of what they have done wrong, together with a minimal social network, can lead to sensory overload, loss of cognitive function and a long-lasting sense of pervasive exhaustion that may impact on their capacity for independent living and quality of life. It is known that people on the autistic spectrum have higher rates of suicidal ideation and suicidal behaviour than neurotypicals (Cassidy et al., 2014), and getting the knock, especially in a very public kind of way, can tip them over the edge.

Impact on the families

The impact of all this on the non-offending partners (NOPs) of the accused is massive (Grant, 2021b). Overnight they lose their relationship with their partner, any income and stability that they may have provided, and are often manipulated into a decision by the social services to either divorce their partner or lose their children by them being taken into care. Some NOPs are blamed by the child protection services as being collusive. Others are forced into being the supervisor of the offending partner to prevent the risk of reoffending, as a cheap option compared to formal supervised access to the children, a practice described by some as exploitative (Wager, Wager & Wilson,

2015) as child protection services fixate on reducing risk at the expense of fulfilling the need of the NOP (Thompson, 2017) and their children. NOP's also face courtesy stigma (Goffman, 1963; Farkas & Millar, 2007), tainted by the association with their partner's offence, as do the therapists who work with the offenders (Duncan et al., 2022).

The partner typically experiences depression and anxiety and the knock *per se* can elicit post traumatic responses of flashbacks and panic attacks. Fears regarding being involved with the social services are rife under the threat of losing their children into care. Support networks and friendships are lost as the arrest becomes known, and even well before any form of conviction, the family are ostracised, and may find the word 'pervert' and 'pedo' written in red paint across their homes, even though the alleged offender is no longer living there (Condry, 2010). Research suggests that rather than being perceived as an unintended victim of circumstance of the alleged offence of their partner, NOPs experience grief for the lives they have lost and the future they had planned, disenfranchised by their social network leading to social isolation (Bailey, 2018; Duncan et al., 2020). Agencies designed to support the children in the family may often be judgemental, blaming and insensitive to what the NOP was actually experiencing (Calhane, Parker & Duff, 2013) and are rarely viewed as secondary victims. Some feel forced to leave their homes, change their names, and change their children's schools. Some NOPs are forced into poverty, as the alleged offender was the major earner of the family, and as the police seize computers at a person's place of employment, the subsequent dismissal means that the mortgage can no longer be paid for the house in which the children reside. Universal credit may be insufficient to maintain the payments for outstanding bills, and the now single parent NOP is forced into council accommodation, often bed and breakfast accommodation, due to the lack of availability of council homes.

Children can equally be traumatised by the knock. StopSO therapists report incidences of 6 to 10 officers barging into the house, some with dogs, so the children wake to a cacophony of uniformed men rushing around shouting at the occupants and large dogs barking. The terrified wife and children cower as the search is conducted, then peer tearfully through the windows as daddy is being taken away in handcuffs, while neighbours, awoken by half a dozen police cars outside still with their blue lights flashing, stand in groups gossiping about the reasons for the arrest, until an obliging police officer will drop a hint. The arrested man's children then may have to attend school that day or soon after, and will taunted and bullied thereafter. 'Your dad's a pedo. I bet you are too!'

The collateral damage done to the partners, families (parents and siblings) and children of a person arrested for an online offence has huge unintended consequences, experiencing disenfranchised grief and social isolation (Duncan et al., 2022), but these tend to be overlooked by policy makers due to the intolerance of the crime and vilification of the person alleged to have committed it. 'Lock them up and throw away the key.'

Double-stigma: sexual offender and suicide survivor

As discussed above, with amount of loss and shame an alleged offender experiences after getting the knock, suicidality becomes a common response. Rebecca Key et al. (2021) conducted a systematic review of the suicide rates of this offending population and found that the prevalence could be 100 times greater for those who have viewed CSAM compared to other offending populations. They attributed this risk to personal feelings of shame, the unique demographic characteristics of these offenders, the absence of prior criminal contact, and the impact of such a criminal investigation.

Similarly, Hoffer, Shelton and Joyner (2012) found that of those who did end their own lives, 26% had done so within the first 48 hours, and 55% within the first month, of being made aware of the criminal investigation. Steel et al. (2022) emphasised that these statistics of high-level proximal suicidal ideation, often due to a general perceived lack of empathy in the investigative process, have direct practice implications for both law enforcement and clinicians. Also, how much support the individual receives from family and friends (and how much support family and friends receive) can make all the difference between this person living or dying. As families come to terms with the shock of what their husband, partner, son or lover has done, complete rejection of the person may make the difference between passive suicidal ideation and active suicidal plans. This difference should be a significant indicator to a therapist to help with keep-safe planning with their client: a telephone number of the Samaritan's in their contact list on their phone, also an ICE contact – in case of emergencies; talking about calming, safe places to go, or people to be with, and distracting techniques to get rid of the intrusive thoughts. Even before the potential offending can be addressed, this needs to be prioritised. These online offenders' demographics are not the usual delinquent, law-breaking, anti-socially hardened family individuals commonly found in other illegal offences, like violence, burglary or bank-robbing. These are predominantly white (minority Asian), middle-class, well-educated men in their late twenties to middle forties, many in long-term relationships or marriages, some gay but the majority straight, and many with children of their own. They have a long way to fall, and it happens drastically overnight following the knock. For many it is just too much to bear.

The therapist has to help the client decide between the misery, shame and guilt of the client wanting it all to stop, and feeling completely out of control as they come to terms with being labelled as the most vilified individual of our society: 'a child sex offender', as opposed to the ending, quiet and complete removal by death. Although societal attitudes towards suicide have changed over the centuries, there is still an inheritance of an additional stigma associated with those who want to end their own lives. Indeed, we no longer desecrate the bodies of successful suicides, refusing to allowing their bodies to be buried in hallowed ground, with the government seizing all the person's assets. Nor do we prosecute those who have tried to end their own lives and were unsuccessful. But the stigma remains. Families shut down in shame, friends disappear because they don't know what to say, neighbours whisper to one another and cross over the road not to have to speak, as if the suicide and sex offending might be contagious in some way. The Papyrus charity has done a lot to raise the profile of suicide and allow people to talk about it more openly, such as their involvement with three dads who had lost their daughters through suicide walking across the country to highlight their campaign for suicide to be placed on the school curriculum. But there would be little public sympathy for alleged sex offenders taking their own lives.

Usually the first port of call for a suicidal patient would be their GP, who may either reach for the prescription pad to prescribe antidepressants, put them on a 3-month waiting list for six sessions of free counselling, or make a referral to the mental health services for an immediate hospitalisation, and if necessary a 28-day section for their own protection. Or all three, because the GP feels helpless. During this time, it may be only the therapist who can offer compassion and understanding without judgement or criticism of the situation this potential offender finds himself in. Suicidality is not an illness, *per se*, it is a symptom of the chronic alienation and loss that this alleged offender is experiencing. The main understanding of working with a suicidal client is to listen and help them understand and remove their pain, so they don't pass that pain on to members of their family if they die. By offering an attachment to this client, the therapist is offering a lifeline, but in reality, the delay and uncertainty from the Criminal Justice System is a cruel and unusual punishment in its own right; there is no conviction, but the person has been judged and punished by all around him.

The structure of this book

In my book *Infant Losses, Adult Searches* (Hudson-Allez, 2011), I offered a case study throughout each chapter to elucidate the points I was trying to make. The book demonstrated the composite case of Gordon James from his conception until he received the knock for online sexual offending when he was in his thirties. The infant losses I was attempting to highlight was the loss of attachment and individual potential due to adverse childhood experiences and trauma. His adult searches were in trying to feel safe, secure and connected, but his survival strategies eventually led to his inappropriate behaviour.

This book is focused on the online offender throughout, so it made sense to revisit the same case study, and follow Gordon's path from getting the knock until post-conviction; a period of over three years. Although it does not explicitly follow his therapeutic process during all of that time, it allows us to dip into it, to consider the highlights and the challenges for both Gordon and the therapist working with a damaged and potentially volatile client. This is not a book about how to do therapy; I have written about that in other texts.

This book is about the cultural and societal context that facilitates or impedes the therapeutic process of working with an offender to reach a place of desistance and rehabilitation. The next chapter, however, elaborates on the therapist's reasoning and method of collecting the history of the client to put together a formulation of the work ahead, rather than purely focusing on the offence, as one would find with the police or probation service. One needs to understand and deal with the past before we can start changing a future. Chapter 3 revisits our understanding of the neuroscience of attachment, leading to the differing attachment styles in the adult. It then outlines the damage trauma in early years can do to the developing brain, how that damage can manifest itself in adult behaviour, and the ubiquitous problem of repetition compulsion we find in an offending population. In Chapter 4, I elaborate on the presentations of neurodiversity that tend to be over-represented in an online offending population. In doing so, I make comparisons in the behaviour between those with insecure attachments, and those on the spectrum, and the link both have with adverse childhood experiences. I raise the controversial question, were we all wired to be neurodivergent as an adaptive process? In Chapter 5, I address the addictive nature of online pornography, which, when occurring at a young age, can vandalise the sexual template and distort the sexual script of an adolescent. I discuss the controversy over sexual addiction or sexual compulsion, the development of aggression, very much a factor in Gordon's presentation, and again revisit the link between neurodiversity and online offending. Understanding the development of the self when it has been so vandalised from infancy is discussed in Chapter 6, and feeds into the deep wounds as Gordon's therapy moves from first order changes, the risk management of forensic psychosexual therapy, to second order changes (Delmonico, 2002). It also looks at the victim-perpetrator cycle from the perspective of adverse childhood experiences, and tries to emphasise in view of this, how any forensic therapeutic work needs to be trauma-informed. Considering sex surrounds our lives in the media, social media, advertising, magazines etc, there is still a huge amount of ignorance about childhood sexuality. Chapter 7 overviews infant and childhood sexuality, and offers some understanding about how to determine when a child is demonstrating normal sexual curiosity, or whether they have been sexual vandalised and are acting it out. Here, the case study has moved on to Connor, Gordon's young son, who, after being taken into care, has been sexually abused in foster care. In Chapter 8, I look at aetiological theories of sexual offending to ascertain whether they can offer a valid account of online offending. My conclusion is that they don't, so I propose a developmental model of aetiology with neurological, environment and social factors included. In Chapter 9, I review treatments models facilitated by the Criminal Justice System, and argue that their continuous use of one-size-fits-all approaches is neither necessary nor sufficient, and ignores the rehabilitation and desistance literature, with a focus on the Good Lives Model (Ward, Mann & Gannon, 2005). As the case study switches back to Gordon, the realisation is that for those working in the

Criminal Justice System, the rehabilitation of an online sexual offender actually does not exist. They will always be considered a risk. Finally, in the last chapter, I review many of the services that the client encounters through the course of his journey through the Criminal Justice System. I revisit the unexpected consequences of the damage to the families of the offenders, in particular the damage to their children, most likely to promote history repeating itself in the next generation. Our blame and risk-adverse culture has led to the vilification and ostracisation of an escalating proportion of our society, with no second chances allowed. Here is the adult loss of being a valued member of society following the adolescent searches of sex on the internet.

To avoid binary pronouns, the terms 'their', 'them' and 'they' will be used. 'Child pornography' is no longer an acceptable term in the therapeutic or academic world, as they are essentially crime scene images of children being harmed. The most common terms now applied to this material are indecent images of children (IIOC), child abuse and exploitation images (CAEI) or child sexual abuse material (CSAM). I will use CSAM in this book.

Gordon's review

Gordon presented to the therapist in a broken state, his head hanging in shame and his eyes averted as he mumbled through his situation. He had been interviewed by the police for allegedly making indecent images of children. His devices (computer, laptop, Xbox, DVDs, phone and iPad) had all been seized by the police during an early morning raid by six police officers due to his potential for violence, and he had been held in the cells overnight before being charged and released on bail for one month. He had no money to pay a chosen solicitor, so a duty solicitor had been assigned to him, who advised him to cooperate, plead guilty, be put on the sex offender's register and get on with his life. Oh, and by the way, some counselling might help as Gordon was expressing suicidal plans, and a psychological report will help when it comes to his sentencing.

Gordon's marriage to Rachel had already broken down. She was living in a refuge, escaping his violence. He had been charged 6 months previously for stalking her and for a violent assault on her leaving her hospitalised for a week and her baby in foster care. The police informed social services of Gordon's latest arrest under child protection procedures, and the social worker made it clear to Rachel that if she resumed her relationship with her husband, as many female victims of violence choose to do, then they would remove her child into care permanently. Gordon had shown no interest in their child Connor, whom Gordon did not want Rachel to have. The child simply got in the way of Gordon's ability to have sex with Rachel as and when he pleased.

Gordon had already been fired from work, despite being a talented mechanic. He had been given notice to quit his flat for non-payment of the rent. His addictions to alcohol, drugs, sex and violence had been his only 'true' friends – he had no real friends, so did not feel their loss. For the therapist, faced with a client such as Gordon, they need to be skilled in understanding the forensic implications of working with such a client. Some may argue that no therapy work should be undertaken before any trial. But Gordon is not a victim of, or a witness to, an illegal offence, so as such the therapist cannot be accused to changing any potential evidence in the prosecution. It is for the prosecution to provide the evidence to the court, and an alleged offender need not say anything to incriminate their self, hence the most commonly advocated 'no comment' police interviews. Good supervision for the therapist is essential with such cases, as the societal abhorrence to such alleged offenders can also rub off onto the therapist.

Notes

1 StopSO: Specialist Treatment Organisation for Perpetrators and Survivors of Sexual Offending.
2 Stop It Now! A confidential helpline for anyone worried about their online sexual behaviour, established by the Lucy Faithful Foundation.
3 Pornhub is a Canadian-owned internet pornography website, free for the user.
4 Snapchat is an American multimedia instant messaging app.
5 Tumblr is an American microblogging and social networking website.
6 Kik is a Canadian instant messaging mobile app.
7 YouTube is an American online video sharing and social media platform.

References

Bailey, D. J. S. (2018). A life of grief: An exploration of disenfranchised grief in sex offender significant others. *American Journal of Criminal Justice*, 43, 641–667. doi:10.1007/s12103-017-9416-4.

Beech, A.R., Elliot, I.A., Birgden, A. & Findlater, D. (2008). The internet and child sexual offending: A criminological review. *Aggression and Violent Behaviour*, 13, 216–228. doi:10.1016/j.avb.2008.03.007.

B4U-ACT. (2020). Youth, suicidality, and seeking care. Retrieved from www.b4uact.org/research/survey-results/youth-suicidality-and-seeking-care/.

Calhane, H., Parker, G. & Duff, S. (2013). Treatment implications arising from a qualitative analysis of letters written by the nonoffending partners of men who have perpetrated child sexual abuse. *Journal of Child Sexual Abuse*, 22 (6),720–741. doi:10.1080/10538712.2013.811138.

Camilleri, J.A. & Quinsey, V.L. (2008). Paedophilia: Assessment and treatment. In D.R. Laws & W. O'Donohue (eds), *Sexual deviance: Theory, assessment, and treatment*, vol. 2 (pp. 183–212). New York: Guilford Press.

Cassidy, S., Bradley, P., Robinson, J., Allison, C., McHugh, M. & Baron-Cohen, S. (2014). Suicidal ideation and suicide plans or attempts in adults with Asperger's syndrome attending a specialist diagnostic clinic: A clinical cohort study. *The Lancet Psychiatry*, 1 (2), 142–147. doi:10.1016/S2215-0366(14)70248-2.

Condry, R. (2010). Secondary victims and secondary victimisation. In S. G. Shoham, P. Knepper & M. Kett (eds), *International handbook of victimology* (pp.219–250). CRC Press.

Delmonico, D.L. (2002). Sex on the superhighway. Understanding and treating cybersex addiction. In P.J. Carnes & K.M. Adams (eds), *Clinical management of sex addiction.* New York: Brunner Routledge.

Delmonico, D.L. & Griffin, E.J. (2008). Online sex offending: Assessment and treatment. In D.R. Laws & W. O'Donohue (eds), *Sexual deviance: Theory, assessment, and treatment,* vol. 2 (pp. 459–485). New York: Guilford Press.

Duncan, K., Wakeham, A., Winder, B., Armitage, R., Roberts, L. & Blagden, N. (2020). The experiences of non-offending partners of individuals who have committed sexual offences: Recommendations for practitioners and stakeholders. Retrieved from https://huddersfield.box.com/s/1sumdnyq9yjkgwhw0axzvgt7e2rfgcih.

Duncan, K., Wakeham, A., Winder, B., Blagdon, N. & Armitage, R. (2022). 'Grieving someone who's still alive, that's hard': the experiences of non-offending partners of individuals who have sexually offended – an IPA study. *Journal of Sexual Aggression,* 28 (3), 281–295. doi:10.1080/13552600.2021.2024611.

Farkas, M.A. & Miller, G. (2007). Reentry and reintegration: Challenges faced by the families of convicted sex offenders. *Federal Sentencing Reporter,* 20 (1), 88–92. doi:10.1525/FSR.2007.20.2.88.

Goffman, E. (1963). *Stigma: Notes on the management of a spoiled identity.* London: Penguin.

Grant, H. (2021a). Rise in child abuse online threatens to overwhelm UK police, officers warn. *The Guardian,* 9 February.

Grant, H. (2021b). The knock that tears families apart: 'they were at the door, telling me he had accessed indecent images of children'. *The Guardian,* 31 July.

Gray, N.S., Carman, N.G., Rogers, P., MacCulloch, M. Hayward, P. & Snowden, R.J. (2003). Post-traumatic stress disorder caused in mentally ill offenders by the committing of a serious violent or sexual offence. *Journal of Forensic Psychiatry and Psychology,* 14 (1), 27–43. doi:10.1080/1478994031000074289.

Gunter, T.D., Chibnall J.T., Antoniak, S.K., Philibert, R.A. & Hollenbeck, N. (2011). Predictors of suicidal ideation, suicide attempts, and self-harm without lethal intent in a community corrections sample. *Journal of Criminal Justice,* 39 (3), 238–245. doi:10.1016/j.jcrimjus.2011.02.005.

Hoffer, T., Shelton, J. L. & Joyner, C. (2012). *Operational safety considerations while investigating child sex offenders: A handbook for law enforcement,* vol. 1. FBI's Behavioural Analysis Unit III, Crimes Against Children.

Hudson-Allez, G. (2011). *Infant losses, adult searches. A neural and developmental perspective on psychopathology and sexual offending.* London: Karnac.

Key, R., Underwood, A., Farnham, F., Marzano, L. & Hawton, K. (2021). Suicidal behaviour in individuals accused or convicted of child sex abuse or indecent image offences: Systematic review of prevalence and risk factors. *Suicide and Life-Threatening Behaviour,* 51 (4), 715–728. doi:10.1111/sltb.12749.

Levenson, J.S., Grady, M.D. & Morin, J.W. (2019). Beyond the 'ick' factor: Counselling non-offending persons with paedophilia. *Clinical Social Work Journal,* 48 (4), 380–388. doi:10.1007/S10615-019-00712-4.

Mahoney, M. (2009). Asperger's syndrome and the criminal law. The special case of child pornography. Retrieved from https://lqdd521mbw9du60x43e6yp18-wpengine.

netdna-ssl.com/wp-content/uploads/2019/11/Mahoney-Mark-J-Aspergers-Syndrome-and-the-Criminal-Law-2009.pdf.

McEwen, B.S. & Wingfield, J.C. (2003). The concept of allostasis in biology and biomedicine. *Hormones & Behaviour*, 43 (1), 2–15. doi:10.1016/S0018-506X(02)00024-7.

Papanastassiou, M., Waldron, G., Boyle, J. & Chesterman, L.P. (2004). Post-traumatic stress disorder in mentally ill perpetrators of homicide. *Journal of Forensic Psychiatry and Psychology*, 15 (1), 66–75. doi:10.1080/14789940310001630419.

Quayle, E. (2004). The impact of viewing on offending behaviour. In M. Calder (ed.), *Child sexual abuse and the internet: Tackling the new frontier* (pp. 26–36). Dorset: Russell House Publishing.

Raymaker, D.M., Teo, A.R., Steckler, N.A., Lentz, B. *et al.* (2020). Having all your internal resources exhausted beyond measure and being left with no clean-up crew: Defining autistic burnout. *Autism in Adulthood*, 2 (2), 132–143. doi:10.1089/aut.2019.0079.

Ribero, J.D., Franklin, J.C., Fox, K.R., Bentley, K.H. *et al.* (2016). Self-injurious thoughts and behaviours as risk factors for future suicide ideation, attempts, and death: a meta-analysis of longitudinal studies. *Psychol Med* 46 (2), 225–236. doi:10.1017/S0033291715001804.

Steel, C.M.S., Newman, E., O'Rourke, S. & Quayle, E. (2022). Suicidal ideation in offenders convicted of child pornography offences, *Behavioral Sciences and the Law*, 40 (3), 365–378. doi:10.1002/bsl.2560.

Tener, D., Wolak, J. & Finkelhor, D. (2015). A typology of offenders who use online communications to commit sex crimes against minors. *Journal of Aggression, Maltreatment & Trauma*, 24, 319–337. doi:10.1080/10926771.2015.1009602.

Thompson, A.J. (2017). The lived experience of non-offending mothers in cases of intrafamilial child sexual abuse: Towards a preliminary model of loss, trauma and recovery. Doctoral dissertation, Edith Cowan University. Retrieved from http://ro.ecu.edu.au/theses/1972.

Wager, N. M., Wager, A.R. & Wilson, C. (2015). Circles South East's programme for non-offending partners of child sex offenders: A preliminary outcome evaluation. *Probation Journal*, 62 (4), 357–373. doi:10.1177/0264550515600541.

Ward, T., Mann, R.E. & Gannon, T.A. (2005). The good lives model of offender rehabilitation: Clinical implications. *Aggression and Violent Behaviour*, 12, 87–107. doi:10.1016/j.avb.2006.03.004.

Chapter 2

Beginning therapy and history taking

Case study

The therapist sat in front of her supervisor with a manila file on her lap.

'I would like to talk to you about a new client I have, called Gordon. He's a StopSO client, referred to me after getting the knock last week. I have just seen him once but he raises strong feelings within me.'

The supervisor leaned back in his chair, linked his hands and crossed his outstretched legs. 'Go on', he said.

She opened the file. 'He is a damaged young man in his 30s, separated from his wife and child. She lives in a refuge. He lives alone and lacks care for himself, eating badly, no exercise, strong suicidal ideation following getting the knock. He is addicted to online porn, alcohol, tobacco, drugs. He lacks empathy, and clearly has some narcissistic behaviours, although I am not sure at this stage whether it is classic or compensatory. I'm not sure about psychopathy either.'

She stopped and took a breath, while her supervisor waited patiently for her to continue.

'He is unable to take responsibility for his own aggressive behaviour. Everything is someone else's fault. He is emotionally dysregulated leading to violent episodes. He doesn't seem to be able to express how he feels, so he lashes out.'

The supervisor tips his head slightly and asks gently, 'What are the strong feelings he raises in you? He sounds like many of the forensic clients you see. Does he remind you of someone?'

The therapist sighed. 'It's not that. How can you relate to a client who punched and kicked his wife into unconsciousness, and would have done the same to his baby son if a neighbour had not intervened? I find it really hard to be non-judgemental.'

'Do you fear for your own safety? He could have borderline personality disorder.'

'No. I don't think I'm afraid of him.'

'Does what he did to his wife make him a bad person, and make you feel unable to work with him?'

DOI: 10.4324/9781003330899-2

'No, you are right. Of course not. But just reviewing these notes here with you, I am making some connections that I had not noticed before. He seems to have a high IQ level despite his lack of school achievement. He is a loner with no friends; he doesn't seem to know how to make friends. He has a specialised skill set in car mechanics which he has focused on since he was a young boy. I was also wondering about alexithymia; are his emotional outbursts due to his inability to express his feelings appropriately?'

The supervisor smiled. 'I can see where this is going. You are thinking undiagnosed neurodivergence.'

'Yes, yes. Of course. I need to investigate that more in my assessment.'

What is a formulation?

Lucy Johnstone and Rudi Dallos have written extensively about the advantages and disadvantages of using a formulation in clinical practice (Johnstone & Dallos, 2014). For the purposes of this book, a formulation is defined as a summary of the history taken in collaboration with the client, to help understand the client's core problems, to relate those problems into the clinical practice, or method of therapy used with the client, and to provide meaning for the client as a means of helping them move forward into a preferred way of being. This means that the formulation *per se* is an intervention, as is the history-taking to construct it. As a trauma-informed process, understanding the early years is key, particularly the early preverbal years where there may be gaps in the information, so asking the client to ask family and friends who know this information might help piece together the parts of the puzzle. The information collected must always be underpinned with the concept that the client is the expert on their self, especially when there is a difference in race, culture or religion. The therapist must always be curious and interested, rather than making assumptions. The feedback within the formulation should include the biological, or neurological, understanding of the person, as well as the family/relationships, environmental, social, and developmental factors, and the effect of life events.

In my formulation, I tend to use an adaptation of the 5Ps model (Dudley & Kuyken, 2014). These are:

- Presenting problem: written in terms of the issues that need to be addressed in therapy, but not including any diagnoses that may have been brought from interventions when previously working with other practitioners. These presenting issues need to be in sex positive terms, and mindful of the LGBTQI+ communities. This is not about changing diverse sexual behaviour, but addressing illegal or potentially illegal behaviour, or behaviour that the client may find distressing.
- Predisposing factors – looking at previous generations through the genogram, and any trauma factors that may have contributed to cultural or

sexual expectations. Childhood adverse experiences will also be predisposing. As will be discussed in future chapters, being neurodiverse may be predisposing because of its similarities in presentation to an avoidant attachment style, as will most forms of insecure attachments. At this stage I may ask clients to complete online questionnaires, for example the Autism Spectrum Quotient (ASQ[1]) or the Experiences in Close Relationships Scale (ECR[2]).

- Precipitating factors. The events that trigger sexual acting out when the sexual template comes online post-puberty and during adolescence. Often compulsive viewing of online pornography distorts the sexual template and can lead to confusion over sexuality and diverse sexual interests.
- Perpetuating factors are those that maintain the behaviour, for example the cycle of addiction to pornography and struggles within relationships.
- Protective factors. It is essential to highlight the individual's strengths and resilience in the face of adversity, that they can use for helping with their suicidality and subsequent recovery.

I find these formulations do help the client make sense of their experience of their presenting issues, and they often discuss the details with partners or family members to help all make sense of the presenting issues. We need to remember that these formulations evolve throughout the therapy rather than are fixed. To elaborate how the process may work, I will talk through the process of history-taking with the client, and use the case study to highlight how some of the issues may manifest.

History-taking: 1–5 years

Taking a thorough life history is vital to understanding the presenting problem of any client who walks into a therapy room. Often clients will try and skip these first very early years as they have very little explicit memory of them, especially as the hippocampus within the brain isn't fully developed until about 16–18 months of age. But it is worth asking clients to speak to family members about these years, to get an understanding of what can or cannot be remembered, and what someone is choosing to forget. It is also worth remembering that the coherence of the narrative the client provides the therapist with during the history taking gives a window of understanding of the client's attachment style.

In the initial stages, it is useful to start by asking about grandparents and extended family members. Transgenerational transmission (discussed in more detail in Chapter 6) becomes evident in a genogram, as history of trauma trickles down from one generation to the next. Gordon's genogram is illustrated in Figure 2.1. In this case alcohol abuse, domestic violence and sexual abuse starts with the paternal grandparents (and probably beyond), then repeats down the generations. Similarly, sexual abuse and mental health issues appear in Gordon's wife's family side, making her adopt a victim position quite readily. These would be predisposing factors.

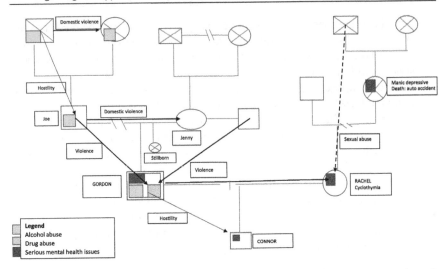

Figure 2.1 Gordon's genogram shows domestic violence through four generations through his paternal line, and sexual abuse and mental health issues on his wife's side.

A child's neurological life commences in the third trimester of pregnancy, so history-taking needs to consider this period before birth too. Stress and trauma experienced by the biological mother will have repercussions for the infant's developing brain as mother's stress hormones reach the infant through the umbilical cord. Of course, the client will have no memories of this period, but it is helpful to encourage the client to ask family members about it, so that the client and therapist can collaboratively build up a picture of what the family of origin was actually like. It is also important to understand that we are looking in these early years for a response to parenting, not to parents (Maté, 1999). Thus, two siblings can have a completely different attachment response to the same parents because the contextual situations were different at that time.

Gordon's history is outlined in detail in *Infant Losses, Adult Searches* (Hudson-Allez, 2011). Gordon was an unplanned pregnancy in a fairly new relationship between his parents. His mother was only 16 when she conceived, 17 when he was born. His father was 22; still immature in neurological terms. There was domestic violence between Gordon's parents while he was in-utero, his birth being precipitated by his father's violence towards his mother. His birth is premature and he is jaundiced and placed into an incubator, unable to feel the warmth and care of his mother's skin.

In utero, Gordon was already receiving too high levels of adrenaline and cortisol from his mother's stress of the unplanned pregnancy. This would have sensitised him to levels of stress when he is born, making him hyperaroused and hypervigilant. The stress hormones shrink the hippocampus of the developing brain, reducing Gordon's memory capacity, which would interfere with his later learning. His amygdala will have increased in size and be overactive, making him hyperactive and over-alert.

Gordon's mother was emotionally unavailable as a depressed victim of domestic violence. This has a devastating effect on the subsequent emotional development of the child (Green, 1996), producing rapid and overwhelming fast-track physiological responses with heightened sympathetic (fight and flight) activity. Insecure or unavailable mothers have been shown to respond in the insula and other disgust centres of the brain to a crying baby (Piallini, De Palo & Simonelli, 2015) and show lower oxytocin levels (Strathearn et al., 2009), the hormone that provides the care and nurturance. By the time of his first birthday, Gordon's mother is pregnant again, but she loses this child as a consequence of her husband's violence. This places her in a deeply depressed state as she grieves for the loss of one child, and is incapable of connecting to the one she already has. It is suggested that parental disengagement seems more developmentally injurious to the infant than the intrusiveness of a poorly attuned mother. As Siegel (2003) emphasised, the lack of resolution of grief or trauma in a parent places the child in a paradoxical, unsolvable and problematic situation. The process of attachment development will be discussed in greater detail in the next chapter, but essentially we are talking about the child using an innate strategy for survival, using the SEEKING CARE systems, to seek proximity to the mother, to feel safe and secure in that proximity, and to feel that is the safe base where the child can return when life gets scary. The paradox of Gordon's seeking proximity is that his mother does not respond to him, shakes him off in her hurt and her shame, and leaves him to fend for his self, with nowhere to go. He does not have the neural infrastructure to know how to do this, so for him the terror is facing life alone, meaning death.

Persistent fear can alter the structure of a child's brain, and this might be one of Gordon's predispositions, in being a victim of violence, being a witness of violence toward his mother and the emotional violence of humiliation, degradation, and neglect in his household. Sometimes, in these situations, trauma is not a specific event but an ongoing aversive experience of life, receiving intentional injuries, unintentional injuries and the witnessing of abuse within the household. Children have two primary interactive response patterns to violent situations: hyperarousal as described above, or dissociation in a dorsal-vagal tuning out as a self-protective mechanism (Porges, 2003).

In a child before the age of 3 years, this is all happening only in the right hemisphere of the brain, as the left hemisphere with language and logic has not yet come online (Schore, 1994). This leads to a right-brain shame response in the body from a BAD-ME circuit. The child is kept in a state of shame as it assumes responsibility for the bad things that happen: 'if I was good, if I was loveable, these bad things wouldn't happen to me', but without the narrative or explanation. It is a body-brain experience, and gives rise to Bessel van der Kolk's view that the body keeps the score (van der Kolk, 2015).

History-taking: 5–9 years

The right hemisphere of the brain is dominant for the first two and a half to three years of life, until the child acquires about half a dozen words, and then it pauses while the left brain assumes dominance for the acquisition of language. Once the child has become reasonably fluent in vocabulary, the Right hemisphere has another growth spurt. Focusing on the client's history during this period will not only give a clearer understanding of the person's attachment style, but also any indication of trauma that might have vandalised the developing child's sexual template, which comes online prior to puberty. I will say more about attachment in the next chapter, but we do know that the quality of the attachment style in the child is correlated to the attachment style of the parent (van Ijzendoorn, 1992), giving a clear indication of the need to investigate transgenerational transmission.

In Gordon's case, Gordon's father left the home when Gordon was 5 years old. Although Gordon experienced a sense of relief as the violence stopped, he also felt abandoned by him as an attachment figure; a negative and aversive attachment figure is better than no attachment figure at all. His mother became more depressed at first, then after taking anti-depressants, she got herself a full-time job working in a supermarket, and a new boyfriend. Both of these new events made her less available for Gordon, which he perceived as rejection: his subtext would be: 'she can make time for a new man, but she cannot make time for me'. Gordon starts to build an avoidant style, with a developing passive-aggressive anger from his RAGE circuit.

As a young boy with no friends, Gordon spent long periods of time on his own wandering the streets, particularly during the school holidays without food or drink, from 8am in the morning when his mother left for work, until 7pm in the evening, when she got home. Instead of nutritious meals, she would opt to give him something quick and easy, like beans on toast, as she prepared to go out for the evening with her boyfriend. This form of neglect is pervasive in the developing child's mind, leading them to feel completely unlovable (BAD-ME). Gordon started to steal sweets and chocolate from other children at school; luxuries he could never have. And he would often bunk off from school at lunchtime rather than watch all his peers eating their school dinners and packed lunches. His teachers called his mother into school and accused him of having a conduct disorder. His mother was furious with school, arguing that they were being unsupportive to a single parent.

As Gordon wandered in the park one school lunchtime, he was picked up by a man and taken to his home. In return for food, crisps and other treats, the man sexually abused him. Gordon told no-one, as he did not feel he had a safe base to share this information. He revisited the man on many occasions when he was feeling particularly lonely, hungry, or when the weather was bad. Gordon hated what the man was doing to him, and vowed he would get his revenge one day, but the need for food was greater than his shame and disgust at the man's behaviour toward him.

The last pre-programmed circuit, the LUST circuit, comes online at 8 or 9 for boys, 6 or 7 for girls. Any abuse, trauma or loss, during this pre-pubescent right hemisphere growth when the child's sexual template is activated can distort behavioural pathways. Gordon's sexual template had therefore been vandalised by the sexual abuse (Money, 1986). From seeing the sex magazines at his abuser's home, Gordon became over-interested in sex, and later turned to watching it on videos and then online. He started compulsively masturbating before he was physically or neurologically ready for it, and his frequent returns to his abuser confirmed in his avoidant attachment style that closeness and physical intimacy is a risk but worth taking to get the rewards.

Gordon was unable to make friends with his peers at school. The others seemed to identify that he was different from them. His clothes were often dirty, and sometimes he was unwashed. He wasn't interested in the sorts of things they were interested in, like football and television programmes. And he had red hair. Gordon became a target for the bullies, so Gordon became unwilling to take the risk of trying to make friends in primary school. But by the time he reached senior school, however, Gordon had learned from his stepfather that aggression and violence was a norm. So in his senior school, Gordon became the bully, mirroring the bullying he received at home from his stepfather. That way others left him alone; friendships were too much of a risk.

History taking adolescence

Adolescence is also a vital time in neural development, and it is a long process going from ages of 11/12 to a fully developed adult brain at age 25. The brain has a huge job to do over this time, disorganising, reorganising and pruning away neural pathways. As an infant is born with twice as many potential neural connections as an adult, the brain does a form of system analysis and defragmentation, checking which pathway connections have been covered with a myelin sheath. This is a form of fat that covers the neural axon in order to protect the connection. Because of the myelin sheath, any further activity required to go through that pathway will be enhanced, and therefore become easier and faster; it is how an individual learns. Neural connections that have not been myelinated will be pruned away. It's a bit like pruning a rose bush: by trimming off lengthy, wispy shoots from a bush that would make it weak and spindly, the pruning consolidates the bush making it strong and rounded. The same with neural connections.

This neural system analysis brings up lots of historical information in the person in the form of memories and flashbacks, as the brain subconsciously reviews past events. This whole process takes a lot of energy for the adolescent, which is one of the reasons why they sleep a lot and eat a lot. It also contributes to their risky behaviour as they are testing boundaries they have learned as children. It also explains why teens do not always understand the consequences of their behaviour, in particular risk-taking. They are operating in the here and now and have little understanding of future consequences. It helps explain why they might interpret social situations differently and respond with different emotions. It is a period of intense self-preoccupation and pressure to consolidate a sense of self. To gain acceptance from their peers, who become their new attachment figures, they are strongly motivated to present themselves in a favourable light. Sometimes this will be done falsely, suggesting they have attributes or views that are not their own, but are designed to impress the others. Judith Lewis Herman (1992) pointed out that the three main tasks of this adolescent period are the formation of their identity, to separate from their family of origin and to explore the wider social world, and any form of trauma during adolescence compromises those goals.

Any form of trauma, loss or damage that occurs to a teenager can have consequences for later attachment processes and their subsequent sense of self, so again a therapist needs to ask detailed questions about what life was like for the client when they were in their teens. In Gordon's case, Gordon's mother and her boyfriend were now living together, and Gordon felt displaced in his mother's affections. Fights had regularly occurred between Gordon and his stepfather, vying for dominance. But an adolescent growth spurt led Gordon to be the bigger and stronger of the two. The blows to the head Gordon frequently received when this man first came into his mother's life are less frequent now, and Gordon realises his larger physique has moved him from a powerless to powerful position. For the first time in his life he has some confidence.

Throughout his intermittent schooling, Gordon was failing academically. But he had one skill that he could excel in. As a young boy he would hang around a local garage and watch the car mechanics at work. He would go to the local library and read about engines and how they operated. The mechanics at the garage got used to him hanging around and would show him different procedures they undertook with the cars. They were impressed with his interest and eventually offered him an apprenticeship. Before he had passed his driving test, he was able to strip a car engine down and rebuild it. Gordon was aware of his superior skills compared to the other apprentices and even some of the long-standing mechanics, and would brag and sneer at his contemporaries in the garage. It is at this stage Gordon is metaphorically covering himself with a grandiose cloak so that others will not see how weak and feeble he felt when he was younger; he has developed compensatory narcissism, a need to portray himself as strong and clever, rather than let others see how weak and feeble he feels inside.

Detailed enquiry about internet use should always be included in any clinical assessment of young people at risk of self-harm or suicide. This is particularly important given evidence that exposure to others who are self-harming is a major risk factor for self-harm (Daine et al., 2013); the subtext being: 'if others do it, then perhaps I should too'. The internet may normalise self-harm, or provide access to suicide content and violent imagery, and create a communication channel that can be used to bully or harass others. Similarly, it is essential when undertaking assessments of individuals with social anxiety, depression, impulsivity or performance anxiety that overuse of internet pornography is considered (Wilson, 2017), and to ascertain not just that they are looking at pornography but details of its content.

It may well be that at the initial sessions with such a forensic client, as shame is so great in their presentations, that the therapist may not hear the whole of the forensic history until trust has been developed over a few meetings. It is not uncommon for clients to drip-feed information of illegal activity, testing the water of the therapist's response. This will include information about what has happened to themselves in their own victimisation, as they take responsibility and blame themselves for the bad things that happened to them in their past. And, as Willmott and Jones (2022) point out, it is not the historical trauma *per se* that leads a person into committing a crime, but the chronic sense of threat and lack of safety that it produces that is fundamental to the coping strategies that a person develops in later life, which may lead them to offending.

Gordon's review

As a therapist, can you like this client? Even in the first session, Gordon's narcissistic approach to the world and sense of entitlement interfered with his ability to relate to his therapist as he tried to justify his behaviour as being all Rachel's fault, and if she hadn't vexed him so much and did as she was told, the violence would not have happened.

He said his employer was a 'wanker' in firing him, when he was the best mechanic in the garage, so much so that the customers asked for him to service their cars, so it was his boss's loss, not Gordon's. Now unemployed, Gordon had let himself go, spending all his money on drink, drugs and online gaming, so much so that he could not pay his rent. He continued that the landlord was a 'twat', because given time, according to Gordon, he would have won sufficient money playing online gambling to pay all his arrears in rent. This blaming of others shows defensive externalisation, which is a victim-specific empathy deficit. Shame restricts Gordon's empathy because he is so absorbed with his negative evaluation of himself through the negative judgement of others (Tagney, 1995), and can promote victim-blaming (Bumby, 2000).

The therapist has to see past all this negativity, and as she starts taking the history, it becomes clear why Gordon has developed such a strong negative strategy of not allowing himself to feel so hurt and let down by those around him. His history tells us he was born into a situation of domestic violence, so much so that his sister is stillborn. First, Gordon had a mother who is deeply depressed, and then she reinvents herself with a new life and a new man and has little time for, or interest in, him. It led to emotional and physical neglect as he became an overlooked child, making him ripe to become a victim of a sexual predator. And then domestic violence returns to the household with the stepfather as he and Gordon vie for dominance. Gordon demonstrates betrayal trauma, which Freyd (1996) argued was more damaging than other forms of abuse or trauma, as it is perpetrated by the one person who should have cared for him the most as a young child. It leads to emotional numbing and an inability to know or understand how to care for himself or others, as he was never cared for. His only coping strategy that worked for him was to keep people away by being argumentative and aggressive.

Before initiating the deep psychological assessment process, there are some introductory processes that the therapist needs to incorporate which are vital for someone so emotionally dysregulated as Gordon. They need to:

- Listen and hear his expression of rage and fear following the criminal justice system response to his violence towards his wife and his online viewing, rather than argue or discount it.
- Provide some information regarding the criminal justice process that he is about to face over the following months or years.
- Provide some stress management strategies for dealing with the long-term uncertainty of whether he will lose his freedom when he finally does come to court.
- Help him with a keep safe plan for his suicidal ideation.
- Gently support his shame as he looks into the mirror at his own behaviour; the window of opportunity of working with someone with narcissistic overlap.
- Encourage right-brain soothing strategies to help with his distress: mindfulness exercises, taking himself to water to walk alongside or to immerse himself in the shower, bath or swimming pool.
- Provide basic psychoeducation regarding diet and exercise to help him think in a clearer way.
- Encourage him to acknowledge his addictions but point out that will be the focus for later work.

This client presentation needs an experienced therapist with appropriate forensic training to understand the Criminal Justice System. Most importantly, this client must want to do the work and be able to trust and relate to the therapist. The therapeutic alliance is vital to its success. And, as Harris and Fallot (2001) point out, mental health practitioners need to stop asking 'what is wrong with you?' and start asking 'what happened to you?'

Notes

1 See https://psychology-tools.com/test/autism-spectrum-quotient.
2 See http://openpsychometrics.org/tests/ECR.php.

References

Bumby, K.M. (2000). Empathy inhibition, intimacy deficits, and attachment difficulties in sex offenders. In D.R. Laws, S.M. Hudson & T. Ward (eds), *Remaking relapse prevention with sex offenders: A sourcebook* (pp. 143–166). Thousand Oaks, CA: Sage.

Daine, K., Hawton, K., Singaravelu, V. & Stewart, A. *et al.* (2013). The power of the web. A systematic review of studies on the influence of the internet on self-harm and suicide in young people. *PLOS ONE* 8, e77555. doi:10.1371/journal.pone.0077555.

Dudley, R. & Kuyken, W. (2014). Case formulation in cognitive behavioural therapy: a principle-driven approach. In L. Johnstone & R. Dallos (eds), *Formulation in psychology and psychotherapy: Making sense of people's problems*. East Sussex: Routledge.

Freyd, J.J. (1996). *Betrayal trauma: The logic of forgetting childhood abuse.* Cambridge, MA: Harvard University Press.

Green, A. (1996). *On private madness.* London: Routledge.

Harris, M. & Fallot, R. (2001). *Using trauma theory to design service systems: New directions for mental health services.* San Francisco, CA: Jossey-Bass.

Herman, J. L. (1992). *Trauma and recovery: From domestic abuse to political terror.* London: Pandora.

Hudson-Allez, G. (2011). *Infant losses, adult searches: A neural and developmental perspective on psychopathology and sexual offending.* London: Karnac.

Johnstone, L. & Dallos, R. (eds). (2014). *Formulation in psychology and psychotherapy: Making sense of people's problems.* East Sussex: Routledge.

Maté G. (1999). *Scattered minds: The origins and healing of attention deficit disorder.* London: Penguin.

Money, J. (1986). *Lovemaps: Clinical concepts of sexual/erotic health & pathology, paraphilia, and gender transposition in childhood, adolescence, and maturity.* Amherst, NY: Prometheus Books.

Piallini, G., De Palo, F. & Simonelli, A. (2015). Parental brain: Cerebral areas activated by infant cries and faces. A comparison between different populations of parents and not. *Frontiers in Psychology,* 6, article 1625. doi:10.3389/fpsyg.2015.01625.

Porges, S.W. (2003). Social engagement and attachment: A phylogenetic perspective. *Annals of the New York Academy of Sciences,* 1008, 31–47. doi:10.1196/annals.1301.004.

Schore, A. (1994). *Affective regulation and the origin of the self.* Hillsdale, NJ: Lawrence Erlbaum.

Siegel, D.J. (2003). An interpersonal neurobiology of psychotherapy. In D.J. Siegel & M.F. Solomon (eds), *Healing trauma: Attachment, mind, body & brain* (pp. 1–56). New York: Norton.

Strathearn, L., Fonagy, P., Amico, J. & Montague, P.R. (2009). Adult attachment predicts maternal brain and oxytocin response in infant cues. *Neuropsychopharmacology,* 34, 2655–2666.

Tagney, J.P. (1995). Shame and guilt in interpersonal relationships. In J.P. Tagney & K. W. Fischer (eds), *Self-conscious emotions: Shame, guilt, embarrassment and pride* (pp. 114–139). New York: Guilford Press.

van der Kolk, B. (2015). *The body keeps the score: Mind, brain and body in the transformation of trauma.* London: Penguin.

van Ijzendoorn, M.H. (1992). Intergenerational transmission of parenting: A review of studies in nonclinical populations. *Developmental Review*, 12, 76–99. doi:10.1016/0273-2297(92)90004-L.

Willmott, P. & Jones, L. (2022). Introduction. In P. Willmott & L. Jones (eds), *Trauma-Informed Forensic Practice*. London: Routledge. pp 1–11.

Wilson, G. (2017). *Your brain on porn: Internet pornography and the emerging science of addiction* (2nd edition). Kent: Commonwealth Publishing.

Chapter 3

Understanding attachment injuries and their effect on neural development

Case study

Gordon attends for his weekly therapy session. The therapist has been gently taking him through his childhood history, asking him about his grandparents, his parents and his stepfather. Gordon is starting identify his difficult beginnings. At first it again evokes his anger, but his therapist has encouraged him to stop his automatic volatility and to try and understand some different feelings that may be inside, by encouraging some mindfulness exercises at the start of each day. Gordon is also using a mind-body connection by watching his hands, as when he is angry, they automatically turn into fists.

'I didn't like that meditation lark,' he retorts. 'I felt a twat! But what I have been doing is going for a walk before breakfast every morning, and trying to not think thoughts, but just try and enjoy the park or the walk along the river.'

'Oh, that's good Gordon.' She smiles warmly. He risks a bit of eye contact with her now, and he blushes slightly. 'What have you learned from doing that?'

'I am starting to think that I don't need to push people away all the time. I meet an old lady in the park every day. She smiles at me and talks about her little dog. I'm thinking of getting a dog. I miss her if I don't see her, if she doesn't come for some reason. I helped her carry her shopping for her the other day. She asked me in for a cup of tea, but I thought I'd better not.'

'I think that was wise, Gordon. You don't want people to misattribute your intentions at this stage. I am not trying to discourage you from making friends, I just feel you need to be mindful about how others would perceive you making friends with an old lady, and whether they would consider you had an ulterior motive.'

'Yeah, I know. I've done some terrible things in the past. Once I came out of a pub and threw a rock at a bloke in that very same park. He didn't do anything to me, only I thought he looked at me funny, and I felt so mad. I just wanted to hurt him.' Gordon's fists curled, then he examined them and stretched out his fingers.

'What is your view now, Gordon, of what you felt then, now that you are starting to put words to your feelings?'

DOI: 10.4324/9781003330899-3

Gordon shuffled in his chair and looked at the floor. 'When I think about it, I was in the pub, watching telly. And I think what I was really feeling was, "How sad am I? Alone in this pub, with no-one to go home to."'

'That is a thought, Gordon, what are the feelings inside that go with that thought?'

Gordon frowned as he struggled to name his feeling. 'Where on your body are you feeling this?' His hand goes to the bottom of his rib cage. 'What does that say to you?'

'Empty ... Alone,' he said finally. Then with a deep sigh, 'I was really lonely.'

'Do you think you felt a little bit ashamed of being alone, and you couldn't bear for the man to see that?'

'Yeah. I bet 'e 'ad someone to go home to.'

The development of attachment pathways

This next section reviews the work elaborated in *Infant Losses, Adult Searches* (Hudson-Allez, 2011), to help put the discussion of neurodiversity in the following chapter into context. We know an infant is born with seven pre-programmed emotional brain circuits found in the periaqueductal grey in the brain stem (Panksepp, 1998). Only the right hemisphere is online at this stage (Schore, 1994). These neural circuits are SEEKING, CARE, FEAR, PANIC, RAGE, PLAY and LUST. This is the physiological attachment system designed for survival of the child. The SEEKING process provides active arousal, curiosity, excitement, engagement, motivation, and the desire to explore. Without the SEEKING circuit, we would still be living like Neanderthals in caves. CARE provides the nurturance to be fed and the warmth and tenderness when with attachment figures, developing empathic concern. It uses the ventral vagal system of the autonomic nervous system, encouraging rest and enjoyment. This system is not necessarily active at birth, but develops through the social engagement system, which is PLAY. To play with others is to feel joy and laughter, encouraging social bonding, social communication and social support. It develops reciprocity, connectedness, and co-regulation. It is through PLAY that fathers develop their strong bond with the infant, with the father's production of beta-endorphins, which Machin (2018) calls the chemical of parental love. PLAY, through the ventral vagus complex, is therefore a biological imperative to spontaneously engage with others using social cues, which in turn, helps us to self-soothe (see Figure 3.1).

PANIC is the fear of separation from important others, initially the biological mother, and includes anxiety, loneliness and sadness. In Fig: 3.2, FEAR is the flight mechanism of the sympathetic nervous system, with the fear being expressed often as hot anger. RAGE is the sympathetic nervous system producing the 'fight' response, a self-protection mechanism and can lead to passive aggressive seething, but also to a parasympathetic dorsal vagal flop of freeze; the fear of the fear itself (Porges, 2003). What underpins fear and rage, which are not

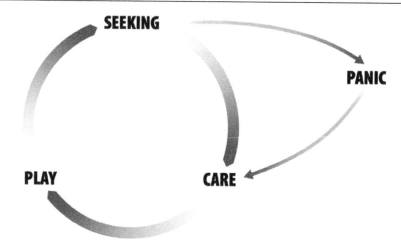

Figure 3.1 The optimal process of a secure attachment.
Source: Hudson-Allez (2011), reproduced by permission of Taylor & Francis Group

negative emotions, but are there for survival purposes, is the sense of loss. Without our attachment figures, our ability to survive is compromised.

Mother and baby communicate via their retinas, processing their mutual visual and auditory communicative signals. As mother and infant gaze reciprocally into each other's eyes, the infant's right-brain limbic system of the

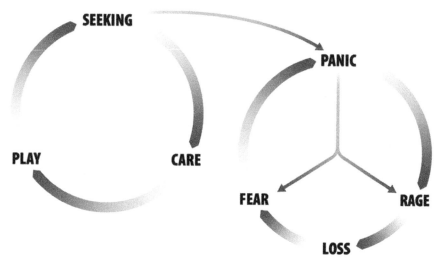

Figure 3.2 The panic of misattunement precipitates feelings of FEAR or RAGE, designed to precipitate action for survival.
Source: Hudson-Allez (2011), reproduced by permission of Taylor & Francis Group

brain is developing a database of visual snapshot images (schemata) using mirror neurons with attached emotional tags, absorbing and learning mother's emotions using nuances of non-verbal communication. It is these loving eyes in protoconversations (Trevarthen, 2001) that are considered the primary trigger for developing a secure attachment (Porges, 2017). Daniel Stern calls these microevents, as mother and baby communicate for short periods, and mother responds to baby's babbling conversation or pointing at things in the environment (Stern, 1995). At this stage, mother and baby are a symbiotic unit which requires attunement, although misattunement with appropriate repair is also required for the child to learn resilience (Winnicott, 1960). The quality of CARE predicts the quality of the attachment relationship. The influential work of Ed Tronick highlights this with his still face experiment, which demonstrates how distressing it is, even for a secure child, not to get the attunement they are looking for (Weinberg, Beeghly, Olson & Tronick, 2008). Using the muscles of the face and head, these reciprocal face-to-face interactions regulate the vagal regulation of the heart, thus regulating the internal state. These attachment experiences mediate the development of the orbitofrontal regions of the brain, which starts to mature in the infant toward the end of the first year, and create the executive structure for later affect regulation. So important is this eye-to-eye contact between mother and infant, that disconnected interactions can disrupt the opportunity for co-regulation, and can trigger the infant's fight and flight system, as the uncertainty of the disconnect creates a sense of threat in the infant. This does not have to be in abusive or neglectful situations. Think of an infant sat in a bouncy chair near their mother, whose eyes are constantly on her mobile phone scrolling through social media; the child will clearly express their distress.

Adoption creates a significant attachment injury in an infant, whether it be from birth, at 6 weeks or early infancy. For years there was an incorrect assumption that newly born infants had no concept of who their biological mother was until about six weeks old (Schaffer & Emerson, 1964), and so long as they were fed and nurtured, it was irrelevant who did it. Neuroscience has taught us that this is not the case. An infant, hears, tastes and feels their mother *in utero,* and this knowledge is present at birth. So taking a child away from everything that this infant has experienced in their short confinement triggers the fear and terror of the attachment system. This is why Nancy Newton Verrier called it the primal wound (Verrier, 2009). And this is also why we have a large proportion of adoptees in our client caseload.

Although in Western society, we are moving against the binary understanding of sex and gender, these social mores are tending to move faster than our neurological system's ability to evolve. Thus, our brains exhibit sexual dimorphisms, that is feminised or masculinised brains, and this can have implications for gender and psychopathology during childhood and adolescence. For example, early-onset conduct disorders or autistic spectrum disorders tend to show a marked male preponderance, whereas adolescent-onset disorders like anorexia and depression show a marked female preponderance (Zahn-Waxler, Shirtcliff & Marceau, 2008). These differences seem to be rooted in the curve of neural development of the infant commencing *in utero*. Androgen and oestrogen surges sculpt the developing brain during critical periods of cortical development, giving rise to either male or female stereotyped behaviour in adulthood. During pregnancy, the increase of chorionic gonadotrophin reaches its peak at 60–90 days gestation. Testosterone surges between 8 to 24 weeks gestation, and then again in the first months after birth, is sometimes called mini-puberty, and it is these surges that are considered to result in gender-typical juvenile play (Hines, Constantinescu & Spencer, 2015). The development of the prefrontal cortex, the caudate, and the temporal lobes mature faster in females than in males, as is their physical and psychological development (Taylor, 1969). Kigar and Auger (2013) propose that the different hormonal and experiential influences produce differences in the epigenome, the network of chemicals that surround the DNA sequence, and that these differences contribute to the gate between risk or resilience in later neurological or psychological disorders. As such, elaborating on infant and mother retinal communication, it has been found that boys are less responsive to eye contact and auditory stimulation than girls (Schneider et al., 2011). They smile less, are more irritable, cry more, and are less able to regulate their affect to repair interactive misattunement by self-comforting (Weinberg et al., 1999). Bingham et al. (2011) similarly discusses the masculinisation of the HPA axis (hypothalamus, pituitary, adrenal – our stress response), making boys more susceptible to acute stress.

Research following Bowlby's seminal work on attachment (Bowlby, 1988) has demonstrated identifiable styles of behaviour in children and later adults as a consequence of their attachment, linked also to their perception of the self and their inner working model of the world in terms of resilience and coping strategies. A secure attachment between infant and child provides a child with a strong sense of self; our sense of self emerges from these self-other interactions. It provides a resilience in the face of adversity, and a confidence to know where to go for help when the going gets tough. However, there are physiological consequences of an insecure attachment. The PANIC circuit physically starves emotional and cognitive nerve and brain systems allowing continued affective dysregulation, leading to constant fears of rejection and abandonment and the need to search for CARE. The child will have an inability to regulate their raw and intense emotions and cope with stressful situations as a consequence of the FEAR and RAGE. This will lead to snapshot images in the Right hemisphere of the brain with an open pathway to the fight and flight circuitry of the HPA axis. Lashing out aggressively when infants hit the FEAR circuit, especially around the age of two years before the cognitive functions come online, is not uncommon, particularly for boys (Tremblay et al., 1999), whereas girls tend not to be quite so aggressive. This is the age that attachment to the father is so important, as it helps boys, through rough and tumble play, to manage their aggression as their left hemisphere comes online (Schore, 1994).

We don't have to think we are scared, for our bodies to act scared; the dorsal vagal complex takes over outside conscious awareness in the process of neuroception, scanning the world for potential threat, triggering threat responses. Trauma in childhood can over-stimulate the dorsal vagal nerve producing a 'stuck-on' or habitual freeze response. It can also remove the vagal brake on the heart that promotes defensive behaviours. This can be particularly seen with children (or adults) who have a disorganised attachment style, with strong feelings of shame without words to express it. Habitual freezing can lead to dissociative states, feelings of hopelessness and helplessness, or a quiet 'phasing out' – not being in the here and now. We know that insecurely attached children at the age of 2, especially the later developing boys, are less persistent and enthusiastic at solving problems. At 11 years they are less able to recall specific incidents from earlier in their life, and less able to reflect on their own mental processes, and they also perform less well on tests designed to measure their ability to understand the mental states of others (theory of mind – spectrum disorders).

Affect regulation and the role of shame

Depue and Morrone-Strupinsky (2005) proposed three major interacting affect regulation systems within the autonomic nervous system: the threat system, the drive-resource acquisition system, and the contentment-affiliative and soothing system. *The drive-resource acquisition system* is the SEEKING system, which I feel is the primary motivational system of survival. It gives us positive feelings of activation, pleasure and excitement, and motivates us to seek out and secure resources (e.g. food, sex) that increases our chances of survival and prosperity. *The threat system* is the PANIC circuit, which is the primary protective system, focused on detection of threats via the thalamus to the amygdala in the mid brain and connected to the HPA axis, to lead to the rapid activation of defensive emotions (e.g. anxiety, anger, disgust) and behaviours (e.g. fight, flight and freeze). The third affect regulation system is *the contentment-affiliative and soothing* CARE system, the primary need system, providing warmth, soothing and well-being elicited by endogenous endorphins and oxytocin. Depue and Morrone-Strupinsky (2005) proposed that when we are not under threat and not seeking resources, then we are in a state of satisfied contentment. This affect regulation system, linked to the self-regulatory role of the pre-frontal cortex, is thought to have evolved alongside the attachment system, being stimulated by signals of care and compassion from others. So, attachment and affiliative relationships can foster feelings of safeness, connectedness and warmth and reduce distress in response to threats (Matos & Pinto-Gouveia, 2014); this essentially is the affect of a secure attachment. The need to PLAY and socialise is missing from this theory. When we are in a state of contentment, we rarely just 'be'; most commonly people will want to 'be together'; to socialise and have fun.

Being loved, cared for and wanted is part of our social cognition that makes our world feel safe, so we are highly motivated to create positive images of ourselves in others (Gilbert, 1998), to make us feel secure and for us to make predictions about what others think and feel about us. The feeling of shame has a socialising function in this impression-management process that promotes humility, autonomy, humour and competence, and precedes sympathy, empathy and compassion (Wurmser, 1995). Shame and sex are inextricably linked. Sanderson (2014) highlighted how disinhibited we become during sexual encounters, many preferring to do it in the dark and to close their eyes, protecting themselves from the scrutiny of their partners. She elucidates: 'the ensuing battle between sexual arousal and societal expectations becomes a crucible for unbearable shame' (p. 122).

Matos and Pinto-Gouveia (2014) argue that shame is an emotion crucial to one's social existence and self-identity. They highlight two sorts of shame: external shame based on how one experiences oneself in the minds of others (looking in), for example, worthless, inadequate, or inferior; and internal shame linked to our childhood memory systems of being shamed or humiliated too harshly (looking out through the eyes of the other). Understanding these two processes of shame are important in a therapeutic context. The external shame is the good shame which we all have to encourage us as a social being and to prevent ourselves from becoming narcissistic. It encourages caring and consideration for others, as it involves the physiological process of a parasympathetic flop, blushing face, and lowered gaze which elicits a cognition of guilt; an awareness that something that the person has said or done has hurt or caused to pain to another in an empathic understanding of what they are thinking or feeling (theory of mind). It is also a warning signal of a social threat that one is perceived by others as being flawed, worthless, of low rank, a failure, unattractive or deficient in some way. These shame memories can influence our internal workings of the self and link with the internal working memories of attachment and thus interfere with our socialisation with others.

Internal shame is a toxic shame as it can corrode the individual's sense of self with the associated BAD-ME circuit recorded in autobiographical memory. Sanderson elaborates:

> 'when shame is too harshly imposed it can become toxic and imprison the individual in an abyss of self-hate and self-blame ... To avoid further shame they withdraw into an iron fortress to keep themselves safe and others at bay ... Such shaming experiences produce a deep sense of alienation from self and others.
>
> (Sanderson, 2014, p. 19)

Thus, too much shame in early years, not just from abuse, but from critical parenting or incessant teasing, can lead to a hyper-sensitivity to shame and a default defensive position from being humiliated. Paul Gilbert (2011) saw humiliation as more intense than shame, as the focus is less on the self and more on the harm done by others. He proposed that the defensive strategies of shame and humiliation differ; the former producing avoidance whereas the latter can precipitate more intense rage and even violence.

Development of the sexual template

Between the ages of 6 and 10 years, again occurring earlier for girls than for boys, and depending on the developmental trajectory of the child, the sexual template comes online, what Jaak Panksepp (1998) called the LUST circuit. The six primary circuits already discussed are online at birth for the protection of the child. This last circuit is for the protection of the species. Thus if an adolescent is operating within a secure circuitry, then the LUST circuit is incorporated as part of the attachment process: loving couples, SEEK CARE from one another, they PLAY together, they have sex together (LUST), and if one or the other gets triggered into PANIC for some reason, they again CARE and support one another. If, however, they are operating on an insecure tra-jectory, the LUST circuit will be intermingled and bounce between feelings of FEAR and RAGE. Sex will become a means of changing how one feels, a form of self-soothing (see Figure 3.3). The result is the formation of insecure attachment styles: FEAR eliciting a preoccupied style, RAGE eliciting an

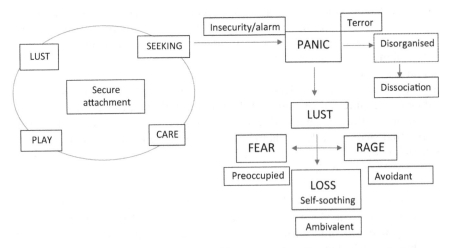

Figure 3.3 Adult secure attachment is a cohesive process of seeking care, playing, and making love. Alarm and insecurity in the relationship trigger panic, leading to fear or rage states, and using sex to change the feelings of shame and loss. Too much fear triggers dissociative states.

avoidant style, or those swinging between FEAR and RAGE becoming ambivalent in their relationships.

Interestingly, those children, soon to be adolescents, who have neurodivergent processing often struggle to be in a secure attachment, predominantly because the PLAY circuit tends to be bypassed, preferring instead their own company. PLAY is not a frivolous circuit. We are a social species, and PLAY is vital for social bonding. However, if the child struggles to interact and connect with others, and struggles with making eye contact through which the SEEKING system operates, then the ability to play with others is reduced as the circuit atrophies (neurones that no longer fire together, no longer wire together). Anticipating rejection and abandonment from one's peers leads to a self-fulfilling BAD-ME circuit. Many adults on the autistic spectrum will recall not fitting in with peers at school, maybe being bullied for being different, and therefore choosing to spend long periods of time alone in solitary play. Losing out on the vasopressin of peer play means that sex subsequently becomes dysfunctional, and the person may choose to have solitary sexual encounters via the internet, or even choose to be asexual. More will be discussed regarding these neurodivergent processes in the next chapter.

Another major attachment injury that may occur at this stage of development is being sent to boarding school. The secure base is wrenched away from a child, as it is the home environment and the parenting that creates the secure attachment. Being placed in an alien environment, into dormitories where a lot of sexual acting out takes place, surrounded by peers who use bullying as a means of maintaining pecking order, may be terrifying for an already insecure child. It would compound their feelings of being unwanted, unlovable, worthless, with a strong sense of rejection and abandonment. The child may feel they have no right to feel unhappy, as the parent may have sacrificed a lot financially to provide what it considered to be a superior education. Duffell (2014) calls this privileged abandonment, which ridicules vulnerability, and demands self-reliance. These children soon learn that they cannot express their distress and have to remain silent about any abuse that takes place within the dormitory for fear of being shamed and humiliated by their peers. Sanderson (2014) emphasises that the paradox of this pseudo-adult behaviour is that it blocks normal developmental maturation, pushing emotional needs outside of conscious awareness, leading to the person becoming mentally 'stuck' at this age despite the body maturing. Again, this is a real risk situation especially for boys, who will not have the social maturity of their female peers.

Insecure attachment behavioural styles

Secure, avoidant, preoccupied, ambivalent and unresolved/disorganised attachment styles have all been identified in adult relating (Feeney, Noller & Hanrahan, 1994).

Secure adults are like secure infants. They express need and distress in clear and communicative ways, and have coherent access to positive and negative feelings about their attachment experiences. They use the SEEKING, CARE, PLAY and PANIC circuits appropriately, allowing the brain to develop the ability to form attachments, regulate intense emotions, learn empathy reciprocity, learn about shame and to respond to it appropriately (Schore, 1994), reduce the narcissism and omnipotence of infancy, and to develop a strong sense of self. So, a secure attachment system physically nourishes emotional and cognitive nerve and brain systems to support affective self-regulation.

Adults with a preoccupied attachment style have hyperactivation of the attachment system, feeling overwhelmed and flooded with emotions associated with early attachment experiences. They are unable to contain and regulate memories and emotions associated with these experiences leading to hyperactivating or heightening emotional cues so that they will get looked after. This adult cannot contain the feelings of loss, even though the loss was in infancy or childhood. Their sense of self is so lacking, they feel so unimportant, they only feel 'whole' when they are with their attachment figure, thus they will constantly demand reassurance, and will be constantly checking to make sure the attachment figure is available for them. No matter how much reassurance is offered, it will never be enough. The preoccupied adult will overuse the FEAR circuit which is defended against with hot anger; thus they will often be described as volatile, with loved ones describing walking on eggshells, as demands for validation and desirability are made for the reassurance that is never satiated.

Adults with an avoidant attachment style demonstrate deactivation of the attachment system psychologically and physically, as a result of feeling that shame and humiliation of not having their needs met in infancy. They may as an adult idealise early relationship experiences, especially of a departed parent, yet describe painful memories in a detached often contradictory way. They tend to minimise and over regulate their emotions that may disrupt their functioning with structures for containing and suppressing emotion, refusing to respond to their body's signals of distress. They are rigid and highly organised, designed to minimise or deactivate emotions that disrupt attachments. Adults who are avoidant find intimacy too threatening. They have lost before; they are not willing to let others close enough to be hurt again. When in sexual relationships, reduced oxytocin release in sexual climax may lead to sex being experienced as a mechanical, unloving experience, rather than something that is accompanied by warm loving feelings. This may explain why individuals with an avoidant or disorganised attachment style often report that they regard sex without love as a pleasurable experience.

An adult with an avoidant attachment style tends to overuse the RAGE circuit, which is a seething, passive-aggressive anger. Their sense of self has a strong BAD-ME circuit, which they may cover with a compensatory narcissistic overlap, which protects them from the humiliation of needing a caregiver who cannot or will not offer CARE. Thus, the narcissism is a cloak that covers the sense of self, puffing up the self in importance, and they may develop sneering attitudes to those the person considers needy. Unlike the classic narcissist, whose hubristic pride goes to the very core of their sense of self, always viewing themselves as superior in mind, intellect and prowess, the compensatory narcissist always has subconscious knowledge of their BAD-ME, so goes to great lengths and many adaptations to cover up their dependency needs. That is why I may refer to it as a cloak of many colours and many layers. The window of therapeutic opportunity to start removing the layers to find the real person beneath is when the individual metaphorically looks in the mirror to see the person that they have become, and for a brief moment, may not like what they see. That is the opportunity to start therapeutically removing the layers slowly and gently to prevent a defensive attack of narcissistic rage.

Some adults demonstrate an ambivalent attachment style, swinging between preoccupied and avoidant triggered by emotional or stressful events. They often remember their parents as unfair. They fear rejection and abandonment and are preoccupied and ruminate in worrying about their relationships. They can show heightened displays of distress and anger with a tendency to catastrophise, flipping from being very needy to being cold or rejecting. Or perhaps solicitous and compliant to gain acceptance, but showing passive aggression to their attachment figures.

Lastly, some individuals have experienced trauma during the first three years of life when the attachment circuitry is developing. These people commonly develop a disorganised attachment style. Sometimes called 'type D' (Main & Solomon, 1986), it is very common in children with traumatic or abusive histories. But trauma need not be a single event, but a pervasive life of not getting their appropriate needs met. Loss can traumatise a child, especially if they have lots of negative experiences as a consequence, as does domestic violence within the family and its unpredictability, migration from one community to another, and more so from one culture to another. Green (1983) argued that if the mother is suffering with depression when her child is born, it can have a devastating effect on the emotional development of her child, leading to emotional neglect. Such children can absorb their mother's depression, and increase the child's risk of depression in their adult life (Taillieu et al., 2016). The children are six times more likely to experience emotional difficulties and eleven times more likely to be hyperaggressive (Chemtob, Nomura & Abromovitz, 2008). It can also lead the child to being pre-programmed to over-identification with sadness, making them less responsive to it in others (Lopez-Duran et al., 2012). Kathryn Stauffer (2021) argued that this emotional neglect is just another form of abuse; that neglect and abuse are interchangeable, as the breakdown in empathy and the lack of attention are common to both, leading to an undermining of the individual's resourcefulness in coping with any further traumatic events that may occur through the person's lifetime.

Abused children often ask themselves two questions: 'Why?' and then 'why me?' (Terr, 1990). They will try to answer these questions by providing personal deficits as to why the abuse occurred; they will not focus on the deficits of the abuser, and this will often lead to a narrative of personal guilt. Blaming yourself for the abuse takes away the concept of perceived vulnerability in the eyes of the other. When the abuser of the child is the significant attachment figure, the child is placed in a conflict, what Siegel and Solomon (2003) called a biological paradox. Strong emotions need to be excluded for fear that the attachment will be lost, creating strong attachments to their abuser, seeking their proximity, even being parental toward the abusing parent, accompanied by avoidance and fear, an unsolvable dilemma. These children not only blame themselves for the abuse, internalising their shame, especially if they found they had pleasurable bodily sensations, but ashamed of wanting or needing CARE, and fear the consequent rejection and abandonment. They also absorb the projected shame of the abuser (Sanderson, 2014). And the demand for secrecy can elicit even more shame from the collusion of keeping that secret; it is common for abused children not to tell, as the fear of what might happen if one tells is scarier than the abuse that is known. These children, when adults, show sequential displays of contradictory behaviour; they may display disorientated wandering, dazed expressions, rapid changes in mood, blank faces, glazed looks and stilled activity (Main & Solomon, 1990). Their experience of grief, loss or trauma (fright without solution plus feeling helplessness) leads to physical shutdown and dissociation; this immobilisation is a defence strategy. It is the dorsal vagal response of disorganised attachment (Schore, 1994). Their sense of self may be totally fragmented, and may even manifest in multiple selves. This can lead to a diagnosis of complex post-traumatic stress disorder (C-PTSD), now recognised by the ICD-11, which they identify as manifesting strong feelings of shame or guilt, emotional dysregulation, destructive and risk-taking behaviour with suicidal ideation. Most importantly, there is an inability to trust in significant relationships (including with a therapist).

The neuroscience of trauma

Chronic stress, whether in a developing child or the mother, can produce structural changes in the brain (De Bellis et al., 1999). The brain will reduce in size, as will the corpus collosum, the band of fibres that allow the two hemispheres to communicate with each other. The hypothalamus will be reduced and the amygdala enlarged (Teicher, 2002), which is specifically a risk factor for male infants as they show a stronger right amygdala activation than females (Schneider et al., 2011); the right brain being the place where early trauma is stored without words to describe it. The connections between the amygdala and basal ganglia in the mid brain and the cognitive executive functions in the prefrontal cortex deplete with catecholamines, our stress hormones; excessive cortisol can produce neural cell death. The consequence of this is less top-down cognitive responses and strengthened bottom-up emotional responses which take precedence (Arnsten et al., 2015). As these neural systems do not hold a concept of time, the responses to past trauma are the same as if the trauma is occurring now. Perry et al. (1995) found that because the young brain is so malleable, severely traumatised children revealed various adaptive mental and physical responses to trauma, including hyperarousal, intrusion of the indelible imprint of the event, and constriction, the numbing response of surrender (Herman, 1992), leading to dissociation. As the brain uses a use-dependent neurological pathway process, re-stimulation of a past event can lead to sensitisation to the trauma, an exaggerated response to it, or maladaptive behaviour patterns, like a hypervigilant watchful state in a frozen body. Trauma can also interfere with the interpersonal flow and communication between two brains (or more), which is the thought processes of two minds, effecting an individual's relationships with others. This may be in a positive way, as with therapy, or in a negative way, as in abuse. Changes in the structure of the brain can produce changes in the process of the mind; and changes in the process of the mind can produce structural changes in the brain (Siegel, 2003), so our early experiences shape the connections that make our sense of self from our maturing mind.

Studies show that there is a higher rate of trauma and childhood aversity in people who commit sexual offences than the general population. It is for this reason that any therapeutic work with a forensic population needs to be trauma-informed. Thornberry, Ireland and Smith (2001) found that persistent maltreatment during childhood and adolescence, has stronger and more consistent negative consequences for the adult than does maltreatment experienced only in childhood. However, having one trusted adult as a significant attachment figure, who is mostly or always available to a child or adolescent, significantly influences the development of resilience for them in the face of adversity (Bellis et al., 2017).

Repetition compulsion

One ubiquitous feature of children and adults who have experienced trauma, is the subconscious re-enactment of a specific traumatic event, either in obvious or subtle ways (Moore & Callender, 2022). From her comprehensive research into psychic trauma in young children, Terr (1990) found that behavioural (implicit) memory (fears, play, re-enactment or dreams) was almost universal, and that the children would repeatedly behave in a fashion consonant with the abuse they themselves experienced, even if it was in early infancy. Children will return willingly to their abuser for it to continue, or re-enact the abuse event with other children or toys. Adolescents may search for similar events online, and watch it again and again. Adults may reproduce the event in their behaviour, without any acknowledgement that it was this event that victimised themselves.

First identified by Freud in 1925, he thought repetition compulsion was an unconscious attempt to get control of a trauma and resolve it. However, Bessel van der Kolk (1989) held that repetition compulsion not only inflicts more pain and self-loathing, but can reinforce preoccupation and fixation on the event(s). Judith Lewis Herman (1992) pointed out its 'daemonic quality'; that even if the behaviour had been consciously chosen, there was something involuntary and compulsive about it. I believe this is a phenomenon of how the brain files away the data of life – or, in this case, doesn't file it away. Particularly through adolescent neural pruning, the brain is doing a neural reorganisation process, pruning out unused neural connections. It develops an orderly database of schemata to aid memory-saving and retrieval; chunks of information that when put together, the brain can weave to make a memory. This database will have a metaphorical filing system, where similar items go together to form a narrative of an event. So, for example, if the brain was filing the process of catching a bus, there would be a schema for what the bus looks like, another for the route, another for the bus stop, and maybe another for the fare. It will not remember each individual bus journey, but weaves together these schemata when necessary to provide a narrative of a memory of the event, conjured up with both a label that will cluster all of these schemata chunks, together with emotional tag, depending whether we enjoyed riding on a bus or not. When an event traumatises the child, the brain struggles to find a place to file it, so subconsciously it replays it in implicit memory images (flashbacks), emotions (anxiety, dread, fear), and compulsive behavioural repetition of the traumatic scenario (van der Kolk, 2003). If we were filing papers away into a filing cabinet using the English alphabet, we may happily do so until we come across a file that is headed by, say, a word from the Greek alphabet. We may cast that file to one side in our confusion, or look through all our files to find somewhere relevant to put it. We may revisit it frequently in case the idea comes to us where to put it. This is what the brain is doing. It is trying to make sense of trauma by repetition, by re-running it to see if the filing place becomes clearer. But in doing so, it can subconsciously lead people into the path of inappropriate repetitive behaviour. For example, Veneziano, Veneziano and LeGrand (2000) found a correlation between how offenders were offended against as children, compared to their adult offences. So, if an offender was abused before 5 years old, they were more like to target under 5s themselves. It is the hippocampus in the limbic system of the left brain that aids our memory processing, contextualising a memory in a timeline with a beginning, a middle and an end (Rothschild, 2000). If the foetus or infant has been exposed to high levels of cortisol from the triggering fear systems of the enlarged amygdala, the hippocampus fails to develop sufficiently to provide the contextual ending of a traumatic event, as an infant has no concept of future, only past and present (Heard, Lake & McClusky, 2009), so therefore it keeps repeating it subconsciously in the present. Thus, people are influenced by their past and may re-enact it without ever consciously remembering that they are doing so (Schacter, 1996) as the saving of an implicit memory, the storage of it, and its retrieval are all separate neural process in a damaged and underdeveloped hippocampus.

Gordon's review

When the therapist considers Gordon's childhood history, some of the trauma processes are self-evident: the domestic violence between his parents, the experience of loss of his biological father, the sexual abuse from the stranger in the park, and the physical abuse from his stepfather. But what is not so self-evident is that he was an overlooked and emotionally neglected child, and some would argue that this pervasive chronic injury is a desecration of the self, giving a sense of shame that is catastrophic, overwhelming and all-consuming, as Stauffer argues:

> An ignored child may feel they are disgusting, or greedy, or just 'wrong' – deep down, lacking in some essential human quality. Their shame will have an all-pervasive quality, as if the person's identity and their very soul is shameful.
>
> (Stauffer, 2021, p. 18)

This sense of shame is so impregnable, that Gordon's strategies for his very being subconsciously will be focused on hiding the shame that he feels others can see. And the additional self-evident physical traumas he experienced will be attributed to his lack of worth, that he somehow deserved the bad things that happened to him, that he was not worthy of love and care. So, as a child, he stole food and money because he was hungry, or exchanged sex for food, because he felt he was a bad person, and that's what bad people do. He will not be angry with his mother for not taking appropriate care of him, it will be his fault, and if he were a better son, then that wouldn't have happened.

How does one face the world with such a burden of shame? Some people implode with corroding anxiety and depression, or both, leading to long-term mental health issues. Others, like Gordon, develop a false self, a metaphorical cloak that they will wear to hide what they feel others will see if they allow themselves to be known. This false self might be in the form of constant care-giving of others, hiding their own needs and putting everyone else's needs above their own, so that people cannot see how unworthy they are. This fits in with a preoccupied attachment style, constantly on the look-out for a way to prove to others that they are of worth. Gordon, however, wore a cloak of avoidance, keeping himself away from the penetrating eyes of others, focusing on proving his worth at how clever he was with engine mechanics, and in doing so, developed a sneering, disparaging view of others who could not achieve what he achieved. This is the cloak of compensatory narcissism.

In his therapeutic assessment, Gordon is already starting to identify his previous behaviour as being inappropriate, and is starting to learn how to express himself in different ways. He is taking small steps, but they are going in the right direction. In psychodynamic terms, his therapist is becoming his 'good enough mother', as she coaches him in mindfulness techniques, and he reports back his progress. But she is also gently steering him away from potentially dangerous situations; if you like, doing an ongoing risk assessment. It is not that she feels he would be a risk to the old lady he has made friends with, but attack from others, if they misperceived his intentions, may retrigger his potential for lashing out. Also, she identified another issue: repetition compulsion. She identified that his finding a friend with an old lady in the park repeated his childhood of finding a friend in the park leading to his abuse. It is vital that these two events do not cross in his mind, leading him to subconsciously act out toward the old lady, as he has said he would like to do toward his abuser. She made a point of discussing this with Gordon, so he could clearly distinguish between the two events in the here and now.

References

Arnsten, A.F.T., Raskind, M.A., Taylor, F.B. & Connor, D.F. (2015) The effects of stress exposure on prefrontal cortex: Translating basic research into successful treatments for post-traumatic stress disorder. *Neurobiol. Stress*, 1, 89–99. doi:10.1016/j.ynstr.2014.10.002.

Bellis, M.A., Hardcastle, K., Ford, K., Hughes, K. *et al.* (2017). Does continuous trusted adult support in childhood impart life-course resilience against adverse childhood experiences – a retrospective study on adult health-harming behaviours and mental well-being. *BMC Psychiatry*, 17 (1), 110.

Bingham, B., Gray, M., Sun, T. & Viau, V. (2011). Postnatal blockade of androgen receptors or aromatase impair the expression of stress hypothalamic-pituitary-adrenal axis habituation in male rats. *Psychoneuroendocrinology*, 36 (2), 249–257. doi:10.1016/j.psyneuen.2010.07.015.

Bowlby, J. (1988). *A secure base: Parent–child attachment and healthy human development.* New York: Basic Books.

Chemtob, C.M., Nomura, Y. & Abromovitz, R.A. (2008). Impact of conjoined exposure to the World Trade Centre attacks and to other traumatic events on behavioural problems of preschool children. *Archives of Paediatrics and Adolescent Medicine*, 162 (2), 126. doi:10.1001/archpediatrics.2007.36.

De Bellis, M., Keshavan, M., Clark, D., Casey, B., Giedd, J., Boring, A., Frustaci, K. & Ryan, N. (1999). Developmental traumatology Part II: Brain development. *Biological Psychiatry*, 45(10), 1271–1284.

Depue, R.A. & Morrone-Strupinsky, J.V. (2005). A neurobehavioral model of affiliative bonding. *Behavioural and Brain Sciences*, 28, 313–395. doi:10.1017/S0140525X05000063.

Duffell, N. (2014). *Wounded leaders: British elitism and the entitlement illusion. A psychohistory.* London: Lone Arrow Press.

Feeney, J.A., Noller, P. & Hanrahan, M. (1994). Assessing adult attachment: developments in the conceptualisation of security and insecurity. In M.B. Sperling and W.H.

Berman (eds), *Attachment in adults: Clinical developmental perspectives* (pp. 128–152) New York: Guilford Press.

Freud, S. (1925). *The unconscious: Collected papers*. London: Hogarth.

Gilbert, P. (1998). What is shame? Some core issues and controversies. In P. Gilbert & B. Andrews (eds), *Shame: Interpersonal behaviour, psychopathology and culture* (pp. 3–36). New York: Oxford University Press.

Gilbert, P. (2011). The evolution of social attractiveness and its role in shame, humiliation, guilt and therapy. *British Journal of Medical Psychology*, 70 (2), 113–147. doi:10.1111/j.2044-8341.1997.tb01893.x.

Green, A. (1983). The dead mother. In *Private madness* (pp. 142–174) London: Rebus.

Heard, D., Lake, B. & McClusky, U. (2009). *Attachment therapy with adolescents and adults: theory and practice post Bowlby*. London: Karnac.

Herman, J. L. (1992). *Trauma and recovery: From domestic abuse to political terror*. London: Pandora.

Hines, M., Constantinescu, M. & Spencer, D. (2015). Early androgen exposure and human gender development. *Biol Sex Differ*, 6 (3). doi:10.1186/s13293-015-0022-1.

Hudson Allez, G. (2011). *Infant losses, adult searches: A neural and developmental perspective on psychopathology and sexual offending*. London: Karnac.

Kigar, S.L. & Auger, A.P. (2013). Epigenetic mechanisms may underlie the aetiology of sex differences in mental health risk and resilience. *Journal of Neuroendocrinology*, 25 (11), 1141–1150. doi:10.1111/jne.12074.

Lopez-Duran, N.L., Kuhlman, K.R., George, C. & Kovacs, M. (2012). Facial emotional expression recognition by children at familial risk for depression: high-risk boys are over-sensitive to sadness. *The Journal of Child Psychology and Psychiatry*, 54 (5), 565–574. doi:10.1111/jcpp.12005.

Machin, A. (2018). *The life of dad: The making of the modern father*. London: Simon & Schuster.

Main, M. & Solomon, J. (1986). Discovery of an insecure-disorganized/disoriented attachment pattern. In T.B. Brazelton & M.W. Yogman (eds), *Affective development in infancy*. New York: Ablex Publishing.

Main M. & Solomon J. (1990). Procedures for identifying infants as disorganized/disoriented during the Ainsworth Strange Situation. In M.T. Greenberg, D. Cicchetti & E.M. Cummings (eds), *Attachment in the preschool years* (pp. 121–160). Chicago, IL: University of Chicago Press.

Matos, M. & Pinto-Gouveia, J. (2014). Shamed by a parent or by others: The role of attachment in shame memories relation to depression. *International Journal of Psychology and Psychological Therapy*, 2, 217–244.

Moore, C. & Callender, N. (2022). Trauma, psychosis, and violent offending. In P. Willlmot & L. Jones (eds), *Trauma-informed forensic practice* (pp. 197–211). Abingdon: Routledge.

Panksepp, J. (1998). *Affective neuroscience: The foundations of human and animal emotions*. New York: Oxford University Press.

Perry, B. D., Pollard, R.A., Blakley, T. L., Baker, W. L. & Vigilante, D. (1995). Childhood trauma, the neurobiology of adaptation, and 'use-dependent' development of the brain. How states become traits. *Infant Mental Health Journal*, 16 (4), 271–291. doi:10.1002/1097-0355(199524)16:4<271.

Porges, S.W. (2003). Social engagement and attachment: A phylogenetic perspective. *Annals of the New York Academy of Sciences*, 1008, 31–47. doi:10.1196/annals.1301.004.

Porges, S.W. (2017). Vagal pathways: Portals to compassion. In E.M. Seppälë (ed.), *The Oxford handbook of compassion science* (pp. 189–204). Oxford: Oxford University Press.

Rothschild, B. (2000). *The body remembers: The psychophysiology of trauma and trauma treatment.* New York: Norton.

Sanderson, C. (2014). *Counselling skills for working with shame.* London: Jessica Kingsley.

Schacter, D.L. (1996). *Searching for memory: The brain, the mind and the past.* New York: Basic Books.

Schaffer, H.R. & Emerson, P.E. (1964). The development of social attachments in infancy. *Monographs for Research in Child Development*, 29 (3), 1–77. doi:10.2307/1165727.

Schneider, S., Bromberg, P.U., Brassen, S., Menz, M.M. *et al.* (2011). Boys do it the right way: sex-dependent, amygdala lateralisation during face processing in adolescents. *NeuroImage*, 56 (3), 1847–1853. doi:10.1016/j.neuroimage.2011.02.019.

Schore, A. (1994). *Affective regulation and the origin of the self.* Hillsdale, NJ: Lawrence Erlbaum.

Schore, A. (2003). Early relational trauma, disorganised attachment and the development of a predisposition to violence. In D. Siegel & M. Solomon (eds), *Healing trauma: Attachment, mind, body and brain.* New York: Norton.

Siegel, D.J. (2003). An interpersonal neurobiology of psychotherapy. In D.J. Siegel & M.F. Solomon (eds), *Healing trauma: Attachment, mind, body & brain* (pp. 1–56). New York: Norton.

Siegel, D.J. & Solomon, M.F. (2003). Introduction. In D.J. Siegel & M.F. Solomon (eds), *Healing trauma: Attachment, mind, body & brain* (pp. xiii–xxi). New York: Norton.

Stauffer, K.A. (2021). *Emotional neglect and the adult in therapy.* New York: Norton.

Stern, D. (1995). *The motherhood constellation.* New York: Basic Books.

Taillieu, T.L., Brownridge, D.A., Sareen, J. & Afifi, T.O. (2016). Childhood emotional maltreatment and mental disorders: Results from a nationally representative adult sample from the United States. *Child Abuse & Neglect*, 59, 1–12. doi:10.1016/j.chiabu.2016.07.005.

Taylor, D. (1969). Differential rates of cerebral maturation between sexes and between hemispheres: Evidence from epilepsy. *The Lancet*, 294 (7612), 140–142. doi:10.1016/S0140-6736(69)92445-92443.

Teicher, M. H. (2002). Scars that will not heal: The neurobiology of child abuse. *Scientific American*, 286 (1), 54–61.

Terr, L. (1990). *Too scared to cry: Psychic trauma in childhood.* New York: Harpers & Row.

Thornberry, T.P., Ireland, T.O. & Smith, C.A. (2001). The importance of timing: The varying impact of childhood and adolescent maltreatment on multiple outcomes. *Development and Psychopathology*, 13 (4), 957–979.

Tremblay, R.E., Japel, C., Pérusse, D. & McDuff, P. (1999). The search for the age of 'onset' of physical aggression: Rousseau and Bandura revisited. *Criminal Behaviour and Mental Health*, 9 (1), 8–23. doi:10.1002/cbm.288.

Trevarthen, C. (2001). The neurobiology of early communication: intersubjective regulations in human brain development. In A. F. Klaverboer & A. Gramsbergen (eds), *Handbook on brain and behaviour in human development.* Dordrecht: Kluwer.

van der Kolk, B. A. (1989). The compulsion to repeat the trauma. *Psychiatric Clinics of North America*, 12 (2), 389–411.

van der Kolk, B.A. (2003). Posttraumatic stress disorder and the nature of trauma. In D.J. Siegel & M.F. Solomon (eds), *Healing trauma: Attachment, mind, body & brain* (pp. 168–195). New York: Norton.

Veneziano, C., Veneziano, L. & LeGrande, S. (2000). The relationship between adolescent sex offender behaviours and victim characteristics with prior victimisation. *Journal of Interpersonal Violence*, 15 (4), 363–374. doi:10.1177/088626000015004002.

Verrier, N. N. (2009). *The primal wound: Understanding the adopted child.* Baltimore, MD: Gateway Press.

Weinberg, M.K., Beeghly, M., Olson, K.L. & Tronick, E. (2008). A still-face paradigm for young children: 2 ½ year -olds' reactions to maternal unavailability during the still-face. *J. Dev. Process*, 3 (1), 4–22.

Weinberg, M.K., Tronick, E.Z., Cohn, J.F. & Olson, K.L. (1999). Gender differences in emotional expressivity and self-regulation during early infancy. *Developmental Psychology*, 35 (1), 175–188. doi:10.1037//0012-1649.35.1.175.

Winnicott, D. W. (1960). The theory of parent-infant relationship. *International Journal of Psycho-Analysis*, 41, 585–595.

Wurmser, L. (1995). *The mask of shame.* Northvale, NJ: Aronson.

Zahn-Waxler, C, Shirtcliff, E.A. & Marceau, K (2008). Disorders of childhood and adolescence: gender and psychopathology. *Annual Review of Clinical Psychology*, 4, 275–303. doi:10.1146/annurev.clinpsy.3.022806.091358.

Chapter 4

What is neurodiversity?

Case study

The therapist noticed that Gordon looked cleaner now. He was starting to take notice of his appearance. He had had his hair cut and was cleanly shaven. His skin looked less spotty and the dark rings around his eyes had almost vanished.

'Gordon, we need to talk about the results of the ASQ that you filled out online. You scored 45 out of a possible 50, which is quite a high score, indicating you may have Asperger's syndrome, or what it is often known as high functioning autism. Have you done any research into this on your own?'

'Yes.' He shuffled in the chair. 'I spent hours going round and round on Google. But I am not sure what it means for me. Does it mean that I have some form of problem, like? Have I got a screw loose?'

'No, not at all. I would like you to think of it as a difference, rather than a problem or deficit. It generally means that your thinking processes are different from others. For example, you told me that when you are repairing a car engine, you visualise the parts you need, rather than naming them, so you use a catalogue with images in to find the bits that you need.'

'Yes, but I know my way round that book so well now. It's rare that I need to look something up.' He risked a quick look at the therapist's face to check she approved.

She nodded. 'This is extremely common for someone who thinks like you, to think in pictures rather than words. It is probably what makes you such a skilled mechanic. You can "see" what is wrong and how it needs to be repaired perhaps in a way that others might take longer to do. This means it is, for you, a strength, not a weakness.'

She allowed him some silent space to absorb this information.

Then she continued, after he gave a sharp nod, 'It may also account for why you have struggled to make friends, and have difficulty in social situations. Indeed, it also may account for why you cannot put your feelings into words, although in fairness, I think from your upbringing, you were never taught or encouraged to do that.'

DOI: 10.4324/9781003330899-4

'Nah.' He grimaced. 'Wasn't allowed to say much or I'd get me 'ead bashed against the wall.'

The therapist closed her eyes momentarily. 'This score isn't a definitive diagnosis, as such, Gordon, but we don't need that to work out how to make things easier for your way forward. By having a general understanding of your neurodivergence, it will help us build on your strengths that it brings, especially your ability to think outside the box, and to improve on your weaknesses, like your struggle with eye contact and making friends. If things make sense to us both, that makes your recovery so much easier.'

What is neurodiversity?

Neurodiversity is a group name used to refer to a cluster of presentations of people who are on a spectrum of divergent thinking and behavioural styles, that have common difficulties in sensory-emotional social communication; for example, presentations on the autistic spectrum (ASD), or issues of dyslexia or dyspraxia. These neurodivergent styles, or neurodivergent strategies, are thought to be due to variations in how the pathways in the brain, commonly manifested during early infant development, lead to differences in adult cognitive methods of structuring and analysing our world. A caveat is in order here. It is essential when considering whether a person is on the spectrum to appraise the presentations as to whether the child/adult is male or female, as the behavioural patterns that they manifest tended to be gender specific, whereas most research and behavioural accounts are based on males with ASD.

These different cognitive processes are thought to be innate, or genetic, whereas others are thought to be due to childhood trauma, or long-term use of recreational drugs. As a consequence, such individuals, as they grow older may have differences in learning and attention, may have difficulty in making friends and later loving relationships, struggle with making eye contact and small talk, have mood swings and sometimes obsessive-compulsive obsessions and extreme emotional attachments. As discussed in Chapter 3, at school they are frequently bullied, as other children identify that they don't quite fit in, even when their parents can't or won't identify it. The essential issue with this presentation is that each individual has a different level of ability on IQ, cognitive inference, sensory tolerance, visual-spatial and verbal reasoning, attention span and focusing, and social and relationship levels, making it more complex than a simple continuous spectrum from high to low. As such, there is much criticism of the term 'high functioning autistic', as it can deny support to those who are deemed as having high IQ and also restrict agency and autonomy to those classified as 'low functioning' (Alvares *et al.,* 2020). Although the term may not be specifically about IQ as suggested, it does appear that those with a phenotype of high IQ, poor social functioning, and obsessive-compulsive cognitive processes can fall into a trap of online offending, and it is to this presentation that I will refer when discussing being on the spectrum of ASD throughout this book.

Neurodiversity includes presentations such as Asperger's syndrome, dyslexia, dyscalculia, dyspraxia, attention deficit (ADD) and attention deficit and hyperactive disorder (ADHD), but also mental (ill) health concepts like bipolar and schizophrenia. If a person is neurotypical, it means that their thinking/ behavioural neural style mechanisms function in a conventional way. Alternatively, a person may have a divergent thinking style. For example, those with ASD may have encyclopaedic memories for facts and are often highly intelligent, but that does not register in some sections of an IQ test. They may be capable of focusing for long periods on tasks that take advantage of their natural gift for focusing on computerised data, or detecting flaws in visual patterns, especially if their thinking pattern occurs visually instead of verbally, whereas neurotypical people tend to be easily distracted and can lack the attention to detail that neurodivergent people can do. But their subjective experience of the world may be chaotic and intense which compounds social difficulties and impedes social development (Walker, 2014).

The term 'neurodiversity' was coined in 1998 by Australian sociologist Judy Singer in her Honours thesis, herself on the autistic spectrum. She argued:

> For me, the key significance of the 'autism spectrum' lies in its call for and anticipation of a politics of neurological diversity, or neurodiversity. The neurologically different represent a new addition to the familiar political categories of class/gender/race and will augment the insights of the social model of disability.
>
> (Singer, 1999, p. 64)

This concept was taken up by journalist Harvey Blume, who helped popularise the concept: 'Neurodiversity may be every bit as crucial for the human race as biodiversity is for life in general. Who can say what form of wiring will prove best at any given moment? Cybernetics and computer culture, for example, may favour a somewhat autistic cast of mind' (Blume, 1998b). He had previously argued:

> in trying to come to terms with [a neurotypical-dominated] world, autistics are neither willing nor able to give up their own customs. Instead, they are proposing a new social compact, one emphasizing neurological pluralism. [...] The consensus emerging from the internet forums and Web sites where autistics congregate [...] is that NT [neurotypical] is only one of many neurological configurations – the dominant one certainly, but not necessarily the best.
>
> (Blume, 1998a)

It was Blume's belief that the internet was the only way that people on the autistic spectrum could improve their lives, in allowing them to communicate freely in a way that they cannot under usual social conditions, and the internet provides the perfect forum for them. The concept was later taken up by Kassiane Sibley, (later known as Kassiane Asasumasu) who coined the term neurodivergent to describe an individual and neurodivergence to describe these atypical cognitive/behavioural styles (Sibley, 2004).

The neurodiversity paradigm is also gaining momentum in special education by helping students make the most of their native strengths and special interests, rather than focusing on trying to correct their 'deficits' or 'normalise' their behaviour. This is a more effective method of educating young people with atypical minds so they can make meaningful contributions for themselves, and for society.

> We don't pathologise a calla lily by saying it has a 'petal deficit disorder'. We simply appreciate its unique beauty. We do not diagnose individuals who have skin colour different from our own as suffering from 'pigmentation dysfunction'. That would be racist. Similarly, we ought not to pathologise Australian children who have different kinds of brains and different ways of thinking and learning.
>
> (Armstrong, 2012, p. 9)

Neurodiversity advocates denounce the framing of autism, attention deficit, dyslexia, and other neurodevelopmental divergent disorders as requiring medical intervention to cure or 'fix' them, and instead promote support systems such as positive inclusion-focused services. The intention is for individuals to receive support that encourages human diversity rather than treatment which focused on them to adopt a perceived view of the norm. Neurodiversity advocates point out that neurodivergent people often have exceptional abilities alongside their deficits. In particular, people on the autistic spectrum may have a savant, or exceptional ability, in a specific narrow domain like mathematics or building design, but equally cannot manage their time, their phones or their organise their lives.

Neurodiversity advocate John Elder Robison agrees that neurological difference may sometimes produce disability, but at the same time he argues that the disability caused by neurological difference may be inseparable from the strengths it provides.

> 99 neurologically identical people fail to solve a problem, it's often the 1% fellow who's different who holds the key. Yet that person may be disabled or disadvantaged most or all of the time. To neurodiversity proponents, people are disabled because they are at the edges of the bell curve, not because they are sick or broken.
>
> (Robison, 2013)

Asperger's syndrome

The prevalence of Asperger's syndrome is thought to be 1 person in 250. Lorna Wing was the first to use the term Asperger's syndrome when considering children with autism might be on a spectrum of ability (Wing, 1981), noting Hans Asperger (1944) who identified a pattern in developing children considered then to have autistic personality disorder. He noticed that their social abilities were delayed, making it difficult to make friends or understand the rules of social interactions. They would be very pedantic and some had an unusual tone in their speech, being flat and emotionless. Their empathy was immature, showing difficulties of understanding a theory of mind (Baron-Cohen, 1995). Some showed themselves to be clumsy and needed ongoing help and support from their parents in organising day-to-day skills. They also demonstrated high sensitivity to particular senses especially sounds and lighting. They also would have very specific preoccupations with specific topics differing from the topics common in young children, over which they can discuss at an adult level, whereas they may be immature talking about other topics common in young children (Aronowitz et al., 1997). Some of these personality characteristics can be shared by other members of the family, especially the fathers, suggesting that the condition might be genetic or neurological, although it is vital to consider that genes are designed to adapt to the environment, and the environment has the capacity to alter genes. Gabor Maté (1999) argues that this is a genetic predisposition rather than a genetic inevitability.

Asperger's syndrome or high functioning autism (hfASD) (DeMyer, Hingtgen & Jackson, 1981) are terms these days that are considered to be interchangeable in clinical practice (Attwood, 2007) but was proposed originally to distinguish between those who have language and intellectual difficulties and those with a greater level of intellectual ability and communicative ability, often greater than the norm. However, many people object to the term hfASD, as it is thought to be discriminatory and demeaning to those of lower functioning. It is true that being on the spectrum is just not about intellectual and languages capability, but is a spectrum of features that can produce a spikey profile on the Wechsler Intelligence Scale (WAIS):

- communication difficulties;
- social impediments;
- intense focus or interests;
- sensitivities; and
- routines and repetition.

Each individual would have a differing level of skill in each category. Whereas the objection to the terminology hfASD is understandable, it does present difficulties in a clinical setting if the presentations cannot be readily distinguished.

Co-occurring conditions that often are identified alongside Asperger's syndrome are attention deficit hyperactivity disorder (ADHD), semantic pragmatic language disorder, Tourette's syndrome, anorexia nervosa, non-verbal learning disability, obsessive compulsive disorder (OCD), and/or generalised anxiety disorder (GAD) (Attwood, 2007). These varying diagnoses suggest the range of behavioural presentations, all neurodivergent in their own right, where each co-occurring condition has similar presentations as those with Asperger's syndrome. For example, it is extremely common for those with Asperger's syndrome to experience high levels of anxiety and depression (GAD), especially when routines are disrupted, when experiencing social difficulties with peers, or when experiencing high levels of sensory stimulation. Similarly, those with Asperger's syndrome may have behaviour or vocal tics which resemble Tourette's syndrome (Ringman & Jankovic, 2000). Or a child who wants to focus attention on their own specific interest, may be totally disinterested in learning about other educational topics as exhorted by teachers or parents (attention deficit), and may get extremely anxious and even hyperactive when pressurised to do so – hence a diagnosis of ADHD, which then means that being on the autistic spectrum can be missed. Rigid and obsessional thinking is common, not just in the form of classic OCD, inviting behavioural rituals to relieve the anxiety, but also rumination of obsessive and unwanted thoughts causing considerable anxiety and distress, sometimes referred to as Pure O. Interestingly, these obsessive thoughts are often the very antithesis of the person's behavioural style, for example, a person may experience a terrible fear that they might be a paedophile if one looked at children inappropriately, even with a lack of sexual arousal toward children. One or several of these co-occurring conditions are considered to be the neurodivergent rule rather than the exception (Attwood, 2007).

Attention deficit hyperactivity disorder and attention deficit disorder

These presentations are usually split into two issues of inattention and hyperactivity, where ADHD comprises both issues whereas attention deficit disorder (ADD) is mainly inattention. To be inattentive, the person demonstrates an inability to focus on tasks for a sustained period of time, can be careless and slapdash in what they are doing, would have their mind elsewhere when someone is speaking to them, and has difficulty in organising and finishing tasks. They are easily distracted, forgetful and sometimes are accused of being lazy and aimless. Hyperactive people are unable to sit still, constantly fidgeting and moving themselves, may often jump out from the seat when they think of something else instead of being able to focus on any task in hand. They may talk excessively, talk over people because they cannot listen and need to get their point across, and blurt out secrets that they are unable to keep to themselves. For someone with ADD, an analogy would be having all the apps on one's smart phone open all at once, and the brain is jumping from one to the next, not wishing to miss anything, yet not really taking anything in.

Brown (2013) sees these as a failure in the executive functioning of the cerebral cortex. That being the case, the issues would not be identified other than rudimentary observation in early childhood, but would become more fixed and apparent as the neural pathways develop and myelinate over the developmental years, although many parents would describe the hyper-activity of their toddlers, who do not necessarily have ADHD. So, observers would be looking to see if a child's behaviour is obsessive and intense in terms of being unable to keep still, unable to focus, or unable to stop making noise. But at such an early stage of neural development, the executive functioning of the cerebral cortex is minimal. What seems to be going on here is an inability to regulate themselves at this early stage, which will help them with their impulse control. Tomasi and Volkow (2012) found from ADHD fMRI studies that there tends to be a default pathway to reward networks, suggesting instant gratification, and an inhibition in the cortical networks that would apply the handbrake to allow for analysis and delayed gratification.

Phil Mollon (2015) describes three core features of having ADHD as an adult: a core sense of chaos and disorganisation; prone to high anxiety and/or rage under stress; and a feeling that life is inherently unrewarding. He suggests that there might be some neural lateralisation process going on; they might be either right brain dominant and over-emotional, or left brain dominant only interested in logic and reasoning, but they struggle with engaging both hemispheres equally, which suggests a problem with the corpus collosum between the two. What we do know is that the chaos and disruption that sits alongside someone with ADHD leads to a feeling of not fitting in with neurotypical people, who find the individuals difficult and sometimes unmanageable. Plus the need for additional stimulation, either by creating drama and arguments in relationships, or the visual stimulation of games on the internet, to be discussed in more detail in the next chapter, becomes a common strategy.

Concentration deficit disorder or sluggish cognitive tempo

Often described as a subsection of ADD, is concentration deficit disorder (CDD), which again is an inability to attend but instead of being hyperalert, they are hypoalert, being sluggish, unmotivated, unable to focus through fogginess, sleepy, absent-minded and forgetful (Barkley, 2015). Whereas the hyperalert individual with ADHD seems to have a hair-triggered HPA (hypothalamus-pituitary-adrenal) axis with the fight and flight system, someone with CDD would seem to have an over-active dorsal vagal system, causing the individual to live in a dissociated fugue state. Barkley (2015) argues that some of the symptoms of CDD overlap with ASD, which suggests that this is also a neurodivergent phenomenon involving different neurophysiological mechanisms. Graham et al. (2013) found CDD to be significantly related to prenatal alcohol exposure, and a correlate to social adversity, which would make sense if its mechanism was based in the dorsal vagal system of the autonomic nervous system.

Is it environment or genetics?

We don't tend to have nature-nurture debates anymore; they are gene-environment interactions. We are not just genetically coded. We need epigenetic social experiences. Our genes can affect how we respond to our given environment, just as our environment can alter the shape of the genome through the release of gonadal steroids producing changes in gene expression, cellular interactions, and neural networks. The developmental path is malleable and constantly influenced by numerous interacting external and internal influences, which may be genetic, hormonal, behavioural, or environmental (Leckman and March, 2011).

The development of the sense of self

Nick Walker, who identifies herself as a queer, autistic, scholar and educator offered the distinction that neurodivergencies refer specifically to pervasive neurocognitive differences that are intimately related to the formation and constitution of the self. Cozolino (2006) agrees. He argues that if a person has not got a theory of mind, then they will not have a theory of body and consequent emotional experiences, which will interfere with the development of the self. Phil Mollon (2015) references Kohut (1977) in the development of the self in developing empathy, soothing, recognition and encouragement usually provided by others in early years, and becomes adopted by the individual as part of the self-regulatory system as the infant matures (Schore, 2014), but in neurodivergent individuals this seems to be impaired.

The development of the self is something that occurs in early months of child development through the attachment system (see previous chapter). Using the pre-programmed neural circuits in the brain stem, sometimes called the reptilian brain, these circuits in the periaqueductal grey direct primary affective and motivational systems before the infant's prefrontal cortex is functional, and are designed for the infant to make attachments in order to stay alive (Panksepp, 1998). The brain stem can feel and communicate emotions, and some suggest that the subjective experience of the self lies within it. Mollon (2015) references Goldberg (2001) who blames the frontal lobes of the brain for the high prevalence of ADHD, as it is the frontal lobes that 'defines your identity, that encapsulates your drives, your ambitions, your personality, your essence' (p. 1). But this does not account for the fact that the frontal lobes are not online as the child is developing their sense of self in early infancy. However Bessell van der Kolk (2014) emphasises that our sense of self occurs in our mid-brain structures, starting above the eyes and running all through the centre to the back, to the posterior cingulate, which gives us our proprioception; that mid brain structures (which are online in infancy) focus on the self, whereas exterior brain structures (which come on line during development) focus on the other.

As discussed in the last chapter, driven by the SEEKING system using the visual, dopamine, and vasopressin pathways, the infant searches for CARE, stimulating more dopamine and oxytocin, allowing PLAY (social development), which turns into a secure attachment relationship with the biological mother (Hudson-Allez, 2011). However, if the CARE is not forthcoming as and when the infant expects it, the amygdala triggers the PANIC circuit leading to feelings of FEAR or RAGE, and also triggers endogenous opioid reduction making separation painful. As such, in these infants there would be a reduction of oxytocin as CARE is bypassed, and Insel (2000) has suggested that the reduction of oxytocin may be a contributory factor in autism. Interestingly, however, it has been found that in some cases of autism, the opioid system has been overactive, making separation from attachment figures less painful and make the bonding less important to them. Solms and Turnbull (2002) suggest that the regulation of the PANIC system sculpting the cortical structures plays a key role in autism and Asperger's Syndrome.

FEAR and RAGE are not negative emotions, but are there for a purpose: to get the attachment figure back into close proximity in order for the infant to survive, and the underpinning of both emotions is the experience of loss. This leads to an insecure attachment, and most notably the PLAY circuit, designed for the development of social interaction and communication, is bypassed. This may account for the reduced size found in the brain stem of those on the autistic spectrum (Hashimoto et al., 1995), among many other neural differences discovered, that might occur as a snowball effect (Cozolino, 2006). The struggle with social interaction and social communication is a common struggle that people on the autistic spectrum experience, but may be overlooked if the child/adult is considered to be functioning well. A reduced or missing PLAY circuit will increase the size of the SEEKING circuit, as the infant will know something is missing (see Figure 4.1). An enlarged SEEKING circuit will lead to enlarged PANIC as the child will never feel safe and will have an ongoing pervasive sense of anxiety. As the SEEKING circuit uses the eyes for its frame of reference, this will also be enhanced, and may account for why so many neurodivergent individuals speak of thinking in pictures. With the visual pathways enhanced, some of the cognitive left-brain processes and verbal reasoning may be reduced, leading to less activity between the two neural hemispheres through a diminished corpus collosum. An enlarged PANIC system focusing on fear, rage and loss can lead to the development of a BAD-ME circuit that says, 'I am unloveable'.

Could this bypassing of the PLAY circuit be a contributing factor in the development of Asperger's Syndrome? It was very notable that in Michael Rutter and colleagues' research with Romanian Orphans, they found the prevalence of autistic features, or quasi-autism, in 12 percent of their sample, which was not found in a control study of orphans adopted within the first 6 months of life in the UK (Rutter et al., 1999, 2000), and this finding was based on the malfunctioning end of the autistic spectrum rather than those

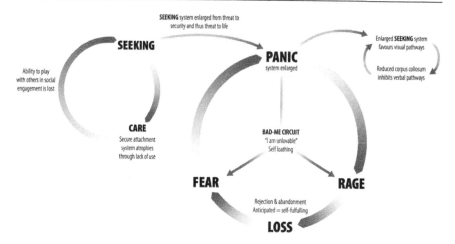

Figure 4.1 It appears with many neurodivergent individuals, the PLAY circuit has been reduced, or bypassed all together. This will enlarge the SEEKING system, which in turn enlarges the PANIC circuit.

who were high functioning. Cozolino (2006) believes that the cerebellum might play a significant role in autism, and Bauman and Kemper (1988) have found structural abnormalities in the cerebellum and limbic forebrain. This area is at the back of the brain stem, which is online at birth, together with the amygdala and hippocampus of the right brain. Similarly, Levin (1991) suggested that the cerebellum houses the sensory-motor memories of 'good mothering' (i.e. the attachment system).

To reiterate, the SEEKING system uses the eyes to search for CARE, and if not available triggers the amygdala in the limbic system of the brain, which in turn triggers the emotional systems of FEAR and RAGE in the attachment system. It has been identified that those on the autistic spectrum struggle with making eye contact with others, thus the usual proto-conversation (Trevarthen, 2001) with mother is not stimulating the child's right hemisphere. Phillips, Baron-Cohen and Rutter, (1992) found through neural imaging techniques that those on the autistic spectrum have no activation in their amygdala. As the amygdala is the gateway to the fight and flight system, this suggests that this PANIC system may fully on, hence the extreme ongoing anxiety that some people on the autistic spectrum sometimes experience, or fully off, suggesting the person may be disengaged from an understanding of potentially dangerous situations.

A very common difficulty experienced by children with ASD is with their peers at school, who seem to identify a difference often before any adult does. Any form of difference to a child will feel threatening unless they have been encouraged by their caregivers in early years to accept difference. Therefore, children are likely to attack what they don't understand, especially during the time of schooling when they are forming a social pecking order. Children with ASD are more likely to encounter teasing, bullying and even sexual assault by their peers than those without ASD (Weiss & Fardella, 2018).

Tony Attwood (2007) identified four compensatory or adjustment strategies that young people with ASD may develop in response to their own realisation on starting school that they are different from other children:

- *A reactive depression*, by being overly apologetic, self-critical and increasingly socially withdrawn (BAD-ME circuit).
- *Denial and arrogance*, to over-compensate for feeling defective in social situations (in therapeutic terms compensatory narcissism). In these cases, the child may perceive themselves more adult than other children and try to discipline or correct them.
- *Imitation.* They often use their high intelligence to observe and mimic those who are socially successful. This is especially the case for girls, and as a consequence their diagnosis can be overlooked, as they experience real problems with trying to convince others that they have a problem with social understanding or empathy.
- *Escape to imagination*, developing complex and imaginary worlds, sometime with make-believe friends.

These adaptive strategies are likely to continue into adolescence and adulthood, with them experiencing further bullying, sexual contact and greater sexual contact victimisation, considered by Brown-Lavoie, Viecili and Weiss (2014) to be due to their lack of sexual knowledge from social sources. This vulnerability is thought to be due to an impaired theory of mind, and an impaired ability to understand the intention of others. Their use of language also provides difficulties, as they tend to make very literal interpretations of what others say, as they don't have the semantic understanding of metaphors or allegories. This would prompt confusion from this lack of understanding and the need to withdraw further to protect themselves, but equally to turn to the internet to seek out what may prove to be malevolent others who claim to be their 'friends', not understanding that there might be a hidden agenda in this 'friendship'. As Tony Attwood (2007) points out, those with Asperger's have difficulty in distinguishing the 'good guys' from the 'bad guys' (p. 99).

When feeling constantly anxious and feeling out of control of situations, or life in general, it is common for individuals to develop very controlling rituals to allow for some certainty in their world. So developing OCD-type rituals is very common place for neurodivergent individuals. Mollon (2015) highlights the paradox for someone with ADHD, who is bombarded by overstimulation of sights and sounds, but equally is under the threat of boredom from the lack of stimulation, leading to an active although unconscious need to elicit arguments and drama, and the threat of addictive pursuits, as we will discuss in the next chapter. He writes: 'Self-esteem is always compromised for people with ADHD, caught between the grandiosity of unmodified narcissism and the reality of impaired achievement and repeated experiences of relational and professional failure' (Mollon, 2015, p. 7).

Links between autism and insecure attachments

There is a closeness between the presentation of autism or Asperger's syndrome, and attachment insecurities, and diagnostic tests have been developed to unpack the differences between the two (McKenzie and Dallos, 2017; Moran, 2010). Coughlan (2018) argues that one of the distinguishing features will be a history of insufficient care, although it is important to trace this history not only pre-natally but to trace the history of the parents and the grandparents because of the transgenerational transmission of unresolved trauma (Coles, 2011). Allan Schore (2014) pointed out that models of autistic aetiology have shifted into an interactive relational model used in other developmental neuropsychiatric disorders, that is the attachment relationship directly influencing the development of the autistic brain. Research has found that infants demonstrating infantile autism have enlarged amygdala in the right hemisphere (Yirmaya & Charman, 2010), which as we have discussed leads to heightened chronic fear states, hyper-reactivity and abnormal fear conditioning that can persist until they are 6 or 7 years old (Kim et al., 2010). Bessel van der Kolk elaborates:

> Having a biological system that keeps pumping out stress hormones to deal with real or imaged threats leads to physical problems: sleep disturbances, headaches, unexplained pain, oversensitivity to touch or sound. Being so agitated or shut down keeps them from being able to focus their attention or concentration. To relieve their tension, they engage in chronic masturbation, rocking, or self-harming activities (biting, cutting, burning, and hitting themselves, pulling their hair out, picking at their skin until it bled). It also leads to difficulties with language processing and fine motor coordination. Spending all their energy on staying in control, they usually have trouble paying attention to things like schoolwork, that are not directly relevant to survival, and their hyperarousal makes them easily distracted.
>
> (van der Kolk 2014, p. 190)

This describes the presentation of a fearful insecure attachment, autistic spectrum and attention deficit hyperactivity disorder.

Guedeney and Fermanian (2001) made comparisons of the behaviour of infants with a disorganised attachment, which they described as a sustained withdrawal, with frozen facial expressions, lack of eye contact, absence of relationships with others, and an impression that the child was beyond reach; this being a classic male presentation of a child on the autistic spectrum. Schore (2014) therefore argued that autism researchers must recognise the contribution of the right amygdala in dissociative states.

We know that a risk factor for autism is within premature babies (Leavey et al., 2013) who are unable to attach to their mothers due to the incubation process. Oxytocin is reduced in premature babies due to the lack of contact with biological mother. Premature babies demand more because they have more needs, so it depends if mother is secure enough and available enough to provide it. Again, this also links to the high prevalence in Romanian orphans, previously discussed, who had no attachment at all.

Coughlan (2018) also points out emerging evidence that children with autism may be more likely to have an uneven cognitive profile, that is, a significant difference between performance and verbal IQ (Melling & Smethurst, 2017). Such profiles tend not to be typically reported in children with attachment difficulties although Coughlan is overlooking that alexithymia, which is a common presentation of a disorganised attachment style and of ASD (Allely, 2022). Clare Allely (2022), referring to the Toronto Alexithymia Scale (Engelbrecht 2022; Bagby, Parker & Taylor, 1994), defines alexithymia as having three components: a difficulty in identifying one's own feelings, a difficulty in describing feelings, and externally orientating ones thinking by ignoring one's emotions. Smith (2009) agrees and argues that it is not a lack of empathy that people on the spectrum experience, rather than the cognitive ability to express it, whereas they can equally have a surfeit of emotional empathy leading to highly aroused states, leading to a significantly higher level of self-harm (Paivio & McCulloch, 2004). In addition, Costa, Steffgen and Vögele (2019) found that parents of children on the autistic spectrum interacted significantly less with their children than parents of neurotypical children. They argued that this reduced interaction was better explained by the children's alexithymia than by children's autistic diagnosis. But there would be a feedback loop, because if children are not encouraged to acknowledge and express feelings, then they would not feel the need to do so. And if the children fail to interact with the parent or fail to give eye-contact, the parent may offer less opportunity or encouragement to do so. This failure to give eye contact stems from a tendency, when looking at faces, instead of looking at the eyes for the perception of emotion to develop empathy, they tend to look at mouths for a perception of anger or threat (possibly due to an abnormality in the amygdala; Adolphs, Sears & Piven, 2001), the consequence being an inability to read facial expressions appropriately, and thus a lack of sympathy, which tends to precede the development of empathy (Heard, Lake & McClusky 2009).

Vivanti and Nuske (2016) point out that while early attachment quality is associated with later social outcomes in neurotypical development, interventions targeting mother interaction with children on the autistic spectrum often show positive effects on parental responsivity and attachment quality, but not on the child's social behaviour. Therefore, improvements in parent-child bonding do not necessarily result in improvements in social functioning of the neurodivergent child. In addition, research into the prevalence of attachment difficulties among children with autism often fails to reflect detailed knowledge of attachment theory (McKenzie and Dallos, 2017), or an understanding of how these two processes interact.

Thorell, Rydell and Bohlin (2012) found a relationship between disorganised attachment and symptoms of ADHD, independently of both executive functioning and conduct issues, arguing the necessity of considering the parent-child dyad to fully understand the child. Similarly, Scholtens et al. (2014) found significantly stronger expressions of ADHD in children with a disorganised attachment style than in those who were securely attached. This connection could not be accounted for either by the overlap between ADHD symptoms with externalising behaviour problems or by cognitive deficits. Phyllis Erdman (1998) argued that insufficient notice of parent-child interactions are taking place in clinical settings, leading to ADHD being misdiagnosed, and even over diagnosed; that a child may display ADHD-like symptoms as a means of obtaining an attachment base, and this discrepancy comes in part from the DSM-V failing to consider the heterogeneity of the presentation of ADHD. Kissgen & Franke (2016) agree, and also point out that insufficient notice is taken on the parental attachment style. It is known that this transgenerational transmission plays a major role in the attachment experiences of the child (van Ijzendoorn & Bakermans-Kraneburg, 1999), and that the prevalence of maternal insecure attachment increased the severity of the child's ADHD symptomology (Kissgen et al., 2009).

If one considers the presentations of neurodivergence and insecure attachment side by side, one can see behavioural patterns emerging (see Figure 4.2).

By virtue of the reduction in protoconversation between the parent and child in early infancy, a neurodivergent child is likely to be operating within an

Figure 4.2 Insecure attachment presentations and neurodivergent presentations offer many similarities.

insecure attachment circuitry. Those who are predisposed to the FEAR circuit, and thus present with a preoccupied attachment style, will be constantly scanning the environment for fear of threat, which means that they can focus less on learning as the visual pathways to the amygdala take preference. The amygdala triggers the HPA axis leading to excess cortisol and adrenaline, making them jumpy, clumsy, anxious and irritable. So here we have the presentations of ADHD and ADD, with the co-occurring presentations of alexithymia, dyslexia, and dyspraxia. Alternatively, with those who are predisposed to use the RAGE circuit present with an avoidant attachment style. They create a distance between themselves and others as closeness is too threatening, as is eye contact. They will disengage themselves from their peers and prefer solitary activities, which leads to their peers targeting them as others identify or feel threatened by the difference. The lack of social connection means that empathy and compassion are minimised, often leading these children/adults to blurt out truths or failings with no diplomacy or empathic tact or consideration of another's feelings. Becoming obsessed and only focusing on what one is interested in leads to high IQ and the development of specialised skills or savants. The price to pay for this, however, is the depressive episodes that occur from the loneliness of the lack of social connection. This is the presentation of people on the autistic spectrum, often described as Asperger's syndrome or high functioning autism.

The link between neurodiversity and adverse childhood experiences

In the previous chapters, I have highlighted that, following the seminal work of Panksepp (1998), an infant would develop either a secure, or insecure, attachment circuit using pre-programmed circuits that are online at birth; six out of seven of these circuits are designed for the survival of the child, while the last is designed for the survival of the species. It does appear, that when a child experiences adverse circumstances either pre- or post-natally during critical periods of their neural development, most particularly during periods of right-hemisphere development, that these circuits, especially the PLAY circuit designed for social development and social communication, gets bypassed. As such the child develops behaviour that has many similarities to those who manifest ADHD. Thorell, Rydell & Bohlin (2012) have demonstrated a strong overlap between a disorganised attachment presentation and ADHD symptoms, although the research is limited due to the researcher's constructs of these two phenomena. Similarly, Bessell van der Kolk (1996) found that the incidence of ADD was 7 times higher for a group of girls who has been sexually abused, compared to those who hadn't been abused. But Maté (1999) argued that it is not the abuse that caused the ADD, but the family environment they are brought up in that allowed the abuse to occur. Mollon (2015) pointed out that neurodivergent adults often report that they were recipients of adverse childhood experiences of parental anger, criticism or violence, and that there is a two-way spiral of interaction between the parent and the child and the way they respond to each other that can lead to an escalation of intense negative emotion.

One issue that is common between both insecure attachment presentations and those with neurodivergent processing is the chronic sense of shame that these children carry, as if they know deep down that they do not fulfil the optimal requirements of development, which is either stuck at some level, or following a different neurological route. This sense of shame is pervasive. Talking about neglected children, Stauffer (2021) highlighted this burden of shame, although exactly the same applies to those who are neurodivergent:

> It feels shameful to be anxious and insecure. It feels shameful to find that they don't enjoy going to clubs and large parties in the same way others do. It feels shameful to be inhibited and socially awkward and unable to make friends easily. It feels shameful to merit the label 'introverted' or 'avoidant'. And in addiction, it feels shameful not to be able to change all this.
>
> (Stauffer, 2021, pp. 18–19)

Could it be, in an infant's developing brain, that the optimal circuitry waiting to be activated and myelinated, is that of the secure attachment process, and as such is a default circuitry for the neurotypical, but there is also a secondary (or even a tertiary) circuit, a neurodivergent circuit, for times when the environment is not optimal? It seems it must be there within us all for the various neurodivergent behavioural processes to present with so many similarities, rather than a kaleidoscope of behavioural differences. This default circuitry to deal with adversity would also protect the child's survival by allowing the development to be conducted through different routes, giving different distinguishing features and talents, rather than allowing all the development to be lost. This may account for how ASD is a difference rather than a deficit; it may take the person longer to reach some aspects of their behaviour, but they may be much quicker at others. This suggests, therefore, that in every human being there is the potential pathway available for neurodivergent processing, and it is our developmental environment that determines which circuitry we would use.

Gordon's review

The therapist was not surprised at Gordon's high score on the ASQ. She had already created a checklist in her assessment for the formulation of the presenting issues that may indicate this. These included a seemingly high IQ despite his lack of educational attainment, which he blamed on dyslexia. He identified a difference in cognitive style, tending to 'think in pictures' rather than words. He has had a lack of friendships throughout his life. Indeed, his wife had been his only friend, which was why her loss was so devastating, even though it was his own behaviour that precipitated it. He had experienced anxiety throughout his life, which he had covered by being argumentative and aggressive. He had a lack of ability to keep still and focus, as his mind flited from one topic to another, leading to teachers suggesting he had ADHD and a conduct disorder due to his aggression. He had also had some deep bouts of depression as he felt alone and alienated from a society that he felt he didn't fit into. Even the bullying at school was predominately because the other children perceived him as different, which he later copied at senior school. He was unable to express his feelings; alexithymia is classic in neurodivergence. And he had obsessive tendencies, which had led to him developing exceptional skills as a car mechanic, the focus of his obsessional information gathering. Finally, he was extremely uncomfortable with eye contact and awkward in his gait.

But is it ASD or is it a disorganised attachment style? Using attachment as a frame, and considering his adverse childhood experiences, his inability to attain any form of educational achievement may be due to the fear he was living under at home, living in a situation of domestic violence. This would have given him an overactive HPA axis, hypervigilance, and a need to constantly scan the environment for threat. Thus, schoolwork and teacher's lessons would have bounced off his protective armour, as he would have been too busy checking out the teacher's nonverbal communication that may have put him in a threat situation. Paradoxically, it often did, because his lack of attention would promote his teacher's wrath, leading to various forms of punishment, and the sniggering and sneering of his fellow schoolchildren. None of the teachers checked out what was going on at his home. They would complain about his stealing and attention-seeking behaviour, but did not consider that he might just have been hungry. They did not ask why he disappeared from school at lunchtime, again presuming bad conduct rather than hunger. His aggression was a protection mechanism that he was role-modelling from both his father and his stepfather in how men should behave, leading him to be the bully when he became big enough and strong enough.

Alexithymia is a common presentation in a person with a disorganised attachment style, as very often they are operating only on a right-brain body-emotional process, with the cognitive narrative switched off; hence no words for feelings. His avoidance in attachment and intimate situations is an early-learned survival strategy; a reluctance to let people close because lowering your guard means taking the risk of being hurt again. No-one can be trusted. The computer provides the only respite. It tells you anything you want to know, you can see anything you want to see, you can make friends under a pseudo-profile, so that no-one knows who you really are. And you can have sex via and with your computer. The internet never lets you down like people do.

Is Gordon's presentation a consequence of neurodivergence, or is it his adverse childhood experiences changing the structure of his brain to automatically use keep-safe mechanisms? It is most likely both. We know that an adverse environment can change the structure of child's brain. We also know that such an environment can alter the gene structure, which can precipitate neurodivergence. And as the outcomes of both are so closely allied, maybe the neural connections and pathways are intertwined, making the similarity in presentation.

When the therapist first discussed the issue with Gordon, he wanted to know if ASD was his diagnosis. He went to his GP, who of course did not know, and reluctantly offered to refer him to a specialist. However, he was advised that the waiting lists were so long, and he wasn't considered a priority case, so it may be three to five years before he was seen. Similarly, if he paid to go privately, there would be a long waiting list and it would be very expensive. When he talked to the therapist about these options, they discussed what difference having a formal 'diagnosis' would make. He therefore decided not to pursue it for the time being, unless something came up that would make the formality an imperative.

References

Adolphs, R., Sears, L. & Piven, J. (2001). Abnormal processing of social information from faces in autism. *Journal of Cognitive Neuroscience*, 13, 232–240.doi:10.1162/089892901564289.

Allely, C.S. (2022). *Autism spectrum disorder in the criminal justice system. A guide to understanding suspects, defendants and offenders with autism.* Abingdon: Routledge.

Alveres, G.A., Bebbington, K., Cleary, D. *et al.* (2020). The misnomer of 'high functioning autism': Intelligence is an imprecise predictor of functional abilities at diagnosis. *Autism*, 24 (1), 221–232. doi:10.1177/1362361319852831.

Armstrong, T. (2012). *Neurodiversity in the classroom: Strength-based strategies to help students with special needs succeed in school and life.* Alexandria, VA: ASCD.

Aronowitz, B.R., DeCaria, C., Allen, A., Weiss, N., Saunders, A., Margolin, L. *et al.* (1997). The neuropsychiatry of autism and Asperger's disorders: Review of the literature and case reports. *CNS Spectrums*, 2, 43–60. doi:10.1017/S1092852900004892.

Asperger, H. (1944). Die Autistisehen Psychopathen im Kindesalter. *Arch. Psych. Nervenkrankh*, 117, 76–136. doi:10.1007/BF01837709.

Attwood, T. (2007). *The complete guide to Asperger's syndrome.* London: Jessica Kingsley.

Bagby, R. M., Parker, J. D. A. & Taylor, G. J. (1994). The twenty-item Toronto Alexithymia Scale-I. Item selection and cross-validation of the factor structure. *Journal of Psychosomatic Research*, 38, 23–32. doi:10.1016/0022-3999(94)90005-1.

Barkley, R.A. (2015). Sluggish cognitive tempo/concentration deficit disorder. Oxford Handbooks Online. doi:10.1093/oxfordhb/9780199935291.013.9.

Baron-Cohen, S. (1995). *Mind blindedness: An essay on autism and theory of mind.* Cambridge, MA: MIT Press.

Bauman, M.L. and Kemper, T.L. (1988). Histoanatomic observations of the brain in early infantile autism. *Neurology*, 35, 866–874. doi:10.1212/wnl.35.6.866.

Blume, H. (1998a). Neurodiversity. *The Atlantic*, 7 November.

Blume, H. (1998b). Neurodiversity: On the neurological underpinnings of geekdom. Retrieved from www.theatlantic.com/magazine/archive/1998/09/neurodiversity/305909/.

Brown, T.E. (2013). *A new understanding of ADHD in children and adults, executive function impairments.* Hove: Routledge.

Brown-Lavoie, S.M., Viecili, M.A. & Weiss, J.A. (2014). Sexual knowledge and victimisation in adults with autistic spectrum disorders. *Journal of Autism and Developmental Disorders*, 44 (9), 2185–2196. doi:10.1007/s10803-014-2093-y.

Coles, P. (2011). *The uninvited guest from the unremembered past*. London: Karnac.

Costa, A.P., Steffgen, G. & Vögele, C. (2019). The role of alexithymia in parent–child interaction and in the emotional ability of children with autism spectrum disorder. *Autism Research*, 12 (3), 458–468. doi:10.1002/aur.2061.

Coughlan, B. (2018). Autism and attachment: A need for conceptual clarity. Retrieved from www.acamh.org/blog/autism-attachment-conceptual-clarity

Cozolino, L. (2006). *The neuroscience of human relationships*. New York: Norton.

DeMyer, M., Hingtgen, J. & Jackson, R. (1981). Infantile autism reviewed: a decade of research. *Schizophrenic Bulletin*, 7, 388–451. doi:10.1093/schbul/7.3.388.

DSM-V-TR. (2022). *Diagnostic and statistical manual of mental disorders, text revision* (5th edition). American Psychiatric Association.

Engelbrecht, N. (2022). Toronto Alexithymia Scale. Retrieved from https://embrace-a utism.com/toronto-alexithymia-scale/

Erdman, P. (1998). Conceptualising ADHD as a contextual response to parental attachment. *The American Journal of Family Therapy*, 26 (2),177–185. doi:10.1080/01926189808251097.

Goldberg, E. (2001). *The executive brain: Frontal lobes and the civilized mind*. New York: Oxford University Press.

Graham, D.M., Crocker, N., Deweese, B.N., Roesch, S.C., Coles, C.D. & Kable, J.A. (2013). Prenatal alcohol exposure, attention-deficit/hyperactivity disorder, and sluggish cognitive tempo. *Alcoholism Clinical and Experimental Research*, 37(Suppl. 1), E338–E346. doi:10.1111/j.1530–0277.2012.01886.x

Guedeney, A. & Fermanian, J. (2001). A validity and reliability study of assessment and screening for sustained withdrawal reaction in infancy The Alarm Distress Baby Scale. *Infant Mental Health Journal*, 22 (5), 559–575. doi:10.1002/imhj.1018.

Guedeney, A., Foucault, C., Bougen, E., Larroque, B. & Mentre, F. (2008). Screening for risk factors of relational withdrawal behaviour in infants aged 14–18 months. *Eur. Psychiatry*, 23, 150–155. doi:10.1016/j.eurpsy.2007.07.008.

Hashimoto, T., Tayama, M., Murakawa, K., Yoshimoto, T. *et al.* (1995). Development of the brainstem and cerebellum in autistic patients. *Journal of Autism and Developmental Disorders*, 25, 1–18. doi:10.1007/BF02178163.

Heard, D., Lake, B. & McClusky, U. (2009). *Attachment therapy with adolescents and adults: Theory and practice post Bowlby*. London: Karnac.

Hudson Allez, G. (2011). *Infant losses, adult searches: A neural and developmental perspective on psychopathology and sexual offending*. London: Karnac.

Insel, T.R. (2000). Toward a neurobiology of attachment. *Review of General Psychiatry*, 4 (2), 176–185. doi:1037/1089-2680.4.2.176.

Kim, J., Lyoo, I.K., Estes, A.M., Renshaw, P.F., Shaw, D.W., Friedman, S.D. *et al.* (2010). Laterobasal amygdala enlargement in 6- to 7-year-old children with autism spectrum disorder. *Arch. Gen. Psychiatry* 67, 1187–1197. doi:10.1001/archgenpsychiatry.2010.148.

Kissgen, R. & Franke, S. (2016). An attachment perspective on ADHD. *Neuropsychiatry*, 30, 63–66. doi:10.1007/s40211-016-0182-1.

Kissgen, R., Krischer, M., Kummetat, V., Spiess, R., Schleiffer, R. & Sevecke, K. (2009). Attachment representation in mothers of children with attention deficit hyperactivity disorder. *Psychopathology*, 42, 201–208. doi:10.1159/000209333.

Kohut, H. (1977). *The restoration of the self.* New York: International Universities Press.

Leavey, A., Zwaigenbaum, L., Heavner, K. & Burstyn, I. (2013). Gestational age at birth and risk of autism spectrum disorders in Alberta, *Canadian Journal of Paediatrics*, 162 (2), 361–368. doi:10.1016/j.jpeds.2012.07.040.

Leckman, J.F. & March, J.S. (2011). Editorial: Developmental neuroscience comes of age. *The Journal of Child Psychology and Psychiatry*, 52 (4), 333–338. doi:10.1111/j.1469-7610.2011.02378.x.

Levin, F.M. (1991). *Mapping the mind: The intersection of psychoanalysis and neuroscience.* Hillsdale, NJ: Analytic Press.

Maté G. (1999). *Scattered minds. The origins and healing of attention deficit disorder.* London: Penguin.

McKenzie, R. & Dallos, R. (2017). Autism and attachment difficulties: Overlap of symptoms, implications and innovative solutions. *Clinical Child Psychology and Psychiatry*, 22 (4), 632–648. doi:10.1177/1359104517707323.

Melling, R. & N. Smethurst, (2017). Taking care with attachment disorders and autistic-like traits: the potential significance of cognitive markers. *Educational Psychology in Practice*, 33 (3), 264–276. doi:10.1080/02667363.2017.1306489.

Mollon, P. (2015). *The disintegrating self: Psychotherapy of adult ADHD, autistic spectrum, and somato-psychic disorders.* Abingdon: Routledge.

Moran, H. (2010). Clinical observations of the differences between children on the autism spectrum and those with attachment problems: The Coventry Grid. *Good Autism Practice*, 11 (2), 46–59.

Paivio, S.C. & McCulloch, C.R. (2004). Alexithymia as a mediator between childhood trauma and self-injurious behaviour. *Child Abuse & Neglect*, 28 (3), 339–354. doi:10.1016/j.chiabu.2003.11.018.

Panksepp, J. (1998). *Affective neuroscience: The foundations of human and animal emotions.* New York: Oxford University Press.

Phillips, W., Baron-Cohen, S. & Rutter, M. (1992). The role of eye contact in goal direction; Evidence from normal infants and children with autism or mental handicap. *Development and Psychopathology*, 4, 375–383.

Ringman, J. & Jankovic, J. (2000). Occurrence of tics in Asperger's syndrome and autistic disorder. *Journal of Child Neurology*, 15, 394–400. doi:10.1177/088307380001500608.

Robison, J.E. (2013). What is neurodiversity? Retrieved from www.psychologytoday.com/gb/blog/my-life-aspergers/201310/what-is-neurodiversity.

Rutter, M., Anderson-Wood, L., Beckett, C., Bredenkamp, D. *et al.* (1999). Quasi-autistic patterns following severe early global privation. English and Romanian Adoptees (ERA) study team. *Journal of Child Psychology & Psychiatry*, 40 (4), 537–549.

Rutter, M., O'Connor, T.G., Beckett, C. *et al.* (2000). Recovery and deficit following profound early deprivation. In P. Selman (ed.), *Inter-country adoption: Development, trends and perspectives* (pp. 107–125). London: BAAF.

Scholtens, S., Rydell, A-M., Bohlin, G., Thorell, L.B. (2014). ADHD symptoms and attachment representations: considering the role of conduct problems, cognitive deficits and narrative responses in non-attachment-related story stems. *J Abnorm Child Psychol*, 42:1033–1042. doi:10.1007/s10802-014-9854-0.

Schore, A. N. (2014). Early interpersonal neurobiological assessment of attachment and autistic spectrum disorders. *Frontiers in Psychology*, 5 (1049), 1–13. doi:10.3389/fpsyg.2014.01049.

Sibley, K. (2004). Help me help myself: Teaching and learning, In S.M. Shore (ed.), *Ask and tell: Self-advocacy and disclosure for people on the autism spectrum* (pp. 33–64). AAPC Publishing.

Singer, J. (1999). Why can't you be normal for once in your life? In M. Corker (ed.), *Disability discourse* (pp. 59–67). McGraw-Hill Education.

Smith, A. (2009). The empathy imbalance hypothesis of autism: A theoretical approach to cognitive and emotional empathy in autistic development. *The Psychological Record*, 59 (3), 489–510.

Solms, M. & Turnbull, O. (2002). *The brain and the inner world: An introduction to the neuroscience and subjective experience*. New York: Other Press.

Stauffer, K.A. (2021). *Emotional neglect and the adult in therapy*. New York: Norton.

Thorell, L.B., Rydell, A-M. & Bohlin, G. (2012). Parent-child attachment and executive functioning in relation to ADHD symptoms in middle childhood. *Attach Hum Dev.* 14:517–532. doi:10.1080/14616734.2012.706396.

Tomasi, D. & Volkow, N.D. (2012). Abnormal function connectivity in children with attention-deficit/hyperactivity disorder. *Biological Psychiatry*, 71 (5), 443–450. doi:10.1016/j.biopsych.2011.11.003.

Trevarthen, C. (2001). The neurobiology of early communication: intersubjective regulations in human brain development. In A.F. Klaverboer & A. Gramsbergen (eds), *Handbook on brain and behaviour in human development*. Dordrecht: Kluwer.

van der Kolk, B. A. (1996). *Traumatic stress: The effects of overwhelming experience on mind, body and society*. New York: Guilford Press.

van der Kolk, B.A. (2014). *The body keeps the score: Mind, brain and body in the transformation of trauma*. London: Penguin.

van Ijzendoorn, M. H. & Bakermans-Kraneburg, M. J. (1999). Attachment representations in mothers, fathers, adolescents, and clinical groups: A meta-analytic search for normative data. *Journal of Consulting and Clinical Psychology*, 64 (1), 8–21. doi:10.1037/0022-0006X.64.1.8.

Vivanti, G. and Nuske, H. (2016). Autism, attachment, and social learning: Three challenges and a way forward. *Behavioural Brain Research*, 15, 251–259.

Walker, N. (2014). What is autism? Retrieved from https://neuroqueer.com/what-is-autism/.

Weiss, J.A. & Fardella, M.A. (2018). Victimisation and perpetration experiences of adults with autism. *Frontiers in Psychiatry*, 9, 203. doi:10.3389/fpsyt.2018.00203.

Wing, L. (1981). Asperger's Syndrome: a clinical account. *Psychological Medicine*, 11, 115–130. doi:10.1017/s0033291700053332.

Yirmaya, N. & Charman, T. (2010). The prodrome of autism: early behavioural and biological signs, regression, peri-and post-natal development and genetics. *J. Child Psychol. Psychiatry*, 51, 432–458. doi:10.1111/j.1469-7610.2010.02214.x.

Chapter 5

The addictive nature of online pornography

Case study

Gordon is starting to feel much more comfortable with his therapist now. He presents for the sessions on time, makes polite conversation on entrance, and is now clean and presentable in his dress. Yet he still struggles to make eye-contact with her, preferring to stay on the edge of his seat, with his long legs outstretched, his hands clasped between them, and his eyes to floor near his feet. The therapist checks in on how he is and whether he has maintained the first-order changes (Delmonico et al., 2002) they have talked about up until now that prevent him from slipping back into old habits.

'It's been six weeks since I've 'ad a drink, a smoke or done drugs', he confirms.

'Very well done, Gordon. Do you feel a sense of achievement at doing so well?'

Well, yeah. D'ya know what I notice? That I'm not so tired – got more energy, and I think I feel less muddled, like. An' I've been eating better, too, not having so much junk food.'

'Good.' They fall into silence. Gordon keeps looking at the floor, his neck and cheeks starting to turn pink.

The therapist notices his discomfort, so chooses to break the silence. 'Why do I get the feeling there is something you are not telling me, Gordon?'

Gordon slumps down onto his knees. 'I've been on the net.'

'OK. Is that with your phone?'

'No, I bought an iPad.'

'Well, good show for telling me Gordon. That was brave of you. Do you want to tell me what you have looking at?'

'I've been looking at porn again. I felt I 'ad to. It's months since I've 'ad sex and I just felt I wanted to enjoy meself.' He raised himself up slightly, and risked a quick look into her face to catch her expression. She smiled gently, and he quickly looked away again.

'I feel I have let you down,' he mumbled, 'but I miss Rachel.'

DOI: 10.4324/9781003330899-5

'First, you haven't let me down, Gordon. You are not doing this for me. And when you say you miss Rachel, are you saying you miss having someone to have sex with, or do you miss her as a person?'

'I miss 'er. I miss 'er being there to talk to. I miss the laughs we used to 'ave. I miss the boy. I should never 'ave done what I did!' For the first time since they had been meeting, Gordon's eyes welled up and tears plopped onto his tracksuit trousers.

Understanding neuroplasticity and adolescence

The repetitive use of a particular form of behaviour over a substantial period of time will produce long-term changes in the structure of the brain, which is constantly adapting to the environment in which it is given. I have likened this process to the path through a grass field. If you keep treading through the same path, it becomes a quick and easy route in which no further grass will grow (neurones that fire together, wire together; Hebb, 1949; LeDoux, 2002). If one realises that this path no longer takes you to where you want to be, and you actively tread a different path, then the original pathway atrophies and the grass regrows (neurones that no longer fire together, no longer wire together). This is how the plasticity of the brain manifests itself. It connects, disconnects, and reconnects, but especially during adolescence. So just as early trauma can predispose a person to addiction in the form of self-comfort, the well-trodden pathways of addiction can predispose changes in neurology that makes the addiction the attachment instead of a loving relationship (Samenow, 2010).

Adolescent searches and internet compulsion

A child is born with twice as many neurones as an adult to allow for adaptability and plasticity. During adolescence, the brain goes through an organisational process, checking out which neural pathways have been used and therefore have the protective myelin sheath, and clearing out unused axonal connections. But any system organisation also requires disorganisation to get there, that is why it is a fairly long process, and as such a person reaches the age of about 25 before the brain reaches its full maturity. This process requires a huge amount of physical energy, so explains why adolescents eat more and sleep more. They are more likely to try out new experiences – especially if they have been viewing those experiences online – and are more likely to take risks, test boundaries, and be emotionally turbulent. Conduct issues like physical aggression, stealing, lying and destruction of property are particularly noticeable in male adolescents, again probably due to the neural immaturity compared to girls (Schneider et al., 2011). The biggest issue with adolescence is that it is predominantly a child-like brain in an adult-like body, and can take 10 years to grow up.

Statistics indicate that 87% of men and 28% of women watch porn at least weekly (Buchholz., 2019). For children, in research commissioned by the British Board of Film Classification, 51% of children aged 11–13 had unintentionally viewed porn, rising to 66% of 14–15-year-olds, with some viewers as young as seven or eight years old (BBFC, 2019). A more recent report from the Children's Commissioner (2023) found that the average age at which children first see pornography is 13. By age nine, 10% had seen pornography, 27% had seen it by age 11 and half of children who had seen pornography had seen it by age 13. Similarly, the Lucy Faithfull Foundation found that 86% of the troubled teenagers they studied (mean age 14) had sent sexual images of themselves to others. Around a third had been coerced to do so by adults or peers, although it was thought this figure was likely to be higher, as some youngsters struggled to talk about the exploitation they had experienced. They added that the categorisation is complex, as at least one respondent had been coerced to share images with an adult, then chose to show those images to peers (Vaswani et al., 2022).

For a young person, what may start as a weak and curious link when streaming sexual erotica, becomes a strengthened, well-trodden pathway on Twitter, YouTube or Snapchat, to soft porn and onto hardcore pornography on Pornhub and beyond. Before the advent of the internet, the child may have searched in the parent's bedroom for information, or maybe the top shelf magazines in the local newsagents. But now there is the internet, and so many youngsters have their own mobile devices that can access the images online. It can lead to the need and desire that requires instant gratification of masturbation (Negash et al., 2016) instead of the long-term gratification of finding a loving relationship for which the neurological system was originally designed. Research has shown that the earlier in age a child starts regularly viewing online pornography, the more likely they will be viewing deviant or diverse pornography in adulthood (Seigfried-Spellar, 2016).

Another issue with children accessing pornography so early is that it gives them an inappropriate understanding of what sex within relationships is all about. Rather than providing youngsters with sex education, it distorts their perception of the sexual encounter, most commonly the objectification and abuse of women, leading the child to think that the encounters they see in pornography are the norm, rather than choreographed scenarios designed to increase the desires and stimulation of the viewer. Consistent viewing of pornography is, after all, voyeurism, so it is introducing a paraphilia (or kink) into a young child's mind before they have had a chance to explore their own sexual interests in the real world. So, a child may not realise that women have pubic hair, or may consider it is perfectly usual in relationships for dominance and submission scenarios, or a woman being penetrated in three orifices all at once, or being ejaculated over her face or in her mouth. The Children's Commissioner (2023) report found that 47% of their young respondents stated that girls 'expect' sex to involve physical aggression, like airway restriction or slapping, and a further 42% stated that most girls 'enjoy' acts of sexual aggression. A greater proportion of young people stated that girls 'expect' or 'enjoy' aggressive sex more than boys do.

The consequence of all this is that the child, soon to be adolescent, wants to try out scenarios that they have seen and assumed to be the norm, thus leading to the development of altered sexual tastes, consumption of increasingly extreme material (Wilson 2017) and various paraphilias at a very early age. Plus, a lack of understanding about the need for intimacy and attachment in loving relationships, or the need for active consent for the sexual encounter to occur. It may explain why girls in school experience repetitive sexual harassment from their male counterparts. Boys are not learning that it is just not right to grab what they want, or to belie the myth that all girls say no, but what they want to say really is yes.

The distortion of the sexual template

The predisposing factor of viewing online pornography from an early age can set the viewer up for an adulthood of compulsively using internet imagery. As a pubertal child or early adolescent, the last of the preprogramed circuits for survival of the species gets triggered online: the LUST circuit (Panksepp, 1998). Driven by the dopamine hit from the SEEKING circuit from the nucleus accumbens in the basal area of the forebrain, the young person's curiosity and arousal leads them to want to know more about sex. It is this seeking and searching that provides the compulsion to see more, not the imagery *per se* (Salamon & Correa, 2012); it is the 'wanting' circuit. fMRI research shows that activity in nucleus accumbens is exaggerated during adolescence, compared to that of children or adults, creating the want for excitement and risk, whereas the prefrontal cortex in an adolescent where cognitions would apply the handbrake for these impulses are still like that of children, rather than the more mature adult (Galvan et al., 2006).

Why can't people just stop?

As mentioned earlier, each time the dopamine pathways, the brain's reward centres, are enervated, it entrenches a stronger, more consolidated pathway to follow that behavioural pattern (Wilson, 2017). Studies using fMRI have demonstrated that the neural network used by viewing pornography are the same as those used with drug cues (Voon et al., 2014). Kühn & Gallinat, (2014) also found that constant use of online pornography actually changes the structure of the brain, particularly in malleable adolescent cortices, which most closely resemble those seen with the use of recreational drugs (Olsen, 2011). Wilson (2017) called these changes the 3Cs: *Craving* and preoccupation (as from the SEEKING circuit described above, and may be called 'hedonic dysregulation'; Gardner, 2011), loss of *Control* increasing frequency and duration, and *Consequences* in physical, social, occupational, financial or psychological domains (Wilson 2017, p. 95). These neural changes can be found in all addictive processes, whether it is alcohol, food, drugs, sex, or gambling (Nestler, 2005).

As the viewing of imagery becomes more intensified, desires for arousal with dopamine highs get stronger, and endogenous opioids are also released from the nucleus accumbens, binding to the dopamine reward system, making the adolescent want to go back for more of the same. This is especially the case if the young person's original insecure attachment system produces low self-worth, and lack of resilience over their past experiences, leading to a deficit of endogenous opioids due to living within an insecure environment (Hudson-Allez, 2011). They will be blown away by the intensity of a feeling they had never experienced naturally before, producing a sense of 'liking', predisposing them to return to the imagery. However, these feelings of wanting and liking originate from different areas of the nucleus accumbens: there is a localised area within the shell of the nucleus accumbens that releases the opioids, whereas the dopamine release is distributed widely throughout it (Peciña, 2008). This suggests that the dopamine or 'wanting' is going to have a much stronger effect than the opioid 'liking' (Berridge & Robinson, 1998), which may deplete over time. Tolerance occurs, needing greater stimulation to get the same feeling. As Wilson (2017) argued, compulsion leads to wanting it more, but liking it less (see Figure 5.1).

In addition to the process of wanting and liking, is the interaction of novelty that the internet consistently provides. The anticipation of the novel reward stimuli enervates the nucleus accumbens with the connective pathways linking to the hippocampus (for memory and learning) and primary visual cortex (Krebs *et al.,* 2011). So, the adolescent spends hours visually 'glued' to the computer screen, tapping, clicking or swiping way in a process of 'what else is there?'. As they do so, the novelty of some of the imagery being viewed can illicit feelings of surprise, shock or even anxiety at the image being viewed. These feelings can illicit stress neurotransmitters of adrenaline, noradrenaline and cortisol, as well as elevating the level of dopamine in a further, circular, wanting to see more, loop; stimulating the search for more rather than satiating it. These stress hormones trigger the HPA axis (hypothalamus, adrenal, pituitary fight and flight system) increasing anxiety in the viewer, but consequently also increasing arousal and alertness. Thus, the viewer continues to seek, wanting more, in a trance-like dissociative psychological state, and in a physiological state of arousal, keeping on the edge of, but not wanting to complete, ejaculation or orgasm. Ejaculation often stops the process, and the wanting prohibits that. So, 'edging' is a common phenomenon of the pornography compulsion.

The search for more stimulating/exciting images, leads to escalation of the imagery viewed, often with the additional consequence of erectile dysfunctions (Janssen & Bancroft, 2007) and loss of libido towards potential real sexual

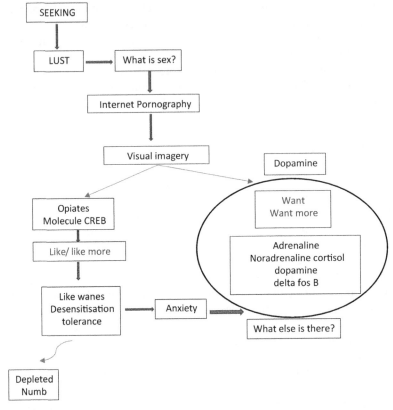

Figure 5.1 The arousal bubble. The nucleus accumbens differentiates between wanting and liking.

partners (Voon et al., 2014). This loss of libido forms a self-fulfilling process of feeling the need for finding even more exciting, stimulating imagery to get that horny again. And when a child/adolescent gets into the habit of constant streaming of porn for hours at a time, they find that absence leads to withdrawal symptoms of restlessness, anxiety, irritability and depression (Fisch, 2014).

Even moderate use of internet pornography can have a physiological effect on the brain. Kühn & Gallinat (2014) found a negative correlation of self-reported pornography consumption with neural volume in the right striatum (caudate) of the brain, less activation in the striatum (putamen) during cue reactivity, and less cross-cortical functional connectivity from the right caudate to the left dorso-lateral prefrontal cortex; thus the more pornography usage, the less grey matter and the less sexual responsivity. They hypothesised that frequent brain activation caused by pornography exposure might lead to a wearing down of the under-lying brain structure, leading to less functionality, and (after habituation) a higher need for external stimulation of the reward system (dopamine pathways) and thus a tendency to search for novel and more extreme sexual material, which switches off the cognitive executive handbrake functioning of the brain (I shouldn't be doing this), and as Doidge (2008) suggests, hijacks the potential of the brain for making social relationships rewarding.

Gardner (2011) proposed that there are three classical sets of addictive craving and relapse triggers:

a   re-exposure to the addiction; involves the nucleus accumbens and the neurotransmitter dopamine;
b   stress, the amygdala releasing corticotrophin and noradrenaline; and
c   re-exposure to environmental cues (people, places, things) involves the basolateral nucleus of the amygdala, the hippocampus and the neuro-transmitter glutamate.

So the inability to stop is not just about the lack of willpower. These adolescent searches, at a time of neural pruning and pathway reorganisation (Weinberger, Elvevag & Giedd, 2005), create neural changes that stay with the youngster into adulthood, reshaping the brain as a consequence. The dopamine and endorphin feeds are too great, so even if there is a conscious evaluation that the behaviour is harmful to themselves and to others, there will be an inability to stop. Gabor Maté (1999) argues that the deficient neurochemistry of addiction, like the deficient neurochemistry of ADD, can be traced back to the very early first year or two of life. The social isolation and early deprivation causing a permanent reduction in the brain's endogenous opiate receptors, and the deeper an individual gets into the addiction, the more emotional emptiness they perpetuate in a never-ending cycle. He emphasises:

> While attention deficit disorder cannot be successfully treated as long as the addiction continues to dominate, neither can the addiction be given the appropriate attention if the ADD is ignored and the common origins of both remain unexplained.
>
> (Maté, 1999, p. 304)

O'Sullivan et al. (2016) found that 78.6% of young men aged 16–21 are reporting problems with real sexual activity, including erectile dysfunction, retarded ejaculation and low sexual desire. As Wilson (2017) points out, it alters the person's mood, their perception and their priorities without any conscious awareness. Meerkerk, Van Den Eijnden and Garretsen (2006) found in a longitudinal study that just one year of high-level viewing of internet pornography was sufficient to develop into a compulsive habit. It can also damage an individual's mental health, as it has been associated with depression (Lam & Peng, 2010), self-harm (Lam, Peng, Mai & Jing, 2009), verbal and physical sexual aggression (Wright, Tokunaga & Kraus, 2015), and suicidality (Daine et al., 2013; Lin et al., 2014). It has also been shown to change a person's sexual preference, as research has found that escalation to alternative forms of sexual encounters are common (Downing et al., 2016). In as little as 7 weeks of weekly exposure to pornography, Zillmann and Bryant (1988) found the exposure strongly impacted the viewer's self-assessment of sexual experience. They reported less satisfaction with their intimate partner's affection, physical appearance, sexual curiosity, and sexual performance, and furthermore assigned increased importance to sex without emotional involvement. Later research has continued to discover that sexual interests are malleable and can be changed, driving escalation to more extreme material (Banca et al., 2016; Gola et al., 2017; Stark & Klucken, 2017). And when one factors in the forthcoming virtual reality process into pornography, one shudders to think of the damage that can do to a generation of young person's sexual templates.

Is it compulsion or is it addiction?

There has been criticism of suggesting that compulsive use of pornography on the internet, or any other compulsive sexual behaviour, is an addiction, as it anti sex-positive and anti sex for pleasure (Neves, 2021). This is particularly aimed at the 12-step approach of working with Sexual Addiction (Carnes, 2001; Birchard, 2017; Hall, 2018) arguing that it is a diseased-based sex-negative medical model. This argument is backed up in reference to the DSM-V-TR (2022) exclusion of behavioural addictions and sex addiction, arguing that there is insufficient evidence to include it. However, gambling is behavioural, but most people would agree that it is addictive and destroys people's lives. The DSM-V-TR highlights four categories (or 'symptoms', which is very medical model) for addictive disorders:

- impaired control;
- social problems;
- risky use; and
- physical dependence (tolerance and withdrawal).

I think the neuroscience overview of internet pornography use described above makes it clear that all of these criteria have been fulfilled. The issue with the DSM-V-TR is it has nothing to offer in our understanding of compulsive online sexual viewing and/or offending in the viewing of CSAM. Ward, Polaschek and Beech have a similar view:

> The DSM-V-TR diagnosis of paedophilia has little relevance in the mainstream treatment of child sexual abuse, and for that matter does not advance our understanding of the aetiology or maintenance of child abuse, or the offence process itself (Bickley & Beech, 2001). Because it

essentially precludes well over half of those who have committed sexual offences against children, it cannot be said to theoretically advance our understanding of child sexual abuse.

(Ward, Polaschek & Beech, 2009, p. 288)

Bessell van der Kolk (2014) is equally critical of the DSM-V, arguing that it lacks scientific reliability and validity, highlighting that the APA would rather produce a 'smorgasbord of diagnoses' (p. 197) to label children with disruptive mood regulation disorder, intermittent explosive disorder, oppositional defiant disorder, dysregulated social engagement disorder or disruptive impulse control disorder, rather than acknowledge that the underlying cause of these issues is developmental trauma. He accuses the APA board of being regressed in early 19th-century medical practice, who have not moved on with our knowledge and understanding of the developing human brain following neuroscientific scanning procedures.

What about the ICD-11? Calling the issue compulsive sexual behaviour disorder (again a medical model), and placing it into the impulse control disorders category, it makes the 'diagnosis':

a persistent pattern of failure to control intense, repetitive sexual impulses or urges resulting in repetitive sexual behaviour … and causes marked distress or significant impairment in personal, family, social, educational, occupational or other important areas of functioning.

(ICD-11, 2022, §6C72)

Interestingly, this category excludes any compulsive behaviour during adolescence due to the rapidly changing hormones during this time making excessive sexual behaviour normal adolescent experiences, although frequent or risky sexual behaviour during this developmental stage may be considered 'abnormal' if it interferes with social or emotional development.

Does it matter what you call it? Silva Neves (2021) says yes it does. That people can adopt negative conations from a disease model of addiction. He also argues that sex always stays pleasurable, and it is rare to meet someone who wants sex experiencing no pleasure from it. This sex-positive argument, which I essentially agree with and subscribe to, as one of my previous pub-lication's attests (Hudson-Allez, 2014), misses the point that it is not the *sex images* that are compulsive but the *searching* for them. Certainly, edging for hours on end to online pornography can be exciting and rewarding. But not if it leads to a disruption in a person's physical and mental health, the risk of losing a person's relationship, their employment, their children, and their will to live because they have escalated their viewing and crossed the line into illeg-ality. Paula Hall (2018) follows a sexual addiction concept, and argues that it doesn't matter what you call it, so long as the client can identify with the behaviour, and that the term sexual addiction is readily identified by the public and the media. However, when one views the neuroscience, it becomes clear that compulsion and addiction are two different processes. Compulsion seems to develop in the individual first and tends to be behaviourally orientated. It's the 'getting' and the 'liking' that makes the person feel good and want more, but then can't stop. But addiction is neurologically based; it the dopamine SEEKING, the 'wanting', 'give me more', 'what else is there?' As with other addictions, it is the searching for the next fix, the next drink, the next fag, the next sexual exploit, that creates the sense of desperation and anxiety, where the compulsive 'getting' calms it.

It is important to emphasise that the regular viewing of pornography does not necessarily lead to escalation and acting out, any more than regularly drinking of alcohol doesn't make everyone an alcoholic; no-one would argue that alcoholism isn't an addiction. In some people, however, there is a transition from 'normal' rewards, like food or sex, to compulsive engagements, and these have been termed behavioural addictions (Olsen, 2011). Thousands of people have been helped and supported by the various forms of Sex Addiction treatments (Carnes, Delmonico & Griffin, 2002; Hall, 2018). But to rely on the DSM-V as grounds for an argument against other models of working is, I believe, essentially flawed. Labelling presenting symptoms of an issue does not provide an understanding of its underlying causes or how the problem is maintained. And certainly, for therapist in the UK, it is an unnecessary detour away from their clinical judgement in holding the client in their pain.

The link between neurodiversity and online addiction

For neurodivergent individuals who, by their very nature, struggle with social and intimate relationships, they can take refuge in sexual fantasy and pornography, hidden from the gaze of another (Sanderson, 2014), and it has been found that neurodivergent men (but not women) show more masturbation, hypersexual activity, paraphilic fantasies and behaviours than the neurotypical (Schöttle et al., 2017). It is thought that neurodivergent women are more socially adapted and therefore present with less spectrum symptomology. The internet is the obvious strategy to try and learn about sexual behaviours and perhaps meet like-minded others. But, as discussed above, the use of internet pornography is a highly addictive process for neurotypical people, and even more so for the neurodivergent, who have no other means of feeling attached and belonging somewhere. Many are secluded from their peers, have no real-life sexual experiences to relate to, and their somewhat obsessive, logical ways of thinking (Mesibov & Sreckovic, 2017) may lead to the online exploration of paraphilias, on the assumption that is what neurotypical people commonly do. It is more likely, therefore, that if someone has ASD when receiving the knock, their devices may contain many CSAM, not because they are turned on in seeing them, but because the obsessive compulsive nature of their presentation, together with their lack of sexual knowledge and impaired social skills means that they want to keep searching for information, leading to what has been described as counterfeit deviance (Griffiths et al., 2013; Allely, 2022) defined as a naïve curiosity. Unfortunately, there is still an assumption made in the criminal justice system that there is a correlation between the number of images on an individual's device, and their level of risk of a contact offence. Correlation does not imply causation, however, and this argument is fallacious and not supported by empirical evidence (Stabenow, 2011).

People who have ASD, ADD or ADHD often have an underlying presence of anxiety (Russell et al., 2005) coming from the dominance of their obsessive-compulsive thinking, feeling different from others and never really fitting in, as well as any aversive experiences throughout their childhood as a consequence their difference. Anxious infants and babies reach for their genitals to self soothe, a habit that adults condition out of them as they grow older, However, neurodivergent adolescents are often behind in their social development. Fear of being shunned by their peers leads to social anxiety and consequent withdrawal. So reaching for their genitals when feeling anxious to self-soothe is a behaviour often maintained well into adolescence, if not later. And, when stimulating material is visually available on the internet, the self-soothing is undertaken at a pre-conscious level.

It is interesting that individuals with ADD or ADHD may not be able to focus on very much away from the computer, but when it comes to pornography or gaming on the Net, they are easily hooked. In addition, many people on the spectrum can't tell the difference between what they see as real and what they see as fantasy, which interferes with a cognitive review of the imagery, not understanding that seeing pictures of naked children isn't acceptable. Some do it because a 'friend' on the internet told them to get the pictures and pass them on, so they will keep being their 'friend'. Forwarding the pictures is the price for the friendship which is so important, as it may mean someone notices them and speaks to them for a while, making them feel special.

Furthermore, Vaswani et al. (2022) found that young people with ASD, LGBTQI+ youngsters and young people with mental health difficulties were more vulnerable to engage in online harmful sexual behaviour, with girls being three times more likely to become victims of it than boys.

To reiterate the earlier discussion of neuroscience, Brand et al. (2011) found that the extent of online addiction was related to the novelty of stimuli presented and the number of screens open, rather than just the length of time viewing. This suggests that the dopamine reward pathways, often called the brain reward cascade, are always demanding something more interesting to get the same thrill and to fulfil the immediate need to self soothe (i.e. to masturbate). This auto-erotic behaviour often, though, is about staying on the edge, the height of arousal before the need to ejaculate – because that is where the addiction is reinforced; being on the edge of arousal, searching to see what else can be found. Ejaculation often means it's going to stop, so that is not place the viewer wants to go.

This production and usage of dopamine by the SEEKING circuit raises another interesting issue, and that is the rising interest of the default mode network (DMN) in the processing of the brain. This is a neuro-network in the midbrain that only becomes active when we are at rest, with no tasks to undertake. Phil Mollon (2015) uses a useful analogy of like a car engine ticking over, waiting to be put into gear and be driven. It is thought that networks in our central brain tend to be self-orientated, whereas networks toward the outside of the brain tend to be other-orientated. Thus, the DMN will activate when our autobiographical memory clicks in remembering events that occurred in our own history, or if we are reflecting about our emotional state, or when we are thinking about other's emotional states in comparison with ours, that is the theory of mind (Donohue, 2022). Studies have shown that early adverse childhood experiences showed reduced connectivity to multiple areas of the DMN, in the parietal brain regions and mediated the effects of social cognition that produce fundamental challenges to accurately recognising and processing socially relevant stimuli. This finding was most notable for individuals who had experienced physical trauma and childhood neglect, leading to poorer emotional recognition (Dauvermann et al., 2021). This neural background activity, which allows an individual to instantly undertake a task, and even undertake more than one activity at a time, as a background supportive network may be misfiring, interfering with the perception of appropriate social stimuli, but also interfering with our thought processing of theory of mind. This DMN is thought to be activated by dopamine, and it has been found that people with ADHD are deficient in dopamine, the consequences of which interfere with brain reward cascade and predispose individuals to have a high risk for addictive, impulsive, and compulsive behaviours (Blum et al., 2008). This suggests another interaction between neurodivergent processing and adverse childhood experiences.

As Sanderson (2014) argues, shame is inextricably linked and plays a central role in addictive and compulsive sexual behaviour, as its role is to regulate emotions. However, if shame is overridden, addiction can take its place as an emotional regulator, replacing frightening or unsatisfying relationships (Khantzian, 2003).

Development of aggression

What underpins the development of addictive behaviour is our understanding of shame. Shame is not a negative concept *per se*. We all need shame and empathy to create a compassionate and caring society. So there is good shame that is our socialising system, and there is a negative/toxic shame from a BAD-ME circuit. An excess of toxic shame leads to maladaptive strategies for covering it up, for example compensatory narcissism, or addictive self-soothing behaviours. The dopamine produced as a result of these strategies changes the way the individual feels, but equally constricts them, and interferes with their concept of self. Anger leading to aggression is another automatic, well-trodden pathway response to cover up their feelings of shame, that blames someone else for making the individual feel bad. This may be the hot anger of the preoccupied attachment style from the FEAR circuit, creating an individual who is volatile, and others feeling they walk on egg-shells around them. Or there may be the cold, calculating, seething, passive-aggressive anger from the person with an avoidant style using the RAGE circuit.

Joseph LeDoux (2002) held that there are two routes to our perceptual awareness of the environment. There is the perception of threat that comes in through the eye, triggers an alarm in the amygdala, and shoots straight through to the HPA axis, setting off our fight and flight system with meta-phorical red lights flashing and sirens wailing. He called this the quick and dirty route, as it offers no analysis through the orbitofrontal cortex. The alternative route was a re-orientation of the visual stimuli, which allowed time for the individual to make an analysis of the threat and process the information; this is the long and accurate route, and may produce a totally different physical response in the perceiver, even though this response still occurs within a matter of seconds. Daniel Siegel (2003) elaborated on this process of autonoetic consciousness as a higher mode of integrated processing of the mind that the orbitofrontal cortex provides. But if that higher mode (or road) is shut down, then the individual will operate in a lower road of automatic con-sciousness and impulse control, flooding the mind with automatic thoughts and ideas and making the rational mind inaccessible. This mental trigger of the low road of the quick and dirty route may be inaccessible to the person's conscious awareness, but the previously learned behaviours can erupt into infantile rage and violent behaviour. This Siegel blames the on frightened and/or frightening behaviours of the parents, which do not allow for sensitive communication in the attachment process, leading to disorganised attachment in the children, and this is how transgenerational transmission of trauma occurs.

The adjudicating and moderating process of the orbitofrontal cortex on the high road of the long and accurate route is thought to be missing or impaired in people with neurodivergence, in particular ADD (Maté, 1999), This leads to a lack of inhibition, as it is the role of the orbitofrontal cortex to inhibit inap-propriate behaviour, not to find the most appropriate response (LeDoux, 1996). This may account for why some individuals to blurt out what they think or feel in Tourette's fashion without consideration of someone else's feelings, or embark on inappropriate impulsive behaviour without thinking, which if discovered to be illegal, they will not try to cover up or dissemble, but will openly admit it naïvely. Haskins & Silva (2006) propose the reason for this is their deficits in the theory of mind, a predilection for intense narrow interests, coupled with deficient social awareness or interpersonal and social constraints on their behaviour.

Schore (2003) suggested that anger and subsequent violence is the fight and flight response dysregulated as a result of childhood trauma. Tremblay et al. (1999) suggested that there may be two main developmental trajectories for the development of physical aggression: childhood limited and life-course persistent. The childhood limited trajectory is where the onset of the peak of aggression may occur at 17 months old, but by the time the child reaches school age, they have developed inhibitory methods of dealing with it. If they do not learn these inhibitions at this critical period, however, the aggression is more likely to be life-course persistent. This may be an indication that there is a sensitive period for learning to inhibit physically aggressive behaviour (i.e. developing the neural pathways to applying the handbrake when the anger feels like it is getting out of control). So, to prevent cases of physical aggression in adolescence or adulthood, which underpins a lot of violent behaviour, we need to help children learn to inhibit their aggression during the preschool years. Also during preschool years, as we try and modify and shape prosocial behaviour in children, we also need to encourage their acceptance and tolerance of difference to prevent the in-group/out-group process of bullying, the memories of which individuals carry with them for the rest of their lives

Gordon's review

The therapist has reached the stage of sharing her formulation with Gordon. Some of the issues presented will be tentative, as they work through them collaboratively. Here are the notes made for the formulation and subsequent therapeutic work:

Presenting issues

- A damaged young man in his 30s, separated from his wife and child. Domestic violence. She and the child are in a refuge.
- Got the knock for CSAM. He had been interviewed by the police for actual bodily harm previously and of making indecent images of children. His devices (computer, laptop, Xbox, DVDs, phone and iPad) have all been seized by the police during an early morning raid by six police officers, and he had been held in the cells overnight before being and released under investigation.
- Lives alone and lacks care for himself, eating badly, no exercise.
- Addicted to online porn, alcohol, tobacco, used to use drugs.
- Lacks empathy, narcissistic (classic or compensatory to be determined), psychopathy to be determined.
- Unable to take responsibility for his own aggressive behaviour, everything is someone else's fault.
- ?ADHD/hfASD
- Emotionally dysregulated leading to violent episodes. ?alexithymia. Seems to have a high IQ level despite his lack of school achievement. Possible Left/right brain conflict.

- A loner with a specialised skill set. ?neurodivergent.
- He had no interest in their child Connor, whom Gordon did not want Rachel to have. The child simply got in the way of Gordon's ability to have sex with Rachel as and when he pleased (repetition compulsion).
- Had been fired from work –despite being a talented mechanic.
- Had been given notice to quit his flat for non-payment of the rent – lack of safety.
- His addictions to alcohol, drugs, sex and violence and been his only 'true' friends. He had no real friends, so does not feel their loss.
- Suicidal thoughts but no plans.

Predisposing issues

- Transgenerational transmission: culture of alcoholism and domestic violence in extended family.
- Domestic violence in family of origin *in utero*. Changes in brain structure, hypervigilance.
- Domestic violence witnessed pre-3 years.
- Loss of father at 3 years.
- Mother depressed and grieving for loss of next child, Gordon's sister.
- Emotionally and physically neglected.
- Insecure attachment. Lack of resilience. Inability to self-soothe.
- Development of an avoidant /disorganised attachment style.
- Vandalisation of his sexual template following sexual abuse by stranger.
- Gordon has 7 out of 10 ACEs (see Chapter 6).

Precipitating issues

- Adolescent turbulence with commencement of compulsive masturbation and online pornography use from age 10 years.
- The use of sexual activity to soothe himself, but avoidant style is manifest in lots of sex for gratification, yet avoidance of intimacy for fear of rejection and abandonment.
- Bullying at school – loner, didn't fit in, red hair, always being told off for lack of attention and stealing (usually food).
- Domestic violence from new stepfather.
- Development of compensatory narcissism, lack of empathy, sense of entitlement, aggressive stance. Bully victim becomes the bully in senior school.

Perpetuating issues

- Always alone. No friends except Rachel.
- Gordon's natural avoidant style is fearing intimacy, but he becomes totally preoccupied with Rachel. From his pornography viewing she has

become objectified as his sex object, ownership, his entitlement. First and only intimate relationship (other than sex workers).

- Gordon's attachment style changes. In transition to adulthood, he switches from avoidant to being preoccupied with everything Rachel does, who she is with, what she wears, etc.
- Paranoid fear of her loss, leading to coercive control and subsequent violence.
- When Rachel disappeared with their son, Gordon started stalking her. This attachment pathology displays empathy disorders; a complete inability to comprehend the effect he is having on her, which links with neurodiversity presentations.
- He is unable to modulate the intensity of his dysregulated affect, including shame, rage, excitement, elation, disgust, panic-terror and hopeless-despair.
- Locked in an addictive cycle: Sex, alcohol, drugs, tobacco, all changing his neural pathways at a critical stage of his neural development.
- Using sex workers and online pornography, continually feeding his SEEKING system.
- Confusion over his sexuality, feeling aroused to gay and trans porn.
- Gordon had no paedophilic tendencies, but he couldn't stop himself looking at the unacceptable.
- The 'what else is there?' phenomenon perpetuates.

Protective factors

- Highly motivated in therapy. Compliant. Wants to change his life.
- Intelligence. Has potential if encouraged academically.
- Strongly motivated to get his family back.
- Enjoys his work. Can be completely focused on solving a mechanical problem.
- Mrs Watson (the lady he met in the park) already becoming a new attachment figure, as is his boss who has given him his old job back. Such ongoing support can make a huge difference to his recovery.

First-order changes during assessment process

- Hearing the fear and rage of the criminal justice (CJ) system response.
- Information-giving regarding the CJ process.
- Dealing with the stress of the long-term uncertainty of whether he will lose his freedom.
- Keep safe plan for suicidal ideation.
- Reducing access to the computer/phone. Self-limiting surfing time.
- Surfing the arousal process. When the wave hits its height, it will inevitably fall and crash over the other side. Surf through the arousal wave.
- Masturbation is normal, but limiting it helps.

- Raising awareness: providing tasks that help break through client's denial: e.g. making lists of consequences, discussing the effects on others, perhaps involving significant others to break through denial.
- Victim awareness. Online viewing is not a victimless crime.
- Identifying triggers. What leads them to the computer? Keep a journal if they are unaware.
- Confronting the myth of anonymity. There is software to identify the surveillance products already on their pc. They are already being watched by many, including undercover police officers. There is also software that can share with others their browsing habits.
- Right-brain soothing strategies to help with his distress, like mindfulness exercises.
- Psychoeducation regarding diet, exercise, attachments, self-soothing.

Moving on to second-order changes

- Keeping him grounded to face dealing with his childhood trauma.
- Gently supporting his shame as he looks into the mirror of his behaviour; the window of opportunity for narcissistic tendencies.
- Attacking the appeal of using the internet for sexual activity. Planning for impulse control.
- Mental health overview. Does he need support from his GP with anti-depressant or anti-anxiety medication in the short term while the difficult issues are being addressed?
- Introducing the family into the work. What is the situation with his relationship with Rachel? Can it be healed? Does she want to?
- Addressing the collateral damage, in particular his son Connor. Working through the shame that this brings and the grief at his loss.
- Learning about healthy sexuality. That pornography taints a loving sexual relationship with an intimate partner.
- Spirituality also needs to be addressed. Does he have a belief system, and how can this support him in his recovery and rehabilitation?

This formulation is developed in collaboration with the client, mostly as a fact-finding exercise and a road map for ways to change. The information is collected by the therapist in an open, curious way of being, without judgement or trying to 'catch the client out' in any potential falsifications. Judgements force the client into a defensive position and may provoke a defensive attack. The client will be more ready and willing to be open with the truth when they are not sensing from the therapist that there is criticism or disbelief behind the questions. The formulation, once collated is reviewed with the client, with warmth, compassion, humour and even love; one can love a person without approving of their behaviour. The client needs to feel capable of being loved if they are going to break down their

BAD-ME circuit, so it should be presented with positivity that they can change their future path. I often give them a copy of the formulation to take away, as there is a lot to take in, and then ask them to consider or write down the kind of person they want to become, their road map for the future.

References

Allely, C.S. (2022). *Autism spectrum disorder in the Criminal Justice System: A guide to understanding suspects, defendants and offenders with autism.* Abingdon: Routledge.

Banca, P., Morris, L.S., Mitchell, S., Harrison, N.A. *et al.* (2016). Novelty, conditioning and attention bias to sexual rewards. *Journal of Psychiatric Research*, 72, 91–101. doi:10.1016/j.jpsychires.2015.10.017.

BBFC. (2019). *New research commissioned by the BBFC into the impact of pornography on children demonstrates significant Support for age verification.* Guidelines Consultation. BBFC.

Berridge, K.C. & Robinson, T.E. (1998). What is the role of dopamine in reward: hedonic impact, reward learning, or incentive salience? *Brain Research Reviews*, 28, 309–369. doi:10.1016/s0165-0173(98)00019-8.

Bickley, J.A. & Beech, A.R. (2001). Classifying child abusers: its relevance to theory and clinical practice. *Journal of Interpersonal Violence*, 17, 371–393.

Birchard, T. (2017). *Overcoming sexual addiction.* Abingdon: Routledge.

Blum, K., Chen, A.L.-C., Bravernan, E.C., Comings, D.E. *et al.* (2008). Attention-deficit-hyperactivity disorder and reward deficiency syndrome. *Neuropsychiatric Dis Treat.*, 4 (5), 893–918. doi:10.2147/ndt.s2627.

Brand, M., Laier, C., Pawlikowski, M, Schächtle, U. *et al.* (2011). Watching pornographic pictures on the internet: role of sexual arousal ratings and psychological-psychiatric symptoms for using internet sites excessively. *Cyberpsychology Behaviour & Social Networking*, 14 (6), 371–377. doi:10.1089/cyber.2010.0222.

Buchholz, K. (2019). How much of the internet consists of porn? Retrieved from www.statista.com/chart/16959/share-of-the-internet-that-is-porn/.

Carnes, P. (2001). *Out of the shadows: Understanding sexual addiction* (3rd ed.). Minnesota: Hazeldon.

Carnes, P., Delmonico, D. L. & Griffin, E. (2002). *In the shadows of the net: Breaking free of compulsive online sexual behaviour.* Minnesota: Hazelden.

Children's Commissioner. (2023). *'A lot of it is actually just abuse': Young people and pornography.* London: HMSO.

Daine, K., Hawton, K., Singaravelu, V., Stewart, A. *et al.* (2013). The power of the web: A systematic review of studies on the influence of the internet on self-harm and suicide in young people. *PLOS ONE* 8, e77555.

Dauvermann, M.R., Mothershill, D., Rokita, K.I., King, S. *et al.* (2021). Changes in default-mode network associated with childhood trauma in schizophrenia. *Schizophrenia Bulletin* 21, 47 (5), 1482–1494. doi:10.1093/schbul/sbab025.

Delmonico, D.L. (2002). Sex on the superhighway: Understanding and treating cybersex addiction. In P.J. Carnes & K.M. Adams (eds), *Clinical management of sex addiction.* New York: Brunner Routledge.

Delmonico, D. L., Griffin, E. & Carnes, P. (2002). Treating online compulsive sexual behaviour: When cybersex is the drug of choice. In A. Cooper (ed.), *Sex and the internet. A Guidebook for Clinicians* (pp. 147–168). New York: Brunner-Routledge.

Doidge N. (2008). *The brain that changes itself. Stories of personal triumph from the frontiers of brain science.* London: Penguin.

Donohue, G. (2022). How adverse childhood experiences shape our brains. *The Psychologist*, 15 August, 42–46.

Downing Jr, M.J., Schrimshaw, E.W., Scheinmann, R., Antebi-Grusza, N. & Hirshfield, S. (2016). Sexually explicit media use by sexual identity: A comparative analysis of gay, bisexual, and heterosexual men in the United States. *Archives of Sexual Behaviour*, 46 (6), 1763–1776. doi:10.1007/s10508-016-0837-9.

DSM-V-TR (2022). *Diagnostic and statistical manual of mental disorders, text revision* (5th edition). American Psychiatric Association.

Fisch, H. (2014). *The new naked: The ultimate sex education for grown-ups.* Chicago: Sourcebooks.

Galvan, A., Hare, T.A., Parra, C.E., Penn, J. *et al.* (2006). Earlier development of the accumbens relative to orbitofrontal cortex might underlie risk-taking behaviour in adolescents. *Journal of Neuroscience*, 26 (25) 6885–6892. doi:10.1523/JNEUROSCI.1062–1006.2006.

Gardner, E.L. (2011). Addiction and brain reward and antireward pathways. *Adv Psychosom Med*, 30, 22–60. doi:10.1159/000324065.

Gola, M., Wordecha, M., Sescousse, G., Lew-Starowicz, M. *et al.* (2017). Can pornography be addictive? An fMRI study of men seeking treatment for problematic pornography use. *Neuropsychopharmacology*, 42, 2021–2031.

Griffiths, D., Hinsburger, D., Hoath, J. & Ioannou, S. (2013). 'Counterfeit deviance' revisited. *Journal of Applied Research on Intellectual Disabilities*, 26 (5), 471–480. doi:10.1111/jar.12034.

Hall, P. (2018). *Understanding and treating sex and pornography addiction: A comprehensive guide for people who struggle with sex addiction and those who want to help them* (2nd ed). Abingdon: Routledge.

Haskins, B.G. & Silva, J.A. (2006). Asperger's disorder and criminal behaviour: Forensic psychiatric conditions. *Journal of the American Academy of Psychiatry and Law*, 34 (3), 374–384.

Hebb, D.O. (1949). *The organisation of behaviour.* New York: Wiley.

Hudson Allez, G. (2011). *Infant losses, adult searches: A neural and developmental perspective on psychopathology and sexual offending.* London: Karnac.

Hudson-Allez, G. (ed.). (2014). *Sexual diversity and sexual offending. Research, assessment and clinical treatment in psychosexual therapy.* London: Karnac.

ICD-11. (2022). *International classification of diseases*, 11th revision. World Health Organization.

Janssen, E. & Bancroft, J. (2007). The dual-control model: The role of sexual inhibition and excitation in sexual arousal and behaviour. In E. Janssen (ed.), *The psychophysiology of sex*. Indiana University Press.

Khantzian, E.J. (2003). Understanding addictive vulnerability. An evolving psychodynamic perspective. *Neuro-Psychoanalysis*, 5, 5–21.

Krebs, R.M., Heipertz, D., Schuetze, H. & Duzel, E. (2011). Novelty increases the mesolimbic functional connectivity of the substantia nigra/ventral tegmental area

(SN/VTA) during reward anticipation: Evidence from high-resolution fMRI. *Neuroimage*, 58 (2) 647–655. doi:10.1016/j.neuroimage.2011.06.038.

Kühn, S. & Gallinat, J. (2014). Brain structure and functional connectivity associated with pornography consumption: The brain on porn. *JAMA Psychiatry*, 71 (7), 827834. doi:10.1001/jamapsychiatry.2014.93.

Lam, L.T. & Peng, Z.-W. (2010). Effect of pathological use of the internet on adolescent mental health; a prospective study. *Arch Pediatr Adolesc Med.*, 164 (10), 901–906. doi:10.1001/archpediatrics.2010.159.

Lam, L.T., Peng, Z-W, Mai, J. & Jing, J. (2009). The association between internet addiction and self-injurious behaviour among adolescents. *Inj Prev*, 15 (6), 403–408. doi:10.1136/ip.2009.021949.

LeDoux, J. E. (1996). *The emotional brain*. London: Weidenfeld & Nicolson.

LeDoux, J. E. (2002). *Synaptic self: How our brains become who we are*. New York: Penguin Books.

Lin, I.-H., Ko, C.-H., Chang, Y.-P., Liu, T.-L. *et al.* (2014). The association between suicidality and internet addiction and activities in Taiwanese adolescents. *Compr Psychiatry*, 55 (3), 504–510. doi:10.1016/j.comppsych.2013.11.012

Maté G. (1999). *Scattered minds: The origins and healing of attention deficit disorder*. London: Penguin.

Meerkerk, G.-J., Van Den Eijnden, R.J. & Garretsen, H.F.L. (2006). Predicting compulsive internet use: it's all about sex! *Cyberpsychol Behav.*, 9 (1), 95–103. doi:10.1089/cpb.2006.9.95.

Mesibov, G. & Sreckovic, M. (2017). Child juvenile pornography and autism spectrum disorder. In L.A Dubin & E. Horowitz (eds), *Caught in the web of the Criminal Justice System: Autism, developmental disabilities and sex offences*. Philadelphia: Jessica Kingsley.

Mollon, P. (2015). *The disintegrating self: Psychotherapy of adult ADHD, autistic spectrum, and somato-psychic disorders*. Abingdon: Routledge.

Negash, S., Sheppard, N. V.N., Lambert, N.M. & Fincham, F.D. (2016). Trading later rewards for current pleasure: Pornography consumption and delay discounting. *Journal of Sex Research*, 53 (6), 689–700. doi:10.1080/00224499.2015.1025123.

Nestler, E.J. (2005). Is there a common molecular pathway for addiction? *Nat Neuroscience*, 8 (11), 1445–1449. doi:10.1038/nn1578.

Neves, S. (2021). *Compulsive sexual behaviours: A psycho-sexual treatment guide for clinicians*. Abingdon: Routledge.

Olsen, C.M. (2011). Natural rewards, neuroplasticity, and non-drug addictions. *Neuropharmacology*, 61 (7), 1109–1122. doi:10.1016/j.neuropharm.2011.03.010.

O'Sullivan, L.F., Byers, E.S., Brotto, L.A., Majerovich, J.A. & Fletcher, J.A. (2016). Longitudinal study of problems in sexual functioning and related sexual distress among middle to late adolescents. *J. Adolesc Health*, 59 (3), 318–324. doi:10.1016/j.jadohealth.2016.05.001.

Panksepp, J. (1998). *Affective neuroscience: The foundations of human and animal emotions*. New York: Oxford University Press.

Peciña, S. (2008). Opioid reward 'liking' and 'wanting' in the nucleus accumbens. *Physiol. Behav.*, 94 (5), 675–680. doi:10.1016/j.physbeh.2008.04.006.

Russell, A. J., Mataix-Cols, D., Anson, M. & Murphy, D.G. (2005). Obsessions and compulsions in Asperger syndrome and high-functioning autism. *British Journal of Psychiatry*, 186 (6), 525–528. doi:10.1192/bjp.186.6.525.

Salamon, J.D. & Correa, M. (2012). The mysterious motivational functions of mesolimbic dopamine. *Neuron*, 76 (3), 470–485. doi:10.1016/j.neuron.2012.10.021.

Samenow, C.P. (2010). A biopsychosocial model of hypersexual disorder/sexual addiction. *Sexual Addiction & Compulsivity*, 17, 69–81.

Sanderson, C. (2014). *Counselling skills for working with shame*. London: Jessica Kingsley.

Schneider, S. *et al.* (2011). Boys do it the right way: Sex-dependent amygdala lateralization during face processing in adolescents. *Neuroimage*, 56(3), 1847–1853.

Schore, A. (2003). Early relational trauma, disorganised attachment, and the development of a predisposition to violence. In. D. Siegel & M. Solomon (eds), *Healing trauma: Attachment, mind, body and brain*. New York: Norton.

Schöttle, D., Briken, P, Tüscher, O. & Turner, D. (2017). Sexuality in autism: Hypersexual and paraphilic behaviour in women and men with high-functioning autism spectrum disorder. *Dialogues Clin Neurosci*, 19 (4), 381–393. doi:10.31887/DCNS.2017.19.4/dschoettle.

Seigfried-Spellar, K.C. (2016). Deviant pornography use: The role of early-onset adult pornography use and individual differences. *International Journal of Cyber Behavior, 6(3), 34–47*. doi:10.018/IJCBPL.20160701034.

Siegel, D.J. (2003). An interpersonal neurobiology of psychotherapy. In D.J. Siegel & M.F. Solomon (eds), *Healing trauma. Attachment, mind, body & brain*. New York: Norton.

Stabenow, T. (2011). A method for careful study: A proposal for reforming the child pornography guidelines. *Federal Sentencing Reporter*, 24 (2), 108–136. www.jstor.org/stable/10.1525/fsr.2011.24.2.108.

Stark, R. & Klucken, T. (2017). Neuroscientific approaches to (online) pornography addiction. In M. Reuter & C. Montag (eds), *Internet addiction: Neuroscientific approaches and therapeutic implications including smartphone addiction (2nd edition)*. Ulm, Germany: Springer.

Tremblay, R.E., Japel, C., Pérusse, D. & McDuff, P. (1999) The search for the age of 'onset' of physical aggression: Rousseau and Bandura revisited. *Criminal Behaviour and Mental Health*, 9 (1), 8–23. doi:10.1002/cbm.288

van der Kolk, B. (2014). *The body keeps the score: Mind, brain and body transformation of trauma*. London: Penguin.

Vaswani, N., Mullen, L., Efthymiadou, E. & Allardyce, S. (2022). *The risk of online sexual abuse (ROSA) project*. Bromsgrove: The Faithful Papers.

Voon, V., Mole, T.B., Banca, P., Porter, L., Morris, L, *et al.* (2014). Neural correlates of sexual cue reactivity in individuals with and without compulsive sexual behaviours. *PLOS ONE* 9 (7), e102419. doi:10.1371/journal.pone.0102419

Ward, T., Polaschek, D. & Beech, A. R. (2009). *Theories of sexual offending*. Chichester: Wiley.

Weinberger, D.R., Elvevag, B. & Giedd, J.N. (2005). *The adolescent brain: A work in progress*. The National Campaign to Prevent Teen Pregnancy.

Wilson, G (2017). *Your brain on porn: Internet pornography and the emerging science of addiction* (2nd edition). Kent: Commonwealth Publishing.

Wright, P.J., Tokunaga, R.S. & Kraus, A. (2015). A meta-analysis of pornography consumption and actual acts of sexual aggression in general population studies. *Journal of Communication*, 66 (1), 183–205. doi:10.1111/jcom.12201.

Zillmann, D. & Bryant, J. (1988). Pornography's impact on sexual satisfaction. *Journal of Applied Social Psychology*, 18 (5), 438–453. doi:10.1111/j.1559–1816.1988.tb00027.x

Chapter 6

Transgenerational transmission and the development of the self

This chapter discusses the formation and neurological development of the sense of self, and how trauma tends to repeat itself across generations. The sense of self can be damaged by adverse childhood experiences and may lead to a vast array of psychological and physical consequences. It discusses the victim to perpetrator cycle, the differences between male and female victims of abuse, and potential protective factors that prohibit history repeating itself. In the case study, the therapist takes the client back to the origin of his aggressive behaviour, and helps him understand that he was acting out memories of the past instead of living in the here and now.

Case study

'I'm getting a dog!' Gordon blurts out as he attends for his weekly session with his therapist. Excitedly he sits on the chair, his face open, eyes wide. The therapist notices he is dressed differently. The usual track suit has gone, and he is wearing jeans and a white t-shirt, both clean and newly pressed. 'Yes,' he continues. 'I am getting a little dog. He is a sort of terrier cross, four years old and I'm getting him from the Dog's Trust. He was badly treated by his first owner, and he became quite aggressive. But they have retrained him.'

'A bit like you really.' The therapist knew she was taking a risk by this tease, but was testing his reaction, which would previously have been a defensive attack.

Gordon turned sharply, then gave a toothy grin. 'Yeah. Like you've trained me.' They both laughed.

Gordon continued excitedly. 'I have been to see him every day this week. At first, he just crawled to me on his stomach, like. But now he has got to know me and he comes running up with his little tail wagging.'

'When you saw him crawl to you on his stomach, how did that make you feel?'

Gordon's excitement drained from his eyes, his leg began to bounce and his fists clenched. 'I thought, I know what that feels like.'

'No, Gordon,' the therapist gently corrects, 'that is not a feeling, that is a thought. What was the feeling? You seemed to identify with the dog's behaviour. What was that feeling for you?'

DOI: 10.4324/9781003330899-6

There is a long pause, with confusion breaking over Gordon's face. His leg stops bouncing and he starts to curl up in the chair, making himself look smaller. 'I can't say,' he whispers, 'I don't know.'

'Can you say the first time you felt like this?'

'Always. I have always had to be like the dog. Keep low, keep small, stay out of the way, hide under the chair, hide under the table, don't get in the way ...'

The therapist notices he is holding his breath. 'Breathe, Gordon'.

He exhales loudly. Tears flood Gordon's eyes and plop onto his cheeks. The therapist pushes a tissue box closer, but he ignores it and sniffs loudly.

'You can't seem to say what you feel, Gordon, but can you say where you feel it, in your body?'

Another pause. Then he places his hand on his chest 'Here' and then on his stomach 'and here'.

'If the pain in your chest could speak, Gordon, what would it say?'

No pause here. He blurted, 'It would say, why don't you love me? Why don't care for me? Why don't you notice me? Why am I so unloveable?' He wails with the pain.

The therapist waits for it to subside, and then asks, 'and the pain in the stomach? What would that say?'

'It would say that I am hungry. It hurts. Why won't you feed me?' More sobs.

'And these questions, are they to your mother?'

He nods dumbly. She watches gently, and becomes aware of her own stomach rumbling. She places her hand on her stomach, and holds it there as she watches.

Then she notices his posture change. His fists curl again he sits upright to make himself look taller, his jaw is clenched and his chin juts out. 'She didn't look after me, so I have to look after meself.' Anger and determination flood his face.

'I understand that Gordon. As a small, overlooked child, living in a house where violence was the norm, you adapted your behaviour to cope, and to survive. And these feelings in your body that you feel now, as a grown up, are memories of when you were tiny, before you had words to describe them. Sometimes, your behaviour today is still responding to the hidden memories of the past; you are not responding to the here and now. Just as the little dog learned to trust you over time, you need to learn to trust other people now. Your defensive attacks have gone past their sell-by date. You are no longer under the threat that you were. Your anger was designed to take away the pain of feeling unloved, but the consequence is that the anger has given you different pain. It has taken you down dark paths, and you have lost your wife and child as a consequence.'

Gordon relaxed into the chair, and looked at the therapist long and hard. 'You know what?' he finally said. 'You are absolutely right. I don't know how old I was when I said this to meself, but I remember thinking I am going to have to fight to live. I let my anger take me over. I've never known what it was like not to be angry.'

'Will the little dog make you angry if he doesn't do what you want him to do?'

'Never!' Gordon was emphatic. 'He's going to be loved, and cuddled, and fed, and loved some more. We are both going to put our bad memories into the past. We'll do it together.'

'Oh, that's nice. Does this dog have a name?'

'Not yet. The original owner just called him Dog. I'm going to call him Rex – after the dinosaur.' Another toothy grin. 'They have checked out my flat, and my boss says I can take it with me when I go to work, so long as he doesn't shit all over the garage floor.' Gordon clapped his hand over his mouth and blushed a little. 'Oops. Sorry'.

The therapist chuckled. 'Well, if he has been trained, he is unlikely to shit on the garage floor.' Her smile dropped and she looked pensive, anticipating a further attachment injury. 'But what about if you end up going to prison, Gordon? What will happen to your little dog then?'

Gordon's shoulders dropped and his smile faded. 'Yes. I know that is likely after what I've done to Rach, and the pictures, and that. I've told Mrs Watkins everything, and she said if that happens, she will keep the dog for me until I am released. She came with me once to see him.'

'Mrs Watkins?'

'Mrs Watkins. Yeah. She's the little old lady I told you about who I met in the park. I do 'er garden for 'er now, but I remembered what you said. I never go in 'er house. I don't ask for pay, but she brings me tea and cake when I'm in 'er garden.'

'Well, Gordon. What a transition you are making. I do believe this is the first time in your life you have actually been doing things for someone else.'

'Yeah. You're right. I would never 've done somat for nothin' before. But I like 'er. And she has always been nice to me.'

'I think you told me that she already has a dog of her own. Will a little old lady be able to manage two dogs if you are sent away?'

'She said it will be OK. She retired about 6 months ago, so she said she has plenty of time on 'er hands now.'

The therapist realised that the 'little old lady' was probably a lot younger than herself. She decided to change the subject.

Development of the concept of self

Willmott (2022) highlighted that the attachment system leads to the development of interpersonal relationships, self-regulation and the concept of the self. If the attachment figure of a child is the source of maltreatment, all these systems can be impaired. Without a sense of self, there is no sense of other, and this can impede the Theory of Mind toward others, interfering with empathy and compassion. In addition, insecure attachment often produces a BAD-ME circuit with an overwhelming sense of toxic shame (see Chapter 3) where the child believes they are unlovable and unlikeable because they are not getting the love and care that they need (Schore, 1994). This has a pervasive and corrosive effect on the child, soon to be adult's, sense of self, and can lead to a habit of self-criticism and self-blame, particularly for children who were emotionally neglected or overlooked. As Kathryn Stauffer (2021) argued, they become a precocious internal parent who is internally harsh and critical to an extreme degree, and who is full of fear and self-loathing. Stauffer splits this self-interpretation into two: if the BAD is located into the sense of self, then the person's presentation can become schizoid, producing a more pervasive and generalised sense of toxic shame. If the BAD is located into a need or want, then that is more oral. We can see here that the former is a right-brain internalisation that corrupts the sense of self, whereas the latter is a left-brain narrative about not having wants and needs met, which can trigger FEAR and RAGE.

The insula in the midbrain is now thought to be the part of the midbrain that provides the link of understanding ourselves as human. Its development is promoted from a secure attachment producing opposing social emotions, like the feeling of lust but also disgust, pride yet humiliation, guilt yet atonement. It is also thought to store our empathetic processes and our moral reasoning. The insula receives signals from the senses, the skin and internal organs and allocates them as social emotions. So, a bad smell would be experienced as disgust; a loving touch might be sensual or it might feel abusive based on the individual's predisposing history. Damasio (2003) suggested that it is varying parts of the insula that receive information from the external parts, making ourselves aware of these in an interoceptive sense, so visceral and genital sensations will be transported and calibrated in this part of the brain. He argues that the paradox is that we cannot understand these feelings without consciousness: 'the machinery of feeling is itself a contributor to the process of consciousness, namely to the creation of the self, without which nothing can be known' (p. 110).

Another contributing factor in the corrosion of the development of the self is an infant trying to attach to a parent who has unresolved trauma, which is conveyed through the eyes in the serve and return (Porges, 2003) proto-communication between the parent and the infant, right brain to right brain (Schore, 1994). Thus, unresolved trauma trickles down from one generation to another, and corrupts the development of the self in the infant. For example, Judy Singer, mentioned in Chapter 4, who has written about her own autism, noted that her mother was a holocaust survivor (Singer, 1999), who also had Asperger traits. Is this unresolved trauma trickling down to the next generation, or is it a genetic component of neurodiversity as some might have us believe? No, it is both. Our genetic coding may pass down the generations, but so does our reactivity and adaptation of the environment in which we find ourselves, which has an interactive effect on the genome. The difficulties children find themselves in is not just a consequence of the parenting they received, but the parents are acting from the parenting they received, and so the perception of trauma can go back generations.

Adverse childhood experiences

It is a well-established fact that childhood abuse and household dysfunction particularly during the prenatal and first 3 years of life are a leading cause of chronic physical illness like heart disease, cancer, chronic lung disease, diabetes and hypertension, and also mental health issues, substance and alcohol abuse in adult life (Felitti et al., 1998; Anda et al., 2006). These adverse childhood experiences (ACEs) are:

- recurrent physical abuse;
- recurrent emotional abuse;
- contact sexual abuse;
- substance abuse taking place within the home;
- a household member in prison;
- a household member suffers with mental illness;
- domestic violence (usually, but not always, to the mother from a partner);
- parental separation/divorce;
- physical neglect; and
- emotional neglect.

Exposure to four or more adverse experiences in childhood increases the likelihood of alcoholism, drug abuse, depression and makes a person 12 times more likely to attempt suicide. They are more likely to be violent, have more broken bones, more drug prescriptions, more depression, and more auto-immune diseases. Those with an ACE score of six or greater predictably die 20 years younger than the rest of the population. High ACE scores have also been linked with some sexual behaviours, for example engaging in sexual activity prior to the age of 15, adolescent pregnancy, or having 50 or more sexual partners, and foetal death (Hillis et al., 2004). In a study of 679 male sexual offenders Levenson, Willis and Prescott, (2016) found that they had twice the likelihood of having suffered physical abuse, three times more likely to have suffered from sexual abuse, four times more likely of coming from a broken home, four times more likely to have experienced emotional neglect, and thirteen times more likely to have experienced recurrent verbal and emotional abuse compared to the general population. They are also more likely to repeat the behaviour they have learned within their childhood scripts when they reach their own adulthood. Similarly, Felitti et al. (1998) found that severe childhood maltreatment showed up to 12 times the risk of alcoholism, drug addiction, depression and suicidal attempts when adult, They also found that women who had a history of sexual abuse and neglect were 7 times more likely to be raped, and if they had witnessed domestic violence in childhood, were more likely to experience it themselves in adulthood. In a similar vein, it has been found that pregnant women who experience violence through their pregnancy, thus having raised levels of cortisol, have children demonstrating psychiatric symptoms up to the age of 9 (Isaksson et al., 2015). Despite this being a well-established phenomenon in the literature, when it comes to evaluating those who commit, particularly sexual or violent, offences, this is rarely taken into account. They are described as mad or bad through the criminal justice system, and any attempt to highlight their own trauma in their own history is discounted as manipulative to get sympathy or a means to get any potential sentencing reduced. Where is the line drawn between a society feeling compassion for a damaged child, to vilification when that child grows up and acts out because the internal damage has been ignored?

The victim to perpetrator cycle

The cycle of abuse between victim and perpetrator is a much-argued discourse. It has been suggested that a cycle of sexual abuse is a phenomenon that is tied to a forensic psychotherapy population which only becomes evident when the clients disclose their earlier experiences and admit to their perpetrator behaviour. For example, Jespersen, Lalumière and Seto (2009) found that sexual abuse was a significant factor in the background of those with atypical sexual interests and sexual offences. Alternatively, some hold that sexual perpetrators may feign sexual victimisation in order to gain sympathy or preferential treatment, calling it, derogatorily, 'the vampire myth'. But the confounding variable in these arguments is the term 'abuse'. In my view, not all victims of sexual abuse become perpetrators, but all perpetrators have experienced some form of trauma in their early developmental history. And there seems to be a societal perception of a sliding scale of trauma that a person may have experienced, for others to make perceived judgements as to whether the event or events was severe enough to be damaging to the psychological well-being of the person. Loss in childhood is a significant traumatiser, whether it be death of a significant other, like a parent, sibling or grandparent, divorce or separation of parents, physical abuse leading to family separation or disintegration, addiction within parents, dysfunctional family relationships especially domestic violence, or parental psychiatric illness. These are the ACEs, and as Finkelhor, Ormrod and Turner (2007) point out, these are multiple victimisations that tend to be over looked in the literature, a phenomenon they called poly-victimisation.

But it is not the trauma, *per se* that causes the damage. It is each individual child's perception of the event that causes the damage, and that may be related to whether the child is in Right-brain or Left-brain development at the time of the event. Recall that the two halves of the brain do not develop simultaneously, but consecutively (Hudson-Allez, 2011). When the child is in Left-brain development, the child develops a narrative or understanding around the complexity of the circumstances in which they live. And even when the child is quite young, (that is, over 30 months when the left hemisphere comes online) and the narrative might be simplistic, the narrative helps regulate the extremes of the emotional damage from processing trauma.

So, if a child is in left brain development, the memory of the event will be stored in the left hippocampus, and will tend to have a narrative around the event, that helps the child make sense of what happened. This narrative may not necessarily be logical or accurate, but it makes sense for the child. Interestingly, children don't tend to adopt the forms of denial of traumatic events that is a common in an adult presentation. They often remember the incident in vivid detail, but this will only occur if the event was a single one. Long-standing, ongoing events are remembered with much less clarity as defensive mechanisms come into play, like denial, splitting, self-anaesthesia and dissociation (Terr, 1990), which is vital to protect the child for the next event, but fragments the memory in terms of its formation, storage and retrieval. Ironically, because of the fragmentation, children who do pluck up sufficient courage to speak out will be less likely to be believed.

If the child is in Right-brain development, the memory of the event will be stored in the right hippocampus, with direct somatic connections, and without words to describe it. As Bessell van der Kolk (2014) emphasised, the body will keep the score. If the child is in Right-brain development, any trauma or loss is encapsulated in a schema with a physiological emotional/body tag, which the child struggles to conceptualise without a narrative. At whatever stage the child is exposed to parental separation or loss in their developmental history, for me, is the key to understanding this. The brain will keep flashing up these schematic experiences, which are chunks of memory without a narrative to make sense of it, and when they go through life and a similar experience happens, these schemata flash back with their own alarm bells ringing. This dysregulation, which is both physical and psychological, is essentially memories of a history that cannot be recalled.

As the child becomes older, when the sexual template (LUST circuit) comes online, again during Right-brain development, it may contribute to sexual abuse victims becoming more vulnerable to either further victimisation or the development of diverse sexual fantasies, leading to re-enactment of body memories with others that cannot be recalled. Bagley, Wood & Young (1994) found that the combination of emotional abuse in a person's childhood, along with multiple events of sexual and emotional abuse, was a relatively good predictor of both poor mental health, and later sexual interest in or sexual contact with children. When emotional abuse was controlled for, child sexual abuse remained a statistically significant predictor of current sexual interest in children.

In a 45-year longitudinal study, Ogloff, Cutajar, Mann and Mullen (2012) correlated 2,759 medically confirmed cases of childhood sexual abuse with police database records up to 44 years after the abuse was confirmed. When this data was compared to a similar number drawn from the Australian Electoral Commission (matched for age and gender), the authors found that 5% of male child sexual abuse victims were subsequently convicted of a sexual offence, which was significantly greater than for men who had not been sexually abused as children (0.6%). The link between victimisation and subsequent sexual offending was even greater among men abused at 12 years of age or older, with 9.2% being convicted of a sexual offence. They found that childhood sexual abuse victims were almost five times more likely than the general population to be charged with any offence compared to their non-abused controls. The most typical offences were sexual offences, violent offences and breach of court orders.

By contrast, female victims of childhood sexual abuse were no more likely than female nonvictims to be convicted of a sexual offence, but the risk of them becoming the victims of rape, sexual harassment or a victim of domestic violence doubled (Herman, 1992). Plummer and Cossins (2018) undertook a literature review to try and untangle the reason why most victims of sexual abuse are female (that we know about) whereas most perpetrators are male. They concluded that there was no cycle of abuse for women, but there was indeed one for men, identifying four significant factors in the perpetrator's history:

- That they were abused around the age of 12 (Ogloff et al., 2012): (right-brain development and vandalised sexual template)
- That they were subject to frequent abuse (Bagley et al., 1994)
- That the abuse was serious (Simons, Wurtele & Durham, 2008)
- The abuse was conducted by an attachment (e.g. father) figure.

They also found a relationship between men's experiences of power and powerlessness as a result of their social relationships with other men in their family and peer groups that predicts a boy's experiences of powerlessness and the extent to which those experiences inform his sexuality. The more power-less he felt as a child, the more likely he will seek out sexual experiences with less powerful objects of desire, such as children, so 'that powerlessness and sexuality become central and defining features of his masculinity, and, hence, his experiences of self-worth' (Cossins, 2000, p. 195).

Similarly, Streeck-Fischer and van der Kolk (2000) argued that childhood exposure to intrafamilial violence and other chronic trauma results in pervasive psychological and biological deficits, which in medical settings usually meet the criteria for numerous clinical diagnoses, none of which capture the complexity of their biological, emotional and cognitive problems. They highlight: 'under stress they pass the dehumanisation that they themselves experienced onto others' (p. 911).

And picking up Cossin's (2000) point about powerlessness, is it that being a childhood witness or victim of domestic violence, or significant loss, makes the child feel totally powerless? What these studies generally suggest is that about a third of men who have been subjected to childhood sexual abuse, particularly by a stranger, rather than familial, will become perpetrators of childhood sexual abuse (Glasser et al., 2018), which of course means that two-thirds don't. Prendergast (1993) argued that as the abusive act is a trau-matic one, the change from being the passive victim to the active perpetrator was a process of identification with his childhood aggressor, and as such is the way in which some victims repeatedly attempt to master their own trauma. This toxic shame elicits a process of self-sabotage, whereby the person's strong BAD-ME circuit promotes a feeling of nonchalance in acting out: 'I'm a bad person anyway, so why not?' colloquially known as the 'fuck it' response. Sanderson (2014) highlighted that men who were sexually abused or raped in childhood by a male perpetrator were more likely to search for gay porn despite being heterosexual, as they are flooded with obsessive memory schemata about men having sex with men. Similarly, she proposed that women would masturbate to images of their own abuse because they feel the shame of responsibility; that they orchestrated or wanted it in some way. She suggested a form of traumatophilia; being submerged and preoccupied by one's own abuse. To me, it just reinforces the point that in such circumstances, men attack out or externalise, whereas women attack in or internalise (Holden, 2005) which equally accounts for why the cycle of abuse is not found in the female population.

Protective factors

As mentioned in Chapter 1, there are many men who describe themselves a minor-attracted persons (MAPs) who have never harmed a child, looked at inappropriate images or indulged in any other offending behaviour. What protects them from themselves? How can they manage their desires and impulses, whereas others cannot? A strong sense of resilience in the face of adversity would be key; hence a secure attachment and strong familial support. MAPs do face a vast amount of social stigma, so most would want to keep their thoughts and feelings to themselves. Many struggle with these feelings, but the fear of disclosure prevents many from seeking therapeutic support. This fear may be warranted, as some argue that disclosure will prevent the abuse of a child in the future. However, this argument is not based on the evidence. Stevens and Woods (2019) analysed posts from the Virtuous Paedophiles forum and suggested four protective strategies: managing the risk, managing the mood, managing preferences prosocially, and family, friends and relationships. Here again we have the need to maintain links within the family, yet our system insists on alienating them from their wives and children.

Being female is a major protective factor from repeating the abuse from your history. Kronner (2015) argued for the end of male supremacy, suggesting that women, in comparison to men, are more trustworthy, more reliable, fairer, work and play better with others and have lower levels of prejudice and bigotry. They also are more cooperative, less aggressive, and less motivated and distracted by sex. It is certainly true that men outnumber women in all of the major criminal offences.

Prendergast (1993) focused on men who do not enter the victim-to-abuser cycle, despite having a history of childhood sexual abuse. He listed a series of factors derived from his own case material which appeared to be protective factors, these being:

- good self-esteem;
- a significant other adult in the child's life besides the abusers, with whom they could attach to;
- religious belief;
- success in schoolwork, sports or activities which reflected the pride of the parents;
- the strength of personality of the child that enabled them to have long-term goals rather than day-to-day short-term goals (delayed rather than instant gratification);
- monitoring by the child's parents, reducing the possibility of further abuse; and
- sexual knowledge at the outset of the seduction, so that any sexual pleasure was less likely to ensnare the child in a downward spiral of shame and guilt.

What this list suggests is attachment and relationship connection are the fundamental protective factors.

Gordon's review

Gordon is starting to undertake social processes he has never undertaken before. The therapist has collaborated with him in planning how he has made his life-style changes, and he is beginning to identify the benefits of doing so for himself. He never really knew how to look after himself before; this is not something he learned from his upbringing, from being a very overlooked and subsequently abused child. He is starting to form an attachment with his therapist, and although there is still some avoidance and fear around this, he is starting to learn to take a risk with this relationship. He is learning to trust, as his therapist never rejects him, and has made him understand that even though he has done bad things, he is not a bad person. As a consequence, his compensatory narcissistic cloak of many colours and many layers, which he has worn all his life to hide his BAD-ME circuit and his shame, is starting to fragment.

Gordon had developed this angry and aggressive cloak from childhood to adolescence as a survival strategy to protect himself against domestic violence in the home, both with his biological father and later his stepfather. Judith Lewis Herman expressed his terror poignantly:

> Repeated trauma in childhood forms and deforms the personality. The child trapped in an abusive environment is faced with formidable tasks of adaption. She must find a way to preserve a sense of trust in people who are untrustworthy, safety in a situation that is unsafe, control in a situation that is terrifyingly unpredictable, power in a situation of helplessness. Unable to care for or protect herself, she must compensate for the failures

of adult care and protection with the only means at her disposal, an immature system of psychological defences.

(Herman, 1992, p. 96)

Gordon's childhood learning was that violence was how relationships were maintained; that the men maintained power and control, the women were submissive, and the children did as they were told or were beaten. But Gordon's simmering adult anger was not directed at his father and stepfather, but at his mother, whom he perceived as complicit in the abuse and abandoned him to his fate. She knew what happening, Gordon argued, and she should have cared enough to protect him. Judith Herman elaborated how this aggression towards others can develop:

When I was thirteen or fourteen, I decided I'd had enough. I started fighting back. I got really rough. One time a girl was picking on me and I beat the shit out of her ... Once a kid starts fighting back and becomes delinquent, he reaches a point of no return. People should find out what the hell is going on in the family before the kid ruins his whole life. Investigate! Don't lock the kid up!

(Herman, 1992, p. 113)

When Gordon transferred his attachment from his mother to Rachel, he transferred his childhood learning into his relationship with her. Fed by his terrifying insecure fear that she might abandon him as his mother had, he used the coercive control he learned in childhood to keep Rachel in her place: by his side. At times when he thought he was losing her, violence erupted and he was unable to regulate the combined anger and fear, and he would lash out.

Now, in his therapeutic journey, some layers of his narcissistic cloak are starting to peel away. He reached out to the internet because he was seeking, searching for attachment and searching for sex, as the SEEKING circuit's primary role is to search for CARE. The attachment circuitry and the LUST circuit are indelibly intertwined; without this union, there would be no survival of the species if humans did not couple together to procreate and raise children. So, as Gordon's automatic thoughts of search for CARE led him to think about pornography on the internet, so he had made a mental association to the only person he had received care from: his estranged wife Rachel, currently living in a woman's refuge. As his metaphorical cloak peeled away, he had looked through his narcissistic mirror, which had allowed the reality of his behaviour to reflect back on him. For the first time he felt remorse, identified his shame, expressed in his own way his guilt, and allowed himself to grieve what he had lost. But first he needed to grieve for himself, and the only path he could find in leading him to understand all that he had lost, was through the appeasement behaviour of a little dog.

References

Anda, R.F., Felitti, V.J., Bremner, J.D., Walker, J.D. *et al.* (2006). The enduring effects of abuse and related adverse experiences in childhood. A convergence of evidence from neurobiology and epidemiology. *Eur Arch Psychiatry Clin Neurosci.*, 256 (3), 174–186.

Bagley, C., Wood, M. & Young, L. (1994). Victim to abuser: mental health and behavioural sequels of child sexual abuse in a community survey of young adult males. *Child Abuse & Neglect*, 18 (8), 683–697. doi:10.1016/0145-2134(94)90018-3.

Cossins, A. (2000). *Masculinities, sexualities, and child sexual abuse.* The Hague, the Netherlands: Kluwer Law International.

Damasio, A. (2003). *Looking for Spinoza: Joy, sorrow and the feeling brain.* London: Vintage.

Felitti, V.J., Anda, R.F., Nordenberg, D.Williamson, D.F. *et al.* (1998). Relationship of childhood abuse and household dysfunction to many of the leading causes of death in adults: The Adverse Childhood Experiences (ACE) study. *Am J Prev Med.*, 14 (4), 245–258.

Finkelhor, D., Ormrod, R. & Turner, H.A. (2007). Poly-victimization: a neglected component in child victimisation. *Child Abuse Negl.*, 31 (1), 7–26. doi:10.1016/j. chiabu.2006.06.008.

Glasser, M., Kolvin, I., Campbell, D., Glasser, A. *et al.* (2018). Cycle of child sexual abuse: Links between being a victim and becoming a perpetrator. *The British Journal of Psychiatry*, 179 (6), 482–494.

Herman, J. L. (1992). *Trauma and recovery: From domestic abuse to political terror.* London: Pandora.

Hillis, S.D., Anda, R.F., Dube, S.R., Feletti, V.J. *et al.* (2004). The association between adverse childhood experiences and adolescent pregnancy, long-term psychosocial consequences, and foetal death. *Pediatrics*, 113 (2), 320–327. doi:10.1542/ peds.113.2.320.

Holden, C. (2005). Sex and the suffering brain. *Science*, 308 (5728), 1574. doi:10.1126/ science.308.5728.1574.

Hudson-Allez, G. (2011). *Infant losses, adult searches: A neural and developmental perspective on psychopathology and sexual offending.* London: Karnac.

Isaksson, J., Lindblad, F., Valladares, E. & Högberg, U. (2015). High maternal cortisol levels during pregnancy are associated with more psychiatric symptoms in offspring at age of nine – A prospective study from Nicaragua. *J Psychiatr Res*, 71, 97–102. doi:10.1016/j.jpsychires.2015.09.016.

Jespersen, A.F., Lalumière, M.L. & Seto, M. C. (2009). Sexual abuse history among adult sex offenders and non-sex offenders: A meta-analysis. *Child Abuse and Neglect*, 33 (3), 179–192. doi:10.1016/j.chiabu.2008.07.004.

Kronner, M (2015). *Women after all: Sex, evolution, and the end of male supremacy.* New York: Norton.

Levenson, J.S., Willis, G M. & Prescott, D.S. (2016). Adverse childhood experiences in the lives of male sex offenders: Implications for trauma-informed care. *Sex Abuse*, 28 (4), 340–359. doi:10.1177/1079063214535819.

Ogloff, J.R.P, Cutajar, M.C., Mann, E. & Mullen, P. (2012). Child sexual abuse and subsequent offending and victimisation: A 45 year follow-up study. Retrieved from www.aic.gov.au/publications/tandi/tandi440.

Plummer, M. & Cossins, A. (2018). The cycle of abuse: When victims become offenders. *Trauma, Violence & Abuse*, 19 (3), 286–304. doi:10.1177/1524838016659487.

Porges, S.W. (2003). Social engagement and attachment: A phylogenetic perspective. *Annals of the New York Academy of Sciences*, 1008, 31–47. doi:10.1196/annals.1301.004.

Prendergast, W. E. (1993). *The merry-go-round of sexual abuse: Identifying and treating survivors*. New York: Guilford.

Sanderson, C. (2014). *Counselling skills for working with shame*. London: Jessica Kingsley.

Schore, A. (1994). *Affective regulation and the origin of the self*. Hillsdale, NJ: Lawrence Erlbaum.

Simons, D.A., Wurtele, S.K., & Durham, R.L. (2008). Developmental experiences of child sexual abusers and rapists. *Child Abuse Neglect*, 32 (5), 549–560. doi:10.1016/j.chiabu.2007.03.027..

Singer, J. (1999). Why can't you be normal for once in your life. In M. Corker & S. French (eds), *Disability discourse*. Bristol: McGraw-Hill Education.

Stauffer, K.A. (2021). *Emotional neglect and the adult in therapy*. New York: Norton.

Stevens, E. & Woods, J. (2019). 'I despise myself for thinking about them.' A thematic analysis of the mental health implications and employed coping mechanisms of self-reported non-offending minor-attracted persons. *Journal of Child Sexual Abuse*, 28 (8), 968–989. doi:10.1080/10538712.2019.1657539.

Streeck-Fischer, A. & van der Kolk, B.A. (2000). Down will come baby, cradle and all: diagnostic and therapeutic implications of chronic trauma on child development. *Aust N Z J Psychiatry*, 34 (6), 903–918. doi:10.1080/000486700265.

Terr, L. (1990). *Too scared to cry: Psychic trauma in childhood*. New York: Harper & Row.

van der Kolk, B. (2014). *The body keeps the score: Mind, brain and body transformation of trauma*. London: Penguin.

Willmott, P. (2022). Childhood maltreatment links to offending. In P. Willmott & L. Jones (eds), *Trauma-informed forensic practice*. London: Routledge.

Chapter 7

Trauma and the early sexualisation of children

Case Study

The therapist's phone rings while she is in session with a client. The caller leaves a message, identifying herself as a child protection social worker, and wants to talk about a family she is working with, as she knows that the therapist is working with the father on his offending behaviour. She identifies Gordon. The therapist phones Gordon and after a discussion about the pros and cons of the therapist having a conversation with this person, he gives his informed consent for her to do so in a letter later on that day.

'How can I help?' the therapist enquires warily when she returns the call, not wanting to give too much away.

'Thank you for calling back,' came the response. 'I was working with the wife and child of your client when they were living in the refuge escaping her husband's violence.'

'Was? Are you not now?'

'Well, the mother, Rachel, was hospitalised after having what looked like a psychotic incident, so she had to be sectioned and we put her child, Connor, into foster care on a temporary basis.'

'Was Rachel having a psychotic incident?'

'I'm not sure, and neither is the psychiatrist. She might be bipolar. We knew her mother was bipolar and killed herself in the end. So we couldn't take any chances with Rachel. She was deeply distressed about being separated from her husband and wanted to return to him. The more we told her she couldn't, that we would have to remove the child if she did, the more out of control she became, lashing out at everyone who came near her.'

'A bit self-fulfilling that was, then.' An awkward silence.

'Anyway,' the social worker continued, 'that was six months ago. About two months ago, we found Rachel a little council flat and have been working with her to be reunited with her son, doing life skills, teaching her budgeting, that kind of thing.'

'I see. I'm still not sure why you are telling me this …'

DOI: 10.4324/9781003330899-7

'Well, Connor has been sent to CAMHS for assessment of a conduct disorder and ADHD. The boy was sent home from his reception class for pulling down the trousers of his classmate, and simulating sexual thrusting. As you're a psychosexual therapist, I thought you might be able to offer some insight into his behaviour, especially as you know his father.'

'I would be happy to offer some insight into the child's sexual behaviour, but not in terms of connection with his father. They have spent very little time together, actually. Is Connor still in foster care, or is he with Rachel?'

'He's in an emergency care placement at the moment. I'm not sure under the circumstances whether I should send him back to Rachel, whether she could cope with him, given her own fragility.'

'Why an emergency care placement?' asked the puzzled therapist. 'Has he been acting out like this at the foster home toward other children?'

The was a long pause, and the social worker sighed. 'Look. I don't want this to be general knowledge, but it seems that a babysitter found the foster carer's older son trying to have sex with Connor. So we had to move him quickly. But that is not really why I am ringing. My question to you is, as Connor's father is a sex offender, is the same thing going to happen to Connor? Does it run in families? Is that why he is doing this? Or do you think, like we do, that he has probably abused his own son?'

Infant sexuality

Biological sexual development begins in utero, as the genitals begin to develop after the 6th week of gestation. As early as 16 weeks, erectile responses in male foetuses have been viewed with ultrasound. It is assumed that is will be similar for female foetuses and that lubrication and clitoral erection would begin this early as well, although the technology for demonstrating it doesn't yet exist (but just watch this space). Babies are active and sensual, even before they are born, as one of the earliest sensory systems of the human body to function is the skin. Thus, infants can experience orgasm even in utero.

In newborn males, spontaneous erections continue to occur, awake and asleep, and female newborn's vaginas lubricate and their clitorises swell. Infants will rub their mouths and their genitals when they want to sooth themselves from high arousal states, providing themselves with comfort. As such, oral-genital behaviour is not that uncommon in younger children and is not necessarily indicative of abuse.

Although the sexual response cycle is present at birth, many parents believe that infancy and childhood is a time of sexual innocence (meaning without sexuality) and that sex is supposed to burst out full bloom at puberty or, hopefully, later. Western cultures seem extremely uncomfortable with the concept of childhood sexuality, preferring to romanticise the concept of childhood innocence. As a result, there has been a lack of appropriate research, lest the research *per se* stimulate children into sexual knowledge and activity. However, children do engage in sexual behaviours throughout their childhood, even before they have reached puberty, because they like the pleasurable feelings that their bodies are designed to elicit. But children are not driven by a desire for sexual arousal, or gratification by orgasm. Genital play is not sexual play.

Childhood sexuality

From the age of 18–24 months, children experience bodily sensations, thoughts and ideas which are nascent sexual effects (Sanderson, 2014). Parental approbation or prohibition will determine whether the child will take pleasure from these or will become subsumed with shame. Prepubescent children play sexual games, like doctors and nurses ('you show me yours and I'll show you mine'; often called the 'bums and willies' stage of child development), but as their sexual template has not been activated, their play does not usually involve sexual arousal. Stimulation of the genital area as a result of climbing ropes, bouncing on tree branches, sliding along beams or rubbing on soft fabrics may produce pleasurable feelings, which the child may enjoy repeating, but will not be erotic at this stage unless interpreted as such by an older child or an adult. At this stage, they are exploring and information-gathering. Sexual activity between childhood friends and siblings is not uncommon. They are curious about sexuality and most of the time it is harmless fun. They are learning and practising gender roles and gender-specific behaviours, and choosing whether they want to follow these roles or to be different. These behaviours are exploratory, comforting, playful, and are not hostile, aggressive or hurtful to self or others (Bancroft, 1995). This is bodily exploration; it is not sexual knowing. It is not driven by sexual desire. The behaviour may diminish if it is discovered, and may create embarrassment and shame, so tends to continue out of the view of adults thereafter. How the adult responds to this discovery is key. If the adult responds with shock, horror or outrage to the children, accusing one of being predatory or a perpetrator, then this is already creating a shame pathway with fear and anxiety that could become a self-fulfilling prophecy.

When does sexual activity between children become abusive? It will be abusive if it involves emotional and physical abuse using coercion by using threats, bribes or promises of special attention in order to maintain the secret. Under these circumstances, one can perceive an older, stronger, more powerful sibling (not necessarily older) coercing a younger, weaker sibling into sexual activity. Willmott (2022) argued that a child who has been the victim of grooming and manipulation will learn to use these techniques on others who are young and vulnerable. An age gap of a minimum of 5 years between the two was thought to be necessary before it was considered abusive, although Health Professionals surveyed considered a two-year discrepancy was sufficient to consider the activity abusive (Carlson, 2011). Considering two years is very small in child developmental variance, this seems to me to be very judgemental, and we need to be more discerning about the maturity between two children and whether one considers themselves more powerful than the other; has one been placed in charge of the other by the parent, expecting the younger to be looked after by the elder, for example. Young children also struggle to differentiate between their sexual feelings and their attachment needs (Zaniewski et al., 2019), which can become intertwined under circumstances of abuse.

Cavanagh Johnson (2002) developed a typology of sexual behaviour in children aged 12 and younger, ranging from normative sexual behaviour to increasingly more troubled behaviour, as follows increasing in severity:

- Natural and healthy, in which children engage in healthy, appropriate and natural sexual experiences.
- Sexually reactive, in which children engage in more sexual behaviours than commonly exhibited by their peers.
- Children engaged in extensive mutual sexual behaviours, including children engaged in frequent and precocious sexual behaviour with a consensual peer.
- Children who molest, including children who coerce or force other children into sexual acts, often aggressively. It is estimated that one-third of child sexual offences are committed by young people.

Cavanagh Johnson (2002) also believed that most or all of the children of the latter category have themselves been sexually or physically abused or exposed to sexually explicit materials or environments. Phil Rich argued that research does not necessarily confirm this, but highlighted that many troubled adolescents did have poor early social experiences and contended that we need: 'to understand the nature and strength of the behaviour, forces that drive the behaviour and protect against it, and the possible trajectory of the behaviour into later childhood and adolescence' (Rich, 2009, p. 178).

The internet is a game-changer for assessing the sexuality of children, many of whom have viewed pornography from as early as the age of 5 on their mobile phones, which can become highly addictive to the youngster and may lead to later erectile dysfunctions, as discussed in Chapter 5. If the children's play is that of mimicking what they have viewed in adult pornography, then the innocence of harmless fun is removed, predominantly because adult pornography rarely exhibits loving sex with discussion about consent, but an objectification and exploitation of predominantly girls, women, boys and young men. Ybarra et al. (2011) found that children and adolescents who intentionally viewed adult pornographic material had a six times higher chance of self-reporting sexually abusive behaviour. Some parents may respond quite negatively toward their child if sexually harmful behaviour is displayed by them, sometimes causing anger and distain toward the child, with negative labelling of 'predator', 'evil person' or 'monster' (Archer et al., 2020), splitting off the aspects of their child's personality to distance themselves from the behaviour. This inevitably may produce a strong BAD-ME circuit in the child and potential for self-fulfilling behaviour. Helping both the child and the parents in these situations would be vital for the future of the child, as the more parents are involved in supporting their children, the greater the likelihood of full behavioural change.

In addition to what might be viewed via the internet, some parents are inappropriately sexually open with their children even though they may not be actually abusive. They may make sexual innuendos, crack overt sexual jokes in front of the child, they may leave pornography magazines or DVD's around for the child to see, may fail to put filters on the television or computers, or actively allow their children to watch them having sex on the grounds that they are being educated. Or indeed, multi-generational families living in small accommodation where they have to share bedrooms and bathrooms, so sex cannot be undertaken in private. Boundaries may also become blurred as a parent indulges in deep kissing with the child, encouraging an older child to stay in bed with them, being inappropriately flirtatious or sexual with the child, or using a 'hands on' method of teaching children about sexual arousal. Children who experience this form of boundary-breaking from their parents are likely to break boundaries with each other. If challenged, boundary-breaking parents often respond with cognitive distortions. They may over- or under-estimate the danger for the child to view sexually explicit material. They may protect their selves at the expense of the child, misleading the child regarding the presence or absence of danger. They may deny or mock any comfort-seeking from the child who may be distressed or frightened. Or they may perceive the child as the source of danger or a rival and therefore collude with inappropriate sexual behaviour by the partner. The danger of such boundary-breaking with the young is that it places them on the trajectory for offending themselves; adult offenders often disclose early sexual experiences with their peers before the age of 10, to have witnessed sexual abuse as a child, and to have had frequent exposure to pornography before the age of 10 (Simons, Tyler & Heil, 2005).

Sexual development in neurodivergent children

When a child follows a neurodivergent neurological path, the physiological processes in the body may be the same, but the child's understanding of how they feel may be different. If the child is operating on a hyper-vigilant, high anxiety default mode network, then when the LUST circuit comes online, it may make the child feel anxious about feelings of sexual arousal, and they may become inextricably linked. Neurodivergent children tend to spend more time in solitary activities as they struggle with social interactions, which gives less opportunity to talk to their peers about their changing feelings. In addition, as they are more likely to be targeted by school bullies as their naivety and gullibility gets identified, this can lead to being bullied with sexual innuendo and even sexual assault. However, the discrepancy in theory of mind and empathy may lead the child into repeating these assaults with more vulnerable friends or relatives, without an understanding of the damage caused, and can lead to labels like 'children with sexually harmful behaviour'.

Neurodivergent post-pubescent children and teenagers will inevitably turn to online pornography as their 'textbook' of choice to learn about sex and relationships, leading to the distorted sexual scripts discussed in Chapter 5. Tony Attwood (2007) suggested a gender difference here, in that boys are more likely to turn to pornography to learn about sex, whereas girls are more likely to copy relationships in soap-operas on the TV, and may feel flattered by the attention of boys in their naivety, not realising that there is a sexual motive behind their interest. Boys will use the pornographic scenarios as role-models of how they believe sexual relationships are initiated, and again are in danger of being accused of sexual assault, as so much violence occurs in adult pornography. They are also in danger of the addictive processes described in Chapter 5, as the pornography *per se* becomes their object of special interest, especially if they are repeatedly reviewing what happened to themselves in earlier childhood (re-enactment). Similarly, a 'friend' or celebrity on social media may become an object of infatuation, leading to inappropriate sexual remarks or behaviour. However, if they are challenged about their behaviour, they are unlikely to dissemble, and will quickly admit their breaking of expected boundaries with a confusion of not really understanding that what they had been doing might be wrong or ill-judged.

Interestingly, Daniel Schöttle et al. (2017) found that those on the autistic spectrum tend to have more hypersexual and paraphilic (kink) fantasies and behaviours than the general population, although their data was mostly driven by male respondents, as they concluded that women with ASD were more socially adapted and had less ASD symptomology. This may account for why so many individuals with ASD fall into the online viewing trap.

What should we do when it is discovered that a child has been engaging in sexualised behaviour with another child?

- First, don't panic, and don't make assumptions.
- No matter how young the child is, a conversation about what they are thinking or feeling in a calm and gentle way is key. It will help determine whether the behaviour is normal, problematic, or abusive. This may be uncomfortable for the adult, but honesty and openness about the behaviour will stop driving it under ground.
- Label the behaviour for the child (don't label the child!) so they know what words to use, and explain about the appropriateness or inappropriateness of the behaviour in the given context: 'I know masturbation feels nice, but it is usual to do it in private in your bedroom or bathroom'.

- Assess the information you have been given from the child. Find out what the actual meaning or function is for the child. Expressions like 'we were just playing' or 'it was fun' suggest exploration, providing there is no power discrepancy between the children, especially in terms of intellect or maturity.

- If concerns are raised about problematic sexual behaviour, check out rationally who has the problem. Is it a problem for the child in that they are distressed? Is it a problem for the adult because it makes them feel uncomfortable or shocked? Is it a problem for the context, for example happening in class? There may also be a gender discrepancy between how adults respond to a male child or a female child experiencing unwanted sexual attention, with less concern being shown to boys.

- Monitor the behaviour. And I don't mean with CCTV, but just keeping an eye out when these children are alone together as to what might be happening really. It is likely to stop naturally after a frank discussion with a grown up, unless it is actually repetition compulsion; a re-enactment of what happened to them. In that case, seek professional help sooner rather than later. Don't let it become a well-trodden pathway.

- If the behaviour is repeated, or it is considered abusive, then it needs to be challenged firmly. However, it should be made clear that it is the behaviour that is wrong, not the child; evoking too much shame is damaging for their long-term mental health.

- Defining where play ends and abuse begins is a difficult issue (Jones, 2022). If it is considered abusive, don't sweep it under the carpet, no matter how much compassion or love you have for this child. Get therapeutic help for the child with the abusive behaviour, and get similar help for their victim. Don't make the assumption that they were too young to remember. The body keeps the score (van der Kolk, 1989).

- Getting help does not mean calling in the police or the social services. Young children should not be getting the knock, as some StopSO therapists have become aware of (T. Van Leeson, personal communication, 2023).

How do we know when a child's sexual template has been vandalised?

Kieran McGrath (2019) has written an excellent paper to help parents and carers decide what is sexually appropriate behaviour for children compared to behaviour that might be considered problematic or abusive. In categorising the behaviour into these three headings, it can help the adult get a clearer understanding of what might be going on with the children, to prevent jumping to inappropriate conclusions.

An indicator often cited as an indicator of abuse is excessive masturbation. A limitation of this as an index of sexual abuse is that most children (and adults) masturbate at some time. Thus, it is developmentally normal behaviour, which is only considered indicative of sexual abuse when 'excessive'.

However, a determination that the masturbation is excessive may be highly subjective. The following guidelines from the National Centre on Child Abuse and Neglect (Coulbourne Faller, 1993) may help to determine whether masturbation is indicative of possible sexual abuse of the child:

- masturbates to the point of injury;
- masturbates numerous times a day;
- cannot stop masturbating;
- inserts objects into vagina or anus;
- makes groaning or moaning sounds while masturbating;
- engages in thrusting motions while masturbating;
- may be observed sucking a dog's penis; or
- makes 'Barbie dolls' engage in oral sex.

The majority of adult offenders will recall excessive masturbation commencing around age 8 or 9, when the sexual template is activated. This is a self-soothing mechanism designed to manage negative feelings, but may also trigger strong negative emotions or memories, creating a maladaptive cycle. The reason sexual knowledge is more compelling when demonstrated by younger children than older ones, is that the latter may acquire sexual knowledge from other sources, for example, from classes on sex education or from discussions with peers or older children. However, younger children are unlikely to obtain knowledge from sources other than abuse (Vizard, 2013); for example, they are not likely to learn the intimate details of sexual activity, nor what semen tastes like, nor what penetration feels like, without direct experience.

Another issue to consider is that of a child understanding that their body may respond to stimulation, but that does not mean they wanted it or enjoyed it. For example, it is not uncommon for a boy child to ejaculate during anal penetration, leading the child to be confused about complicity and even their sexuality, and members of the criminal justice system implying that this proves consent (Jones, 2022). This is simply the body responding the way that the system was designed to do, but it is still abuse nevertheless. Similarly, girls who have been sexually abused mature sexually a year and a half earlier than girls who have not been abused (van der Kolk, 2014), as the abuse speeds up their secretion of sexual hormones, increasing their levels of testosterone and androstenedione by three to five times. As such, they are more open to further victimisation, and may actively seek it out.

Childhood sexuality and the law

It is thought that about a third of sexual offences against children are committed by young men who have experienced abuse, emotional neglect and domestic violence in their own lives (Hackett, 2014). Biologically, a post-pubescent child is capable of reproduction, and therefore has all the development hormones to encourage sexual activity. However, it is illegal before 16 years of age, although many under-16s will admit to being already sexually active. Legally, under the Child Act of 2003, they are still classed as a child until 18 years of age, as a means of trying to protect them from their own vulnerability, although they are not emotionally (i.e. their brains have not yet finished developing) or fully mature until 25 years old. Boys will engage in more sexual behaviours and more often than girls, and we are now seeing an increasing number of boys under the age of 10 referred for therapeutic attention because of their sexual behaviour. Alan Jenkins (2005) is highly critical of arbitral age constraints placed on young people:

> Young people are generally regarded as requiring protection and support. Attainment of a certain age is required to qualify specific adult rights and privileges. When it suits adults needs, they are regarded as children. However, when young people commit serious crimes, many legislatures are empowered to regard them as adults and subject them to adult criminal justice systems and penalties ... When young people offend the powers that be, they may do so at the expense of their childhood.
>
> (Jenkins, 2005, p. 99–100)

Too readily these children are labelled as 'child sexual abusers' so they therefore must be a risk to other children. A girl is less likely to be labelled as such, even though girls can be just as sexually aggressive as their male counterparts. Very often they may be acting out their own sexual abuse; sexual interest and arousal is natural, sexual behaviour is learned. But there are other reasons that children reach out to others sexually: to be intimate, to fill their loneliness, to self-soothe, they may have an overly sexualised home environment as previously discussed, or equally a sexually repressive environment where any form of sexual interest is considered deviant or a sin. Or, as discussed in Chapter 5, they have seen pornography online from a very early age and think that is what they are supposed to be doing with their friends.

In addition to contact offences between children, they may engage in many of the online offences outlined in Chapter 1. For a child to view indecent images of children, even though they may be age appropriate, and even though the child make not have a clear understanding of the law that they are breaking, it is still a criminal offence. In addition, children often engage in sexting between themselves, which may consist of flirting to open sexual talk and the mutual exchange of pictures. But this can also lead to cyber bullying as, without consent, the images can be shared among the school friends, whether innocently or as revenge porn, leading to cyber bullying and physical bullying at school. Muncaster & Ohlsson (2020) found that low levels of family cohesion was a significant predictor of becoming a victim of sexting, which links back to the discussion in Chapter 3 of attachments, with females being more at risk due to the online exploitation seen in pornography and pressure to engage in sexual activity. And as McGrath (2019) argues, there is a strong focus in society on online grooming, but insufficient attention paid to the damage that young people can do to themselves and their peers. This again may come from a societal reluctance to accept that children are wanting to be sexual, and would prefer to blame an adult offender.

Our laws in the United Kingdom against inappropriate sexuality are determined by cultural norms, very often driven by single high-profile cases, which define our construct of sexual offending. There is a danger in labelling children and young people as 'sex offenders', as the majority do not continue to sexually act out post adolescence. Yet the sex offender's register tends to label young people for the rest of their lives. In US, some children as young as 7 years old are registered sex offenders. So we need to watch our language, which can define levels of seriousness in others' perception of childhood sexuality, in particular:

- perpetrator/predator;
- child who sexually assaults other children;
- sexually intrusive child;
- abuse-reactive child; and
- sexually inappropriate child.

Hackett et al. (2022) recommend the term 'children with harmful sexual behaviour'; I like it. It puts the child first. If adult terminology and laws are applied to children's sexual activity, then many misinterpretations can be made, and non-abusive sexual contact between children may be inappropriately criminalised. Since there is no empirical evidence to indicate when children engage in developmentally advanced sexual behaviour at a young age that they will continue to sexually offend, then there can be no guidelines for assessment of children with sexual behaviour problems. Cavanagh Johnson and Doonan (2006) therefore argue that it is a cruel and usual punishment to condemn them to a lifetime stigma as a sex offender. Our knowledge and understanding of the neurological, cognitive, emotional and psychosocial development of young people supports the view that they should not be held to the same standards of criminal responsibility as adults over the age of, say, 25. The ability to engage in sound decision-making and rationale is not developed in children or pre-adolescents, and only comes online during the hormone-pumping adolescence given sufficient and appropriate role-models of behaviour and a sense of safety and security.

The contemporary focus of working with children with harmful sexual behaviour previously followed the adult model of risk and recidivism prevention, using statistical analyses of likely presenting issues across a very broad spectrum of childhood behaviour, ignoring developmental considerations. As Hackett et al. (2022) argue, stopping a child from repeating their abusive behaviour is necessary but not sufficient for the work that needs to be done with these children. They continue:

Simply stopping a child from continuing something that, even without intervention, is not likely to continue, is hardly a triumph, especially if in the process that child's broader life chances are ruined or severely inhibited by the consequences of our interventions and policies.

(Hackett et al., 2022, p. 3)

And, as Laub and Sampson (2003) found in their longitudinal study, the early developmental process is the predisposing factor, but the later adolescent and early adult issues must also be addressed to make the difference for the future of these children.

Therapeutic work with young children

Zaniewski et al. (2019) found that young people who engage in harmful sexual behaviour have complex insecure attachment strategies punctuated by unresolved trauma and loss. They highlighted absences of the ability to self-sooth, lack of emotional regulation and an absence of comfort. Therefore, slow and steady therapeutic interventions need to focus on filling many of the hippocampal gaps in the memory as well as possible, without the child going into a freeze state and disassociating. This means, when the child feels sufficiently safe, gently revisiting these right-brain bodily fear states and providing the child with an age-appropriate narrative about what might be causing the fear in the past, and how that fear is no longer in the present. This allows the brain to store the schema of the fear in a different place, allowing it to be laid to rest, so the child is no-longer under the tyranny of experience-dependent flashbacks. A strong therapeutic alliance with the child helps form a secure attachment, which the child can use as a safe base as they allow themselves to experience these fear states. For the therapist, eye contact with the child for proto-conversations, mimicking that of the early years, is important, but constant eye contact may also be deemed as threatening, so it must be in small measured doses, for up to 30% of the time for a secure attachment. Encouraging a child to hold onto their comfort-blankets or favourite toys will help to instil calm, so the child can learn to break secrets and share not only what they have done, but what happened to them and by whom.

In order to achieve their own moral understanding or ethics, the young person needs to internalise a sense of rules of how to behave, to have an understanding that they have been transgressed by others or toward others, which provides a sense of safety for the future. However, a disorganised child is likely to be resistant, chaotic or even attacking within therapy. They may alternate a fear of attachment, with clinging, punitive or sexually controlling strategies, especially after receiving warmth and empathy from the therapist. As with working with adults, the sexually inappropriate behaviour will not be the only issue to address in therapy. The child may be exhibiting stress, anxiety, depression, self-harming behaviours, eating disorders, PTSD or neurodivergence. Left unresolved, these issues will have a negative impact on the work trying address maladaptive self-soothing sexual behaviours.

Shame can be disabling, so the therapist needs to help the child into the recognition that they did a bad thing, not that they are a bad person. Language is important. It will help the child take responsibility for their behaviour and help their passage through shame. Appropriate phrases may include 'what you did', 'what happened with your sister' and 'hurting your sister' (as opposed to 'abusing your sister').

This process of talking provides the all-important left-brain narrative that helps to add meaning and rationale to the therapy and the concept of changing their behaviour.

Other valuable therapeutic techniques are:

- Play therapy – part of attachment circuitry.
- Using emotion cards to help the child express how they feel.
- Good selection of booklets on working with children at www.tcavjohn.com.
- Using a worry monster.
- Art therapy – very helpful for alexithymia.
- High impact imagery – photographs, music, art.
- Family therapy – need to watch family system shifts as the child or adolescent starts to change.

Treatment goals

The therapy needs to focus on the child as a whole and help them resolve their attachment needs, not just assisting on changing sexual behaviour. Compulsive repetition of trauma perpetuates chronic feelings of helplessness and a subjective feeling of being bad and out of control, so children need help to label and evaluate the meaning of sensations and affective states, to discriminate between past and present events, and to interpret social cues in the context of the present rather than the past: a mixture of cognitive and psychodynamic therapeutic modalities. This will increase emotional empathy and emotional intelligence, and working with alexithymia by using emotion pictures, will help the child express their own emotions, especially if they are neurodivergent, and thus understand the impact that their behaviour had on others, which means they learn compassion.

But this treatment should not be constantly reviewing the past and looking at what went wrong. We should not be constantly harping back to behaviour that occurred when they were young, but helping them to leave that behind and move forward with their lives. It is about helping the child build skills and resources for a more successful future, educationally, and socially, and supporting them through present day challenges as they try and build a new way of living, as many of these children may have been removed from their family of origin, so may not have the family network to fall back on. Helping them develop a sense of personal agency, to take control of potential life outcomes in finding meaningful studies and later employment to become a more resilient adolescent and subsequent adult. Teaching them about appropriate ways of behaving within relationships within the community and within intimate relationships, which may have been distorted as a consequence of long-term pornography viewing. And supporting them through the times of crisis, particularly through puberty and adolescence. Hackett et al. (2022) contend that what these children really need help with is: development, development, development; involvement, involvement, involvement; and relationship, relationship, relationship; in essence, this is the Good Lives Model (Ward, Mann & Gannon, 2005), to be discussed in greater depth in Chapter 9.

Tools for working with young children

The Child Sexual Behaviour Inventory (CSBI: Friedrich et al., 2001) focuses on sexualised behaviour indicators unlikely to be found in other traumatised or 'normal' populations. The CSBI was normed with children between 2 and 12, and was found to reliably differentiate children who were alleged to have been sexually abused compared to those not alleged to have been sexually abused. However, a substantial proportion of children in Friedrich's research, determined sexually abused, are not reported to engage in sexualised behaviour. Moreover, children who learn about sex from non-abusive experiences may engage in sexualised behaviour, as discussed above.

The AIM3 (Leonard & Hackett 2019) is an assessment framework designed to help therapists with interventions, therefore it is not an actuarial instrument designed purely to detect risk. Low rates of re-offending of young children make actuarial risk models difficult to produce. In the absence of such a tool, practitioners have had to rely on professional judgement. The AIM3 model seeks to structure decision making using available research, clinical knowledge and research and now includes a trauma-focused lens. It makes deliberate use of the terms 'strength' and 'concern', considering both static and dynamic factors. It takes into consideration the strengths and weaknesses of existing models, making it a 'user friendly model', by helping identify individual/ familial strengths, needs, and concerns. It also helps to formulate further recommendations for intervention leading to co-ordinated management plans, providing a consistent and structured basis for expressing opinions.

Treating a young person who behaves in sexually inappropriate ways as a sex offender is both stigmatising and disproportionate, and demonstrates no understanding of how infants, children and adolescents develop cognitively, emotionally and neurally.

Despite the Department of Health recognising the importance of good assessment and intervention, child and adolescent welfare services like CAMHS are underfunded, and many young people fall on the wayside, or are untrained to work with children who have become sexually reactive. This has been the experience of StopSO therapists who are working with children. Also, the CAMHS services have waiting lists between 12 and 18 months, meaning that the early adolescent behavioural acting out is not nipped in the bud, but left to be entrenched behavioural pathways, with the child now being called an abuser and a sexual predator. Compassionate adults, either as therapists, social workers or child liaison services can alter the long-term outcome of a young person treading a potentially detrimental path.

Gordon's review

The concept that sexual offending is in some way contagious is demonstrated by the way society responds to anyone who is considered to have broken sexual mores: they become pariahs, avoided and alienated at all costs. This applies to the social stigma a child has to carry if the label is applied to their parent. Fellow children will taunt them, accusing them of being 'pedos' or 'perverts' in their own right. Of course, much of this is due to the lack of sex education of the children at the appropriate time. Most often school sex education is limited, and rather than teaching children about how to put a condom on a banana, needs to show an understanding of consent, intimacy, and an awareness that what they see on the internet is not how loving relationships generally are, being inclusive of LBGTQI+ situations. In primary school, most education is around respect and fairness in families, and the real sex education does not commence until secondary school. But for most children, particularly boys, that is much too late, as they have already been watching online pornography for a substantial period of time. They need to learn not to share images of themselves online to peers or to others who are offering 'friendships', especially at times when the child might feel hacked off with their parents. They need to learn at an early age not to share images of themselves to anyone, including their friends.

Connor, at the ripe old age of four years, has already experienced 5 ACEs, with another on the way when his dad goes to prison. History is likely to repeat itself with his upbringing unless someone can take active care of this child and support him through his turbulence. That will not be his father, as the social services will not allow him to have contact with his son. We need to remember that his father has not committed a sexual contact offence. Yes, he has looked at CSAM and as such is labelled as a sexual offender. But he has not demonstrated any form of paedophilia, and therefore any child near him is at low risk (we are not allowed to say no risk) of being sexually offended against. The irony here is that another self-fulfilling prophecy has taken place: the child was removed from his mother in case his father offended against him as he had looked at CSAM, and was placed in an environment where it happened anyway. Foster homes, where there are already biological children living, provides a ripe environment for childhood bullying. In fostering situations, too little notice is taken about the power dynamic of bringing a vulnerable, frightened, sad child who is missing his mum, into a family home where maintaining the pecking order among siblings will always be a key factor. Bullying may often start off in subtle, verbal ways, but may escalate into physical and even sexual abuse as the means of being totally in control.

The other issue that seems to have been missed here is that Rachel is not a bad person for wanting to return to the man that she loves, under the threat of child confiscation. Rachel and Gordon were in a codependent relationship; the addictive nature of these relationships is two-way. She needs him as much as he needs her. He will argue that his violence was justified because it demonstrates how much he loves her. She will agree with that, and feel the intensity of his passion for her. As they are both insecurely attached, they are finding the missing parts of themselves within each other. Neither of them knows how to show their love and trust for the other without someone teaching them how. They have not learned it in their families of origin, and it does not arrive automatically. Instead of insisting on divorce, the social services would have been better off putting them into mandatory couple therapy, helping them to learn how to deal with conflict and the need to compromise. At least that way, Connor may have stayed with his parents, and the transgenerational transmission of violence and abuse might have stopped at his father's generation.

References

Archer, E., Nel, P.W., Turpin, M. & Barry, S. (2020). Parents' perspectives on the parent–child relationship following their child's engagement in harmful sexual behaviour. *Journal of Sexual Aggression*, 26 (3), 359–371. doi:10.1080/13552600.2019.1649479.

Attwood, T. (2007). *The complete guide to Asperger's syndrome*. London: Jessica Kingsley.

Bancroft, J. (1995). *Human sexuality and its problems* (2nd ed.). New York: Churchill Livingstone.

Carlson, B. (2011). Sibling incest: Adjustment in adult women survivors. *Families in Society*, 92 (1), 77–83. doi:10.1606/1044-3894.4067.

Cavanagh Johnson, T. (2002). *Understanding your child's sexual behaviour: What's natural and healthy*. Oakland, CA: New Harbinger.

Cavanagh Johnson, T. C. & Doonan, R. (2006). Children twelve and younger with sexual behaviour problems: What we know at 2005 that we didn't know in 1985. In R.E. Longo & D.S. Prescott (eds), *Current perspectives: Working with sexually aggressive youth and youth with sexual behaviour problems*. Holyoke, MA: Neari Press.

Coulbourne Faller, K. (1993). *Child sexual abuse: Intervention and treatment issues*. National Centre on Child Abuse and Neglect.

Friedrich, W.N., Fisher, J.L., Dittner, C.A., Acton, R. *et al.* (2001). Child sexual behaviour inventory: Normative, psychiatric and sexual abuse comparisons. *Child Maltreatment*, 6 (1), 37–49. doi:10.1177/1077559501006001004.

Hackett, S. (2014). *Children and young people with harmful sexual behaviour*. Totnes: Dartington.

Hackett, S., Darling, A.J., Blafe, M., Masson, H. & Phillips, J. (2022). Life course outcomes and developmental pathways for children and young people with harmful sexual behaviour. *Journal of Sexual Aggression*, online ahead of print. doi:10.1080/13552600.2022.2124323.

Jenkins, A. (2005). Making it fair. Respectful and just intervention with disadvantaged young people who have abused. In. M. Calder (ed.), *Children and young people who sexually abuse: New theory, research and practice developments.* (pp. 98–113). Lyme Regis: Russell House.

Jones, L. (2022). Trauma and sexual offending. In P. Willmott & L. Jones (eds), *Trauma-informed forensic practice* (pp. 212–230). London: Routledge.

Laub, J.H. & Sampson, R.J. (2003). *Shared beginnings, divergent lives: Delinquent boys to age 70.* Cambridge, MA: Harvard University Press.

Leonard, M. & Hackett, S. (2019). *The AIM3 assessment model: Assessment of adolescents and harmful sexual behaviour.* The AIM Project.

McGrath, K. (2019). *Understanding and managing sexualised behaviour in children and adolescents: Guidelines for parents and carers in the cyber age.* [Author] Retrieved from www.kieranmcgrath.com/understanding-managing-sexualised-behaviour-in-children-adolescents/

Muncaster, L. & Ohlsson, I (2020). Sexting: predictive and protective factors for its perpetration and victimisation. *Journal of Sexual Aggression,* 26 (3), 346–358. doi:10.1080/13552600.2019.1645220.

Rich, P. (2009). *Juvenile sexual offenders: A comprehensive guide to risk evaluation.* New Jersey: Wiley.

Sanderson, C. (2014). *Counselling skills for working with shame.* London: Jessica Kingsley.

Schöttle, D., Briken, P., Tüscher, O. & Turner, D. (2017). Sexuality in autism, hypersexual and paraphilic behaviour in women and men with high-functioning autism spectrum disorder. *Dialogues in Clinical Neuroscience,* 19 (4), 381–393.

Simons, D.A., Tyler, C. & Heil, P. (2005). *Childhood risk factors associated with crossover offending.* Poster presented at the 24th Annual Conference of the Association for the Treatment of Sexual Abusers, Salt Lake City, UT.

van der Kolk, B.A. (1989). The compulsion to repeat the trauma. *Psychiatric Clinics of North America,* 12(2), 389–411.

van der Kolk, B. (2014). *The body keeps the score: Mind, brain and body transformation of trauma.* London: Penguin.

Vizard, E. (2013). Practitioner review: The victims and perpetrators of child sexual abuse – assessment and intervention. *The Journal of Child Psychology and Psychiatry,* 54 (5), 503–515. doi:10.1111/jcpp.12047.

Ward, T., Mann, R.E. & Gannon, T.A. (2005). The good lives model of offender rehabilitation: Clinical implications. *Aggression and Violent Behaviour,* 12, 87–107. doi:10.1016/j.avb.2006.03.004.

Willmott, P. (2022). Childhood maltreatment links to offending. In P. Willmott & L. Jones (eds), *Trauma-informed forensic practice.* London: Routledge.

Ybarra, M.L., Mitchell, K.J., Hamburger, M., Diener-West, M. & Leaf, P.J. (2011). X-rated material and perpetration of sexually aggressive behaviour among children and adolescents. *Aggressive Behaviour,* 37 (1), 1–18. doi:10.1002/ab.20367.

Zaniewski, B., Dallos, R., Stedmon, J. & Welbourne, P. (2019). An exploration of attachment and trauma in young men who have engaged in harmful sexual behaviours. *Journal of Sexual Aggression,* 26 (3), 405–421. doi:10.1080/13552600.2019.1678688.

Chapter 8

Theories of online offending sexual offending

Case study

It has been eighteen months since Gordon first got the knock, and had been living with the uncertainty of a potential prosecution as he tried to rebuild his life. Finally, he was called into the police station for a second interview. He attended with his duty solicitor, who told him to respond with 'no comment' throughout. The interviewing police officer told him that the high tech crime unit had found 10 indecent images of children on his phone, 6 were category C (indecent images of children, not necessarily sexual), 3 were category B (non-penetrative sexual activity), and 1 category A video, although they did admit that the latter was found in the deleted folder. They were therefore sending his case to the Crown Prosecution Service (CPS) to determine whether charges should be brought against him. Their view was that he would probably be charged, especially as he had a community service order for violence against his wife, and the waiting time for this decision would be about 4–6 months. Once the CPS had made their decision, his case would be sent on to the magistrates court for hearing, although he needed to anticipate another wait as there is a backlog of cases to be heard. As a second offence, their view would be most likely that he would receive a prison sentence, so it may be transferred from magistrates to Crown Court. If so, he should anticipate a further delay.

Gordon conveyed all this information to his therapist curled up in the chair, almost in a foetal position. His long arms were wrapped around his shins and he frequently buried his head into his knees.

'What's the point!' he blubbed. 'Why have I been doing all this, and trying to make things right, when I am going to get locked up anyway? What about Rex? What about Rachel? She relies on my wages. What about the boy? Will I ever see him again?' He sobbed again.

The therapist sat quietly after pushing the tissue box closer to him. She reflected that this was his first real outpouring of grief that she had seen from him, and that he was identifying the pain he has brought onto others, not just to himself. She also identified that this was a dangerous time for Gordon, that

DOI: 10.4324/9781003330899-8

this 'what's the point' moment could push his prior suicidal ideation into actual plans and/or enactment. Platitudes wouldn't do right now.

'I didn't know,' he continued, searching her face. 'I thought that pictures from Google would be fine. I thought illegal images were on the dark web. I didn't know, and I didn't like those pictures anyway. I was looking for Rachel. She told me her grandfather had posted pictures of her and I wanted to find them to see if I could delete them and get them off the internet. I didn't know what I was doing. I didn't think!'

Theories of sexual offending: why do they do it?

David Middleton (2009) criticised the tendency to group online offenders in similar ways to contact sexual offenders as it is based on assumption rather than an understanding of comprehensive aetiological theories. It might be useful, therefore, to overview the respected theories of sexual offending, to try and formulate where online offenders fit in the literature. It is not my intention to review these theories in detail, for which I would recommend the reader to Ward, Polaschek and Beech's (2009) thorough analysis in the terms of research evidence and clinical utility. What might be more useful here is to look at the face validity of these epistemological theories to try and understand why a man in a long-term relationship with his partner, and perhaps with a couple of children of his own, allows himself to be drawn into viewing child sexual abuse material online, and consequently getting arrested and prosecuted as a sexual predator. It is not my intention to review all theories in detail, especially single-factor theories, as they seem too simplistic to account for the complexity of the multitude of presentations.

The most commonly used theory by police and probation, even though it is an old model, developed well before the ubiquitous issue of online sexual offending, is that of Finkelhor (1984) who provided a four-factor precondition model, temporal in sequence, increasing in its severity, that must exist for sexual abuse of a child to occur:

- Motivation to sexually abuse – emotional congruence to having sex with a child; sexual satisfaction.
- Overcoming internal inhibitors to become sexually aroused by a child; that is, morals, ethics, fear of being caught.
- Overcoming external inhibitors that block the process, as they are unable to meet their needs in socially appropriate other ways. Manipulating the opportunity for privacy, a child with inadequate supervision.
- Overcoming the resistance of the child, which allows them to behave in ways outside of their usual behaviour. Grooming behaviour, gaining trust, using bribes or trickery.

As an aetiological theory it is lacking, because it does not offer an explanation of how people get into stage one, the motivation to sexually offend, in the first place. Nor does the theory have the face validity to be applicable to internet offenders, although he did propose that child sexual abuse material linked together with a male tendency to sexualise emotion could result in deviant sexual arousal toward children. If we look at each factor of his theory in turn, we can see that the first precondition is not met as these men do not necessarily commence with an intention to look at indecent images of children, but may often come across them in the course of their compulsive viewing of adult pornography. The second stage of overcoming internal inhibitors by being sexually aroused by a child is difficult to determine. Many men are sexually aroused when viewing adult pornography online anyway, so it cannot be determined whether images of a child are arousing or not. Many argue that they were not aroused. In addition, any arousal may be pre-primed from an early age by being a victim in sexual abuse when the viewer was a child. The arousal may also be considered to be part of the disinhibition and escalation process, but overcoming resistance suggests an intentional process, whereas the escalation, as described in Chapter 5, is a subconscious physiological process driven by the SEEKING system. Stage 3, overcoming external inhibitors may apply, as the offender will actively search out times when he is alone to conduct his viewing. But, many of these offenders can get their needs met with loving partners, but prefer to stay with the hyper-stimulus of the computer. Many of them will never reach stage four, and have absolutely no intention of meeting up with a child, although some do get drawn into conversations, and an even smaller minority will choose to try and meet with the child.

David Finkelhor did propose that there were different types of child molesters, motivated by differing needs, thereby displaying different patterns of offending and psychological characteristics, but denied that sexual abuse as a child would result in sexual preferences for children as adults (Ward, Polaschek & Beech, 2009). However, this model does not account for the common sexual coping practice of using masturbation to reduce feelings of anxiety, depression or anger (Marshall, Anderson & Fernandez, 1999). It does not account for why non-sexual adverse childhood experiences, like domestic violence, emotional isolation or neglect, can result in diverse or even deviant sexual behaviour. Nor does it offer any insight into why a person with neurodivergent thinking processes might end up committing an offence. As such it lacks explanatory depth from an aetiological perspective, and as Ward, Polaschek and Beech, (2009) argue, should not be used on its own as a guide to assessment and treatment, and that the danger of using it as an explanatory theory could lead to poor clinical decisions, as much of an individual's offending behaviour is missed.

Hall and Hirschman (1992) propose a quadripartite model, based on the empirical research of the traits of sex offenders. Their model is also of four factors: inappropriate sexual arousal, distorted cognitions, affective dyscontrol and problematic personality, which may operate independently or maybe combined. They argue that one of these factors could predominate the others, which they called a primary motivational precursor, and can activate the others. They do not appear to elaborate as to where the inappropriate sexual arousal comes from, unless it is implied from the personality factor, which may be antisocial attitudes, adverse childhood experiences or problematic interpersonal strategies. The distorted cognition would be our understanding of self-serving interpretations of how they have behaved, like rape myths, and maybe a view of whether children are willing participants enjoying sexual activities. This model could fit online offenders if one starts from the personality factor as a primary motivational precursor, or suggesting that ASD might be the primary motivational precursor. This would elicit an inability to control emotional states (dysregulation and alexithymia), so turning to pornography to change the way they feel, thus leading to inappropriate sexual arousal and distorted cognitions. This predisposes that the model can only start from the personality characteristics, which suggests that people offend because they have personality problems, or neurodivergence, which seems counter-intuitive. Not everyone with these issues sexually offend, so where does the desire to offend come from? As such the model tends to be vague and does not account for how some men can watch pornography and never stray from looking at adult porn, whereas others fall down the rabbit hole of looking at illegal images.

Marshall and Barbaree (1999) proposed an integrated theory that gives more attention to the aetiological process of offending. They suggest that early developmental experiences leading to insecure attachments predispose individuals to offending due to their poor emotional regulation, low self-esteem and impulsivity. They may be more likely to turn to masturbation to self-soothe, especially if combined with a history of abuse. This, together with early exposure to antisocial attitudes and misogyny in the home, sets the stage for later inappropriate behaviour when the hormones start pumping at adolescence, which is a critical period for developing sexual scripts. So far, the history of many online offenders seems to fit with this theory, particularly if one adds the concept of viewing of online pornography from a young age. However, they then suggest that the pathways between the hypothalamus, amygdala and septum of the adolescent brain 'fuses' sexual and aggressive behaviours, and together with masturbation, reinforces violent and deviant fantasies (although this has not been supported by the neuroscientific evidence). Under stressful situational experiences, this leads the person onto to committing a sexual offence. It tends to imply that sexual offences are always violent and impulsive, and fails to account for the behaviour of the online offender, or the 'loving' behaviour of an interfamilial offender. They do propose that different types of offence have different pathways, and the one that nearest fits an online offender would be the use of masturbation as a mood regulator, seeking sexual encounters when they feel alienated or alone. If the young man frequently masturbates when feeling alone, then the feeling of loneliness will create sexual arousal *per se* in a conditioning paradigm. Some online offenders do go on to seek out sex workers to connect with, despite having a good relationship with their wife, husband or partner. So this theory fits very well so far, with its integration of developmental, social and biological features, but it assumes that all sexual offending is impulsive, which is not always the case, and it does not account for why the acting out of the adolescent would be sexual as opposed to, say, delinquency. Finally, the model loses the concept of trauma in the mind and behaviour of the offender, and offers no explanation of why internet offenders, neurodivergent or not, would be looking at images of children.

Another popular model of sexual offending are the Cycle models originally proposed by Wolf (1989), later adapted by Eldridge (1998), based on the assumptions that experiences of childhood maltreatment function as 'potentiators' to the development of the sexual acting out, by removing any inhibitory factors. It begins with a negative self-image and an expectation of rejection from loving partners, round in cycle to withdrawal, compensatory fantasies, leading to grooming and acting out with the subsequent feelings of guilt, taking the person back in a cycle to the negative self-image again. This theory proposes links with cognition, behaviour and learning and proposes a pathway between fantasy, masturbation and orgasm in the development and maintenance of sexually deviant behaviour. These cycles, which are very similar to the sexual addiction cycle proposed by Carnes (2001), lend themselves easily to use in clinical practice to help the offender understand the cognitive, affective and behavioural process of his offending. However, such models tend to be rather simplistic considering the complexity of each individual presentation, and leans more to the one-size-fits-all approach of treatment, and any offender who denies fitting into the model could be met with confrontation, which could damage any future work (Carich & Calder, 2003). It also does not account for why so many people who have a negative self-image choose not to offend against children, as the model focuses on maintenance and escalation rather than aetiological processes.

Ward and Siegert (2002), aware of all the problems with the above theories, proposed to 'knit together' the best aspects of each of the theories to offer a more comprehensive pathways model. They proposed that there are five distinct pathways that a person can undertake which will eventually lead to the sexual abuse of a child.

- Intimacy deficit – a preferred adult sexual partner is unavailable, creating problems with loneliness and intimacy. Interpersonal incompetence – social isolation, loneliness, dissatisfaction with life.
- Deviant sexual scripts – a confusion between sex and intimacy and a lack of understanding of when sex is appropriate. Confusion over sexual preferences, arousal and 'deviant' (or diverse) sexual behaviour.
- Unregulated emotions – using sex to change or regulate their emotional state. Difficulty in identifying and controlling emotions, plus a lack of empathy.

- Antisocial cognitions – offence supporting thoughts, distortions, antisocial lifestyles.
- Multiple dysfunctional mechanisms – a catch all process where no specific feature predominates.

They point out that in terms of the profile of a sexual offender and the variations of their offending behaviour, any model needs to take into account of the complexity of the presenting situations. They propose that stressful situations can trigger a person to travel down a specific pathway. In identifying the pathways, they are suggesting Marshall and Barbaree's (1999) proposals that the interpersonal incompetence comes from insecure attachment styles and distorted inner working models of how relationships should be, so it is heavily cognitive, but does not readily explain how thoughts lead to behaviours. It also does not account for how sexual scripts are developed as such. The biggest criticism of this theory is that most offenders, rather than being separated into these various categories, mostly have an element of each pathway (Simon, 2002). Finally, the proposition that offenders with intimacy deficits or emotional dysregulation accessing CSAM at times of loneliness and isolation as a mood elevating strategy doesn't sit well with many researchers, as the implication that the offender may be blameless because they are somehow defective, proved to be discounted (Aslan, Edelmann, Bray & Worrell, 2014).

Middleton et al. (2006) undertook a study of male sexual offenders with convictions relating to CSAM, and then assigned them to the five pathways of the Ward and Siegert model. They found that 60% of the offenders could be assigned to more than one pathway, and the rest they struggled to classify. Middleton (2009) argued that the results suggested that online offenders are not a homogenous group and is diverse within itself as other sex offender groups. In terms of an online offender, the intimacy deficit pathway may apply for a single offender, but very often they are in partnerships, often with children, whom they are choosing not to spend time with. They will have unregulated emotions, and will be using sex to change the way they feel, but they may not have deviant sexual scripts. Viewing CSAM does not mean that they liked what they saw (see Chapter 5 for an elaboration of this). If the person is neurodivergent, they may be in possession of offence-supporting cognitions, not necessarily from the classic understanding of cognitive distortions, but from a naivety: 'It's on Google, and it's free, so it must be legal.'

A recent theoretical aetiological explanation comes from Stinson, Sales and Becker (2008), who propose a multimodal self-regulation theory. Again, this theory integrates many of the developmental, psychological and cognitive processes discussed in other theories. They propose that self-regulatory deficits are the key to sexually inappropriate interests and behaviour. These interests develop in childhood whereby an inappropriate stimulus is linked at a time when the child is sexually aroused, and becomes normalised. So self-regulatory deficits are developed from adverse childhood experiences, which combine with temperamental vulnerabilities, whereby the person is unable to manage or regulate his sexual behaviour, linking arousal to an inappropriate stimulus. Then a conditioning process occurs whereby the sexual gratification, perhaps from obsessively watching online pornography, reinforces the stimulus due to the lack of negative consequences. Cognitive beliefs and personality characteristics mediate the development of inappropriate behaviours, which may also be reinforced by parental role-modelling.

This theory probably relates the closest to the online offender, and the neurodivergent offender, in my view. The temperamental vulnerabilities would be the insecure attachment processes, or neurodivergent thinking processes, predisposing a lack of resilience or self-regulation, combined with feelings of anxiety and low self-esteem. Adverse childhood experiences, like the trauma of a vandalised sexual template following abuse, or bullying, or profound loss, lead the child to sexual self-soothing behaviours, which psychologically link to their experience of trauma. Compulsively watching the vast array of online pornography images as a form of self-soothing at this stage leads to an inability to regulate their compulsive behaviour, with few negative consequences. This leads to distorted perceptions about sex and relationships, objectification of women, girls, boys and young men, and a lack of empathy for the situations viewed. As the child moves into adolescence, the arousal to inappropriate stimuli is well conditioned, but then disinhibition and escalation take place (Sullivan & Beech, 2004). Instead of learning to self-regulate, the SEEKING system demands more. Middleton (2009) highlighted that 86% of his sample of internet offenders scored above average on impulsivity, suggesting that the offenders may be acting without thinking, adding to the perception that their choices are not responsible for their offending. Offence-related cognitions might be 'No one knows what I am doing', or perceiving that the abuse of the child or teenager in the images is historical and therefore is no longer being harmed. Or there may be an element of repetition compulsion as they look for images similar to what happened to them in childhood. This does not suggest a deviant sexual script, but a lack of self-regulatory control in being able to stop the searching.

There are two elements lacking in all of the theories mentioned above. The first is the vandalisation of the sexual template (Money, 1986). Any form of trauma at this stage of neural development pre-puberty when the LUST circuit comes online in the right brain, leads the child to adopt self-soothing behaviours usually around the mouth or genitals. It is this distress that changes what might be childhood misbehaviour and acting out into sexual behaviour. As sexual behaviour of any sort in children is not culturally tolerated, it is pushed underground into secret behaviour covered in shame.

The other process missing in the theories is intent. Forensic theories make the assumption that all offenders intended to offend, presumably following Finkelhor's (1984) first precondition to offending. This will apply to contact offenders, but does not necessarily apply to online-viewing offenders, and making the assumption that viewing CSAM will lead to contact offending is not borne out by empirical research (Marshall, 2000; Wolak et al., 2005; Middleton, 2009). Some will have a paedophilic orientation, or consider themselves as a minor-attracted person, and so target these images. Some do intend to look at CSAM as they may feel aroused and want to see more. Some intend to look as they are curious as they have heard so much about them from the media. But there is also a substantial number of people who had no intention of looking at CSAM, but in the course of down-loading (sometimes a substantial amount of) adult imagery, or in the course of browsing imagery, CSAM comes into their visual space. The paradox here is that one needs to look at an image to determine whether it is inappropriate, and once viewed is stored on the computer. Deleting the image does not help, as the forensic services check for deleted images as well as those saved or easily accessed. Thus, removing the concept of intent in charging individuals with possession or making CSAM, leads to a greater than necessary number of prosecutions, which is contributing to the gridlock in the system, and not necessarily protecting children from risk of harm.

A developmental aetiological model

My aetiological model is outlined in Figure 8.1. It is predominately a developmental model, as each factor in the trajectory builds on the previous factors, but includes biological (neurological), environmental and cultural/societal dimensions as well, as has been detailed throughout this book. It commences before the child is born, with the attachment style and any unresolved trauma of the parents (and grandparents – and beyond), which creates the environment *in utero* and in infancy for the immerging child. Genetic interactions may predispose the child to be neurotypical or neurodivergent, but as I mentioned in Chapter 4, we all have the potential to follow either path. If the child develops an avoidant insecure attachment, and/or if the child is neurodivergent, their infant presentations are very similar, hence, in the model in Figure 8.1, these two dimensions overlap. Developmentally for the child, there follows over a decade in the school system and such groups of children use their animal instincts to delineate a pecking-order based on social skills and sports achievement, and target the weak and vulnerable with bullying and minor sexual assaults. My view is that over the years, academics and researchers have dismissed the long-term consequences of a vulnerable child's time at school, especially boarding school, and it is not therefore put into a trauma category. A securely attached child will have no trouble with this time, as they have personal resilience and a safe base to return to. However, any therapist will highlight that for the insecure, the relationship with school peers, whether as a victim or an aggressor, creates long-term psychological issues for the adult. This would be compounded by any further trauma as the consequence of the child experiencing ACE's (chapter 7).

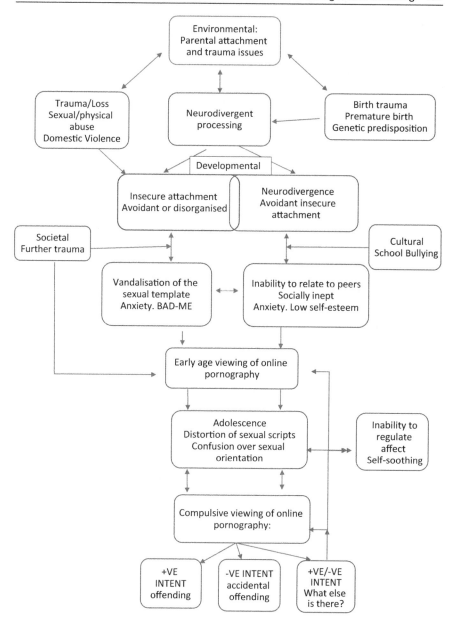

Figure 8.1 A developmental model from pre-birth to adolescence and adult compulsive online viewing with potential sexual offending.

When the child becomes post-pubescent, vandalisation of the sexual template may occur from trauma, and for the neurodivergent, together with an inability to relate to peers, high anxiety and low self-esteem from the perception that they are socially inept. When the child's LUST circuit initiates, for modern-day children, online pornography will be the information source of choice, together with the need to self soothe. These pathways are not individual or separate, as described in other models, but accumulate, as the adolescent SEEKS CARE, yet feels overwhelmed with FEAR and RAGE states. Long-term use of internet pornography, as discussed in Chapter 5, potentiates the dopamine pathways of the brain and produces anxiety and confusion over sexual orientation. The adolescent becomes emotionally dysregulated, triggering a compulsive need to self-soothe, creating the opportunity for other addictive behaviours to take hold; often a combination of several: tobacco, alcohol, gaming, gambling, drugs, food, deepening an already 'well-trodden' dopamine pathway. Addictive fugue states create a downward spiral of emotional numbness, alexithymia and plummeting self-worth. Place this emotional turbulence alongside the early onset (from childhood) pornography use online, where the vast repertoire of choreographed sexual practices is viewed (which hitherto would never had been seen in such graphic detail without the internet) distorts the child/adolescent's sexual script. Many unusual sexual practices viewed may be thought to be commonplace and may therefore initiate paraphilias (kinks), together with the desire to test out some of the practices seen online.

In this trajectory, the left brain of the internet viewer is disengaged, using Joseph LeDoux's (1996) quick and dirty route through the eyes to the insula and amygdala and down the HPA axis, with no opportunity for the long and accurate route from the left brain to put on the handbrake to say 'I shouldn't be looking at this'. As the internet moves from being a choice to a compulsion and on to an addiction, then intent becomes the final factor: positive intent leads to direct searching for illegal imagery as the viewer is aroused by what they see, negative intent can still lead to viewing illegal imagery as the viewer naïvely opens downloaded images and then deletes them, and positive/negative intent is an ambivalence where the viewer is not necessarily aroused by the illegal content, but cannot stop themselves looking at it.

As Ward, Polaschek and Beech (2009) argue, any theory of offending needs to be predictively sound and needs to represent reality, well supported by the evidence. A good theory should underpin the assessment and treatment of offenders following arrest and subsequent conviction. But there is no evidence of a typical sex offender. For example, if we consider the profile of an internet offender, that is a person who has viewed or distributed CSAM, compared to a contact paedophile, the profile of the latter tends to be a middle-aged or elderly man who lives alone, has difficulties with interpersonal relationships, lacks empathy, low IQ, a preoccupied attachment style, and seeks contact with children they know, either through, family, friends or neighbours. However, online offenders tend to be young to middle-aged, white (although some Asian) men who are less sexually risky, more successful, with a high IQ, often married with children, often with an avoidant attachment style (Ward, Hudson & Marshall, 1996), many of whom with undiagnosed ASD. As the profiles of these offenders nowhere near match, why does the criminal justice system assess and treat them in the same way? Why do they still, repeatedly, use a one-size-fits-all approach to their rehabilitation? Indeed, one wonders do these processes actively allow and encourage or interfere with their rehabilitation? Many hfASD online-viewing clients forced to undertake an iHorizon course complain that they are treated like primary school children, as the input needs to be low key for the classic sexual offender. These guys have above-average IQs, and being forced to sit through such processes is patronising, and invariably they switch off and just attend because it is mandatory, but get very little from the course. Such a waste of money and everybody's time. This issue will be discussed further in Chapter 10.

Female internet offenders

The elephant in the room that we have yet to discuss is female internet offenders. None of the theories discussed above will relate to female internet offenders, as their profiles are again substantially different, and probably only account for a very small population of the online sex offending population, making evidence-based research into this field problematic. Grayston and De Luca (1999) classified them into active female perpetrators who physically carry out abuse, compared to passive female perpetrators, who may watch abuse yet not intervene, encourage victims to watch or participate in pornography or prostitution, or procure victims for their partners. Unlike men, they are less likely to offend alone, and tend to be in cooperation with, or under the control of, a male partner or a group (Vandiver, 2006). For active perpetrators, their victims are most likely to be young boys and strangers. Women who co-offend are more likely to abuse girls, particularly familial victims, and to commit multiple sexual offenses (Wijkman, Bijleveld & Hendriks, 2011).

Female offenders are most likely to have the faulty cognitions that the abuse they perpetrated was not harmful and may have been educational, especially toward boys for the teacher/lover dynamic. They often have a history of sexual and/or physical abuse, and/or witnessing domestic violence, especially by women, in their childhoods. They will have dysfunctional adult relationships and attachment deficits, but more likely to be the preoccupied attachment style, whereas men are more likely to be avoidant. For convicted women, their recidivism rates are substantially lower than men at 1% (Cortoni & Hanson, 2005). This data describes female offense characteristics, but essentially does not provide a theoretical framework for the aetiology of female sexual offending, which is still lacking (Logan, 2008).

Gordon's review

Referring back to the internet offender typology in Chapter 1, Gordon fits into the 'curious' group whom Beech et al. (2008) and Delmonico and Griffin (2008) describe as never having exhibited sexual problems until he began using the internet. He shows no paedophilic tendencies, and the number of CSAM on his devices was very low, as for some offenders it may go into the hundreds, or even thousands for collectors. As such, one can assume that children are not necessarily at risk by his presence, as there is no evidence that he would sexually harm a child. However, that is not how the social services will view his case, partly from his prior violent episodes, which quite rightly children need protecting from, but also the incorrect assumption that because he had the images on his phone, he *must* have been sexually aroused by them, and so he *must* be a paedophile. He is going to be, after all, a registered sex offender, so he *must* be kept away from all children. This form of ignorance is not acceptable from professionals, and demonstrates that better training in these areas is required.

The question of intent is another issue that is often ignored by the criminal justice system. Gordon did admit to his therapist that on one occasion when he inadvertently went into a site showing images of post-pubescent girls, he thought about trying to find images of the young Rachel, but gave up as the numbers were too vast and the pictures too upsetting. Of course, the police did not know this, as he gave a 'no comment' interview. So they had fallen back on the concept that possession implies intent. People do make mistakes, and there does not seem to be any allowance for this. And the police interviewer was correct in suggesting that because Gordon has a previous conviction, even for an unrelated case, he will receive a higher sentence than a first-time offender.

During Gordon's distress, he cries out, 'what was I thinking?' As discussed in Chapter 5, Gordon wasn't actually thinking. He was in a trance-like state, eyes glued to the screen, edging, as the SEEKING system demanded more stimulation: 'what else is there?' In this circumstance, the left-brain cognitive system is disengaged as the process goes through a loop between the eyes, the amygdala and the arousal system, which Joseph LeDoux (1996) called the quick and dirty route. So no cognition of 'I shouldn't be looking at this', no understanding of the here and now in terms of space and time, just the heat and intensity of the images and the pumping of his heart.

References

Aslan, D., Edelmann, R., Bray, D. & Worrell, M. (2014) Entering the world of sex offenders: an exploration of offending behaviour patterns of those both internet and contact sex offences against children. *Journal of Forensic Practice*, 16 (2), 110–126. doi:10.1108/JFP-02-2013-0015.

Beech, A.R., Elliot, I.A., Birgden, A. & Findlater, D. (2008). The internet and child sexual offending: A criminological review. *Aggression and Violent Behavior*, 13, 216–228. doi:10.1016/j.avb.2008.03.007

Carich, M.S. & Calder, M.C. (2003). *Contemporary treatment of adult male sex offenders.* Carmarthen: Crown House Publishing.

Carnes, P. (2001). *Out of the shadows. Understanding sexual addiction* (3rd ed.). Minnesota: Hazeldon.

Cortoni, F. & Hanson, R.K. (2005). *A review of the recidivism rates of adult female sexual offenders.* Research report 2005 No. R-169. Ottawa, ON: Correctional Service of Canada, Research Branch.

Delmonico, D.L. & Griffin, E.J. (2008). Online sex offending: Assessment and treatment. In D.R. Laws & W. O'Donohue (eds), *Sexual deviance: Theory, assessment, and treatment,* vol. 2 (pp. 459–485). New York: Guilford Press.

Eldridge, H. (1998) *Therapist guide for maintaining change: Relapse prevention for adult male perpetrators of child sexual abuse.* London: Sage.

Finkelhor, D. (1984) *Child sexual abuse: New theory and research.* New York: Free Press.

Grayston, A.D. & De Luca, R.V. (1999). Female perpetrators of child sexual abuse: A review of the clinical and empirical literature. *Aggression and Violent Behavior,* 4, 93–106.

Hall, G.C.N. & Hirschman, R. (1992). Sexual aggression against children: a conceptual perspective of etiology. *Criminal Justice and Behaviour,* 19, 8–23. doi:10.1177/0093854892019001003.

LeDoux, J.E. (1996). *The emotional brain.* London: Weidenfeld & Nicolson.

Logan, C. (2008). Sexual deviance in females: Psychopathology and theory. In D.R. Laws & W.T. O'Donohue (eds), *Sexual deviance: Theory, assessment, and treatment,* 2nd edition (pp. 486–507). New York: Guilford Press.

Marshall, W.L. (2000) Revisiting the use of pornography by sexual offenders. Implications for theory and practice. *Journal of Sexual Aggression,* 6, 67–77. doi:10.1080/13552600008413310.

Marshall, W.L., Anderson, D. & Fernandez, Y. (1999) *Cognitive behavioural treatment of sex offenders.* New York: Wiley.

Marshall, W.L. & Barbaree, H.E. (1990) An integrated theory of the aetiology of sexual offending. In W.L. Marshall, D.R. Laws & H.E. Barbaree (eds), *Handbook of sexual assault. Issues, theories and treatment of the offender.* (pp257–275) New York: Plenum Press.

Middleton, D. (2009) Internet sex offenders. In A.R. Beech, L.A. Craig & K.D. Browne (eds), *Assessment and treatment of sex offenders* (pp. 199–216). West Sussex: Wiley-Blackwell.

Middleton, D., Elliot, I.A., Mandeville-Norden, R. & Beech, A.R. (2006). An investigation into the application of the Ward and Siegert pathways model of child sexual abuse with internet Offenders. *Psychology, Crime and Law,* 12, 589–603. doi:10.1080/10683160600558352.

Money, J. (1986). *Lovemaps: Clinical concepts of sexual/erotic health & pathology, paraphilia, and gender transposition in childhood, adolescence, and maturity.* Amherst, NY: Prometheus Books.

Simon, L.M.J. (2002). An examination of the assumptions of specialization, mental disorder, and dangerousness in sex offenders. *Behavioral Sciences and the Law,* 18, 275–308. doi:10.1002/1099-0798(200003/06)18:2/3-275:aid-bsl393-3.0.co;2-g.

Stinson, J.D., Sales, B.D. & Becker, J.V. (2008). *Sex offending: Causal theories to inform research, prevention and treatment.* Washington, DC: American Psychological Association.

Sullivan, J & Beech, A.R. (2004) Assessing internet sex offenders. In M.C. Calder (Ed). *Child Sexual Abuse and the internet: Tackling the new frontier* (pp. 69–84). Trowbridge: Cromwell Press.

Vandiver, D.M. (2006). Female sex offenders: A comparison of solo offenders and co-offenders. *Violence & Victims,* 21, 339–354. doi:10.1891/vivi.21.3.339.

Ward, T, Hudson, S.M. & Marshall, W.L. (1996) Attachment style in sex offenders: A preliminary study. *Journal of Sex Research,* 33 (1), 17–26. doi:10.1080/00224499609551811.

Ward, T., Polaschek, D.L.L. & Beech, A. (2009). *Theories of sexual offending.* Chichester: Wiley.

Ward, T. & Siegert, R.J. (2002) Towards a comprehensive theory of child sexual abuse: a theory knitting perspective. *Psychology, Crime and Law,* 9, 319–351. doi:10.1080/10683160208401823.

Wijkman, M., Bijleveld, C. & Hendriks, J. (2011). Female sex offenders: Specialists, generalists and once-only offenders. *Journal of Sexual Aggression,* 17, 34–45. doi:10.1080/13552600.2010.540679.

Wolak, J., Finkelhor, D. & Mitchell, K.J. (2005) *Child pornography possessors arrested in internet-related crimes: Findings from the National Juvenile Online Victimisation Study,* Virginia: The National Centre for Missing and Exploited Children.

Wolf, S.C. (1989) A model of sexual aggression/addiction. *Journal of Social Work and Human Sexuality,* 7 (1), 131–148. doi:10.1300/J291v07n01_10.

Chapter 9

Rehabilitation and desistance

Case study

They filed into the large meeting room and sat round a shiny oak table centrally placed in a bland office with small windows. Attending was the MAPPA manager, who was chairing the meeting, the offender's probation officer, the child protection social worker, the child's guardian, the arresting police officer, a minuting secretary, and the offender's therapist, who had insisted on attending despite her invitation being lost in email cyberspace.

The MAPPA manager opened the meeting and asked everyone to introduce themselves. When it came to the policeman's turn, he added, 'I hope this is not going to take long. I have a busy schedule today, and quite frankly, I don't think there is anything to discuss.'

The MAPPA manager said politely, 'Well, indeed, we all have busy schedules, but we are here to discuss whether Gordon James, who is a category 3 offender by reason of his domestic abuse conviction in addition to making indecent images of children, has the right to be reunited with his wife and child now that he is released from prison. We have a letter from his legal representative saying he has made the application under Article 8 of the European Convention of Human Rights, which entitles him to a private and family life'.

'He gave up all those rights when he beat his wife into a pulp and put her in hospital,' snarled the policeman.

'According to the solicitor, Mr James's wife does actually want this too,' added the MAPPA manager reviewing the letter. 'He says he has spoken to her individually, and there is no evidence of coercion.'

'Well, she would, wouldn't she!' interposed the social worker. 'It's well known that battered women do tend to go back to their abusive partners. It's part of their passive pathology. They can't help themselves but be victims.'

The therapist caught the chair's eye and he nodded his consent for her to speak. 'I would just like to point out that both Mr and Mrs James have done a substantial amount of individual therapeutic work. I have worked with Mr James individually for two and a half years, and I can confirm he is a changed man. My colleague has also undertaken work with Mrs James since she was

DOI: 10.4324/9781003330899-9

released from psychiatric hospital, in addition to the work that was undertaken with her there. And now Mr James has been released from prison, they are both seeing a third therapist working on their couple relationship. They are very committed to making it work and being a family again.'

The probation officer added, 'Yes, I can confirm that Mr James has also undertaken an iHorizon course, a Lucy Faithful internet sex offenders treatment programme, and an anger management course with Mind.'

'Yeah,' sneered the policeman, 'you do-gooders are all the same. These guys are manipulative low-life. They see you coming. He'll bide his time and as soon as you reunite this bloke with his boy, he will be getting his end away and giving his wife two black eyes!'

'May I remind you,' retorted the flustered child's guardian, 'that it was not Mr James who abused his son. That occurred after Mrs James was admitted into psychiatric care and he was placed in a foster home.'

The social worker became defensive. 'We could never have known that was going to happen. We investigate potential foster carers thoroughly, and we did speak to their son who did it.'

'But did you subsequently investigate why this boy abused little Connor James? Did it occur to you that it might have happened to him beforehand?' asked the therapist tentatively.

The social worker reddened. 'Well, it all slipped through the net, really. We were short-staffed, we didn't have an emergency placement for the boy and these people said they were willing to have him. We thought it was a blessing.'

'It wasn't a blessing for little Connor James though,' highlighted the child's guardian.

The MAPPA manager sighed impatiently. 'I think we are getting off the point here. We need to decide whether we consider that Mr James has sufficiently changed to warrant being reunited with his wife and child.'

'These guys don't change,' sneered the policemen. 'I've been in this job 25 years and I know, they don't change. Once a nonce, always a nonce.'

'Oh? And what university did you learn that forensic enlightenment,' sarcastically enquired the child's guardian.

'The university of Real Life, madam,' was the brusque retort.

'I'm inclined to agree with him,' interposed the social worker. 'I did tell Mrs James that if she continues to maintain her relationship with her husband, then we will arrange for Connor James to be adopted, as we will any subsequent children she may have with her husband.'

'Well, you have no right to tell her that,' interposed the child's guardian. 'That is a decision only a judge can decide.'

'Yes, but on our recommendation.'

'But it doesn't appear that you have taken any credence of all the work Mr James has done to change his life for the better. He is fully committed to cease to be the person he was,' said the exasperated therapist.

'Yes,' agreed the probation officer. 'Considering what an angry young man Mr James was, he is now extremely compliant, polite, is never late for his sessions, has maintained his job as a mechanic and his boss has written a letter of support that is in your notes, as is a letter from his landlord saying he has never been behind on his rent, and keeps the inside and out of his premises neat and tidy.'

'And may I add,' said the Therapist, 'that all the work that Mr James has undertaken has been at his own expense. Surely that must say something.'

'Look.' The policeman leaned forward to emphasise his point. 'He's a wife-beater and a pedo. They should have locked him up and thrown away the key.'

'There is no evidence that Mr James is a paedophile,' countered the therapist. 'The images that were found on his phone were all of teenage girls, many of them who looked over the age of 18.'

'Nah.' The policemen examined his fingernails. 'He just sees you all coming and is biding his time.'

MAPPA

The Management of Sexual or Violent Offenders (MOSOVO) is the police-based team who manages the activities of sexual and violent offenders in the community. As a consequence of the Criminal Justice and Court Services Act 2000, their work falls under the remit of public protection by assessing the risk posed by sexual and violent offenders, monitoring their compliance with notification requirements, the safeguarding of adults and children, covert operations, and liaison with partner agencies under Multi-Agency Public Protection Arrangements (MAPPA). MAPPA is the process through which various agencies such as the police, the prison service and probation work together to protect the public by managing the risks posed by violent and sexual offenders released from prison and living in the community. (One wonders why sexual offenders and violent offenders have been lumped together as one heterogenous group in this way, when their presentations are so manifestly different both across groups and within them.) These various agencies will be concerned with the risk assessments, vetting of the individual, and determining the level of contact the parent can have with their child or children. The aim is to manage offenders on a multi-agency basis by working together, sharing information to ensure that effective plans are put in place. Unless someone on that panel is trauma-informed, their coming together can lead to discussions about the present without understanding the past. And while there is no such thing as a typical sex offender, there is a subtext in the minds of many professionals that they are all manipulative, devious, deceptive, misogynistic, secretive, and narcissistic with a sense of entitlement. So many of these offenders are not perceived on an individual basis, but carry with them the stereotype of a registered sex offender, whether they intended to view illegal imagery online or not. The panel's views can be dictated by strong-minded individuals who have their own prejudices, and it is not unusual for there to be conflicting opinions about the person's level of risk to the community or to their children. Considering recidivism rates with individuals convicted of contact sexual offences is so low, the risk of non-contact offenders, that is, online viewing offenders, going on to commit a future contact offence would be even less. If these various members of different agencies kept abreast of the latest evidence-based literature, then one would assume that there should not be disagreements on risk levels. Whether any of the members of these meetings will be trauma-informed will vary, but the issue is that their decision not only effects the offenders in the immediate future, but also for the rest of their lives.

Under the auspices of MOSOVO or their equivalent teams, the police are required to manage and monitor a registered sex offender who has either been given a community service order, a suspended sentence or a custodial sentence and is released on licence. At a time when the number of registered sex offenders is soaring, particularly as a consequence of online offences, the police have had to face huge cuts in their personnel and financial resources. Risk assessment tools (Risk Matrix 2000: Thornton et al., 2003; Active Risk Management System: Kewley & Blandford, 2017; McNaughton Nicholls & Webster, 2014; OASys: Howard & Barnett, 2015) are supposed to consider both the risk and protective factors as to whether an alleged or a convicted sexual offender is likely to reoffend, although there is little evidence to show that this process actually achieves its aim, especially as the risk of recidivism in online offending is so low anyway. However, many such police officers working within these units complain about the length of time is takes to complete such assessments, and they were pleased to hand them over to the probation service when it was re-established from the private sector in 2020, although the quality of completion of these assessments have been found to be poor leading to an over-prediction of risk of those who present with minimal risk, resulting in unnecessary sanctions that are resource intensive, costly and interferes with civil liberties (Kewley et al., 2020). Police officers also complain that taking the lead role is moving them away from policing *per se*, and into the realm of social workers, arguing that the sex offenders they monitor place demands on their time and energy, for example in home visits, which is very often outside of their public protection remit. As a consequence of lack of resources, untrained staff, and the fear of reprisals in a climate of public blame and anxiety (Kemshall, 2009) should they get it wrong, many have adopted a negative and punitive response to any potential move the offender who may want to make to improve their life and move on. So the person may find they:

- Cannot apply for any employment, for example, in the retail or hospitality sectors, in case they meet children.
- Cannot live within 3–5 miles near a school.
- Cannot attend church or community gatherings where children may be present.

- Cannot have holidays or celebration meals with their families which will include children and grandchildren.
- Cannot form new relationships with partners who may have children, even if they are grown up (as the children themselves may have children).

Jones (2022) highlights that while release from prison is what every offender wants, the stress that comes with it is immense. Friends and relations have changed, and even places have changed in the person's absence as new buildings and new roads are developed. Having to start again in job-seeking and forming new relationships can trigger the previous traumas of rejection and abandonment. He argues:

> Placing somebody in a bedsit or in a hostel with negligible income, without the prospect of getting work easily, with no support, with well-intentioned staff who do not have a trauma-informed or diversity-informed perspective, where there is no specialist support for people triggered by current experiences of adversity, and possibly punitive interpretations of ORASC [offence-related altered states of consciousness] – e.g., thinking they are reacting because they are 'evil' or 'bloody-minded', or 'mad' or 'inhuman' - is unfair on the person being released and on those providing care for them.
>
> (Jones, 2022, p. 71)

As already highlighted, it is well established that people convicted of sex crimes have high rates of various childhood maltreatment (Levenson, Willis & Prescott, 2016). High ACE scores have also been linked with risky sexual behaviour, for example, engaging in sexual activity prior to the age of 15, experiencing teenage pregnancy, experiencing foetal death, and having 50 or more sexual partners (Hillis et al., 2004). Similarly, Levenson, Willis and Prescott (2014) undertook a study of 679 male sexual offenders. They found they had twice as likely to have suffered physical abuse,13 times more likely to experience the emotional abuse, and three times more likely to have suffered from sexual abuse compared to the general population. So I struggle to understand those who counter saying that these guys are just trying to get people to feel sorry for them so they do not receive such a heavy sentence.

Contemporary treatment programmes

> People convicted of sex crimes have high rates of various child maltreatment and family dysfunction as youngsters … Early adversity can create distorted thinking and maladaptive coping mechanisms (including violence). It can interfere with attachment and bonding, especially for children who see little modelling of healthy relationship skills (including empathy) in their families or communities.
>
> (Levenson, Willis & Prescott, 2018, pp. 171–172)

Despite our knowledge and understanding about the early lives of offenders from such research as conducted by Jill Levenson and her colleagues, (Levenson, 2016), the UK criminal justice system still persists on a persecutory stance when conducting treatment programmes with offenders, criticising their distorted thinking as being deviant and manipulative. Levenson *et al* continues:

> The historically confrontational approach of many SOTX [sexual offender treatment programs] may inadvertently reproduce disempowering dynamics like those in abusive families … This can easily create a parallel process that reactivates trauma and prompts a client's need to respond with old coping skills that were rehearsed over and over in a dysfunctional home.
>
> (Levenson, Willis & Prescott, 2018, p. 182)

The previous predominant focus has been on relapse prevention (e.g. Core SOTP: Mann, Hanson & Thornton, 2010), that is the prevention of reoffending, despite, as already discussed, the rate of recidivism being so low. The specific risk factors for relapse were considered to be deviant sexual preferences, cognitive distortions, lack of empathy, intimacy deficit and problems regulating their emotions. Using a risk, need, and responsivity model (Andrews & Bonata, 1998), an offender's therapeutic intervention was based on their perceived level of risk, which determined how much therapeutic input was conducted. However, evaluation of this Sexual Offender Treatment and Evaluation Project (Mews, Di Bella & Purver, 2017) found not only no reduction of recidivism rates over an 8-year follow-up, despite this being the *raison d'être* of the programme, but found using a matched controlled non-treatment group that SOTP had actually increased the risk in the treatment group. The obvious criticism of this approach is that it was insufficiently focused on the developmental history and trajectory of each individual offender that lead them down the path of offending; an individual in not just a series of risks, but a human being with a damaged history. Using a manualised, one-size fits all approach overviewing various risk processes is necessary but completely insufficient for the task in hand. Not only did this process overlook the trauma history of the individual, it took no account of the shame that the person would be experiencing, and indeed often evoked further shame, for example, by expecting them to open up to their past when put together to undertake work in groups. Jill Levenson argued that, rather than using their childhood trauma as an excuse for their offending, they were more likely to underreport early adversity rather than advocating it as an excuse for mitigation, because they did not identify the link between their past and their present offending behaviour. Levenson, Willis & Prescott (2018) contend that is time to put therapy back on the agenda for the treatment of sexual offending rather than using workbooks and manuals in rigidly standardised programmes.

Jespersen, Lalumière & Seto (2009) wanted to research the cycle of sexual abuse to sexual abuser hypothesis, and found that there is support for it, in that sex offenders against children are more likely to have been sexually abused than non-sex offenders, and far from it being a vampire myth, found that adolescents who committed sexual offences were more likely to have been exposed to sexual violence, sexual abuse, emotional abuse and neglect. In reference to treatment 'programmes' for young offenders, Ungar and Perry (2012) argued:

> A fifteen-year-old child may have the self-regulation capacity of a five-year-old, the social skills of a three-year-old and the cognitive organisation of a ten year old. And, due to the unique genetic, epigenetic, and developmental history of each child, it is very difficult to apply a 'one-size-fits-all' treatment approach.

There are two additional problems to this one size fits all approach, where offenders are ordered to conduct courses, such as the iHorizon Course for internet Sex Offenders or Kaizen. First, the participants do not necessarily perceive themselves as a heterogeneous group, so may psychologically opt out, going through the motions rather than getting the wrath of probation falling around their ears, with threats of recall to prison. Aslan and Edelmann (2014) compared the demographics of sexual offenders in the Greater London area. They found that the majority of internet viewers were predominantly white, young, single men who were well educated in stable employment, less sexually risky, with no previous convictions (Webb, Craissati & Keen, 2008). Contact offenders were older, more likely to have been accused of a contact offence in their history without being charged, and more likely to report a personal history of childhood sexual abuse. Similarly, Bates and Metcalf (2007) found internet viewers were of a higher level of educational achievement. They had lower scores on sexualised attitudes toward children, emotional congruence with children and empathy distortions toward victims of childhood sexual abuse. Most importantly, they did not support attitudes that explicitly condone or endorse the sexual abuse of children. Yet even with the compulsory treatment programmes that are just for internet offenders, there will be an internal comparison between participants who have been addicted to pornography, who may not recognise themselves as a sexual offender, compared to those who groom and aim to meet children for sexual purposes. Such is the state of shame in the history of any offender, they may be unwilling or unable to reveal their full selves within a group course as they would be required to do. This is especially true for the neurodivergent who cannot bear to be within a group anyway, let alone 'present' his historical timeline to the others.

The second issue is that many of these courses lose sight of the fact that 93% of internet offenders did not generate any new convictions for a sexual offence, as Krone and Smith (2017) found after a 4-year follow up, and 80–90% of internet offenders do not go on to commit contact offences against children (Smith, 2017). Similarly, Seto, Hanson and Babchishin (2011) undertook two meta-analyses of research overviewing more than two and a half thousand cases and found that just 4.6% of their sample of online offenders committed a contact offence over a 6-year period, meaning that 95.4% did not. Yet these sex-offender courses are all focused on the risk of recidivism and relapse prevention, with little individual attention as to why they offended in the first place; their childhood trauma. Aslan et al. (2014) investigated individuals who had been convicted of both online viewing and contact offences. They found differences in developmental factors between the offenders forming two primary themes: childhood attachment difficulties and experiences of childhood abuse, both of which appeared to influence the offending process, and this was escalated by adult relationships, personality problems and substance use. They argued that a better understanding of the offence process would inform clinical practice.

Marshall et al. (2005) agree that exclusive focus on risk can lead to overly confrontational encounters, despite being deemed as to being therapeutic. They add that these encounters, instead of being collaborative to enhance hope, self-esteem and attaining the goal of living a good life, they can lead to a lack of rapport, and fragmented and mechanistic treatment delivery. These confrontational techniques can disempower and discourage clients from owning up to their offences and taking personal responsibility. They elicit more shame and are thus more likely to withdraw into themselves to cover it up. And interestingly, despite the prevention of recidivism being the main goal of these compulsory courses, research shows that for optimal effectiveness, they need to be conducted by qualified registered psychologists with appropriate clinical supervision (Gannon et al., 2019), a fact that in many geographical areas is often ignored. It might be useful to spend some time discussing the primary cognitive foci of these courses; denial and minimisation, and victim empathy.

Denial and minimisation

Andrew Smith (2017) points out that denial and lack of victim empathy are contested risk factors, which is why they tend not to appear in risk assessment tools, yet still form an important part of mandatory treatment programmes. Denial is a process of covering up shame, and although the person may know internally what they have done, will deny it verbally for fear of the consequences or reprisals. But focusing on denial can make engagement in treatment problematic. The aim of therapy is not to increase the level of shame; history cannot be changed. But we need to encourage the client to take personal responsibility for how they are going to change their future behaviour. A person in denial cannot display victim empathy, without admitting to offence (Smith, 2017), so again this is a paradox that keeps an offender locked into their self-protective cognitive mechanisms.

Victim empathy

Identifying with the effect that one's behaviour has on another is thought to inhibit re-offending (Marshall *et al.,* 1995), and therefore held a large place in treatment programmes. One thing that becomes apparent when working within therapy with sex offenders is that one cannot expect them to express any form of victim empathy until they have had their own victimisation, abuse and pain acknowledged and heard. If their own childhood has been so rife with trauma and abuse, it does become normalised in their consciousness, and may therefore not occur to them that the images they have viewed are inappropriate. Williams, Papadopoulou and Booth (2012) undertook a longitudinal survey of prisoners looking at their childhood and family background. Nearly a third of all prisoners (29%) reported that they had experienced some form of abuse and/or neglect in childhood. 41% had observed violence in the home as a child, often when they had a family member with an alcohol (18%) or drug problem (14%). 24% said that they had been in care at some point during their childhood. Nevertheless, the majority of prisoners reported that their families were important to them, and wanted them to be involved in their lives. Many prisoners also believed that support of their family and seeing their children would be important in stopping them from reoffending in the future. This is also important given the effect that parental imprisonment has on their children (one of the ACEs), yet the current default mechanism is removal rather than supervision and support. Levenson, Willis & Prescott (2018) contend that understanding victim empathy does not come from a place of shaming, blaming and confronting clients. It comes from a place of a compassionate validation of their own childhood trauma, which will allow the offender to view their own behaviour from a different perspective.

Cognitive distortions

Cognitive distortions related to offending can take the form of rationalising, justifying, excusing behaviour, as well as victim-blaming (Levenson et al., 2018). The cognitive role is to account for the behaviour, justify it and to reduce or remove shame. Often these maladaptive cognitions are linked to childhood trauma, in that they have not been heard or accounted for in their own victimisation, so become normalised in their own core beliefs. They are both part of the process in maintenance of self-esteem and the product of offending behaviour, but they offer no insight into the aetiology of the offending, as they usually occur after the offence (Abel, Becker & Cunningham-Rathner, 1984).

Deviant sexual interests

It is held that not all sexual offenders have deviant sexual interests or preferences (Ward et al., 2007). However, in our contemporary sex-positive society, who is to say what thoughts and fantasies are deviant anyway? It is well known that there is a substantial population of self-confessed paedophiles who would never consider touching a child, but keep their thoughts and fantasies in their heads. Similarly, there is a large population of people who enjoy BDSM both in their fantasies and within their sexual repertoire, but always keep within the context of consent and safety. So the knowledge that someone may fantasise about coercive sex or sex with children, tells us nothing about any potential risk of offending.

Attachment issues and intimacy deficits

People who have, or are likely to, commit an online or contact sexual offence have commonalities in their presentation, but they also have unique differences. They will struggle with emotional regulation, or maybe even completely disengaged from their emotions. They may be obsessive, impulsive, and if they are neurodivergent, they may also struggle with understanding the perspectives of others in relation to how they have behaved. Their attachment insecurities or childhood traumas may be buried deep within a cage of shame, with either strong defences against their BAD-ME circuit, or wearing it metaphorically on their sleeves as a challenge. As the effects of trauma are often stored in the Right brain and the body without a narrative, verbal therapies may struggle to access it. Therapists need to be more intuitive to the needs of each individual to work on an emotional and physiological level and use techniques that promote cohesion between the two hemispheres, *i.e.* cortical growth in the corpus collosum.

Marshall (1989) was the first researcher to identify insecure attachments as a contributory factor in sexual offending. Thereafter, researchers began to identify specific attachment styles correlated with sexual offending. Ward, Hudson and Marshall (2007) highlighted that a dismissive avoidant style would lead to hostility and the potential to rape. A preoccupied style would lead to the need or sexual approval and to sexualise relationships which may lead to the abuse of children. Baker & Beech (2004) noted that sex offenders were more likely to be disorganised (linking back to childhood trauma) than other offenders, and Jamieson and Marshall (2000) found that extra-familial child abusers were five times more likely to have a disorganised attachment as compared to a control group. Thus, it seems wrong to ignore this vital piece of information in the trajectory of offending because it can't be dealt with in a group setting.

Trauma-informed therapy and desistance

Desistance is the causal process that leads to the termination of offending behaviour; when it actually stops. Laws and Ward (2011) highlight that desistance is not an event, but a process punctuated with lapses, recoveries, relapses, and full recoveries, which ought to be anticipated, rather than used as evidence that no change is possible. Using the age-crime curve, which they argue is 'the most robust finding in criminology for almost two centuries' (p. 36), they found that sex offending peaks in adolescence or early adulthood, and then decreases with maturity, except for a small subset of offenders who show a life-course paedophilic orientation. They outline external conditions that contribute to desistance, for example ageing, marriage, employment stability, military service and education. They add that forensic psychology's contribution to the study of desistance in sex offenders has been negligent. Laub and Sampson (2003) found similarly that even the most persistent offender will desist eventually, albeit at different rates and ages. However, residential instability, marital instability, job instability, failure at school or work, and periods of incarceration, all contribute to the persistence of offending; yet this is the position that those working within the criminal justice system seem to push these potential offenders into as soon as they receive the knock, even before they have been convicted.

An integrative theory of desistance was described by Göbbels et al. (2012) and comprises four distinct phases:

- decisive momentum (initial desistance);
- rehabilitation (promoting desistance);
- re-entry (maintaining desistance); and
- normalcy (successful maintenance over a long period of time).

The probation service identifies three stages: primary, secondary and tertiary desistance. Primary is the behavioural cessation of offending; secondary relates to the person's identity in the adoption of non-offending behaviour; and tertiary is feeling that the person belongs within a non-offending population. The whole ethos behind this is that respect for each individual should be at the forefront of the process of collaboration and that supportive families and intimate relationships support them on their desistance journey. Yet the whole premise of supervision and registration for people who have committed a sexual offence is that they cannot be trusted for the duration that they are on the Sexual Offender's Register: for up to 10 years.

Getting the knock can be the wake-up call, or the turning point, that moves an individual out of offending and into desistance (Laub & Sampson, 2003). It is at this stage that the alleged offender gets jolted out of their addictive fugue offending state into the harsh, cold and shameful reality of what they have been doing. Shame is a major contributory factor in desistance: public humiliation, personal disgrace and private remorse (Leibrich, 1996). Following arrest, many alleged offenders will call StopIt Now! for advice, may undertake courses with the Lucy Faithful Foundation and some find a StopSO therapist to undertake therapy as part of their desistance process. The personal agency is emphasised in this behaviour as these courses are not provided by the criminal justice service, but are self-funded.

Levenson et al. (2016) advocate Trauma Informed Care, conducted collaboratively with warmth, empathy and respect toward their own traumas, needs to be adjusted to reach the client's needs. The argue that it is not a reframing of client's lives as victims, nor is it an excuse for their offending, but a process of emphasising resilience and personal choice; *i.e.* human agency. Marshall et al. (2005) similarly advocate warmth and empathy that is rewarding and directive. Shadd Maruna (2001), using data from the Liverpool Desistance Study, found through interviews that hardened criminals who would be expected to continue on a life of crime, desisted through powerful narratives that aided them in making sense of their pasts, finding fulfilment in productive behaviours, and feeling in control of their future. He emphasised that internal conditions of self-discovery through narrative lead to new understandings that can lead to turning points in the story-telling processes. These researchers tend to suggest that if you listen to what an offender has to say, and the journey they have made into offending, instead of making assumptions about what they think (cognitive distortions), what they feel (deviant sexual arousal), and how they behave (manipulative and devious), then desistance and rehabilitation even for the most hardened criminal can be achieved. Levenson, Willis and Prescott (2018) propose: 'Trauma-Informed Care helps clients make sense of their lives, acknowledge the circumstances they have lived through, understand their choices and patterns of behaviour over time, and identify areas for desired change' (p. 173). This also suggests that this work needs to be conducted on a one-to-one basis, rather than searching for a group option that is cheaper, but less effective.

The link between persistence in offending and desistance, Laub and Sampson (2003) argue, are two sides of the same coin. Persistence in crime is exacerbated by a lack of social controls, a lack of structured routines, and a lack of purposeful human agency. The Good Lives Model–Comprehensive (GLM-C) approach to treatment, rather than focusing on these deficits, promotes human welfare through primary goods or goals that will increase the person's sense of well-being (Ward & Stewart, 2003): states of affairs, states of mind, personal characteristics, psychological well-being, and activities, which are sort for their own sake. Ten types of primary goods have been identified, which are: life, healthy living and functioning; knowledge; excellence at work and play; excellence in agency: autonomy and self-directedness; inner peace: freedom from emotional turmoil and stress; relationships and friendships, including intimate, romantic and family; community: happiness; spirituality, having a meaning in life; and creativity (Ward et al., 2007). Secondary goods are the instrumental ways and means of securing these primary goods, either through certain types of work or relationships. It is assumed that sexual offenders pursue these primary goods through inappropriate means. So, to rehabilitate an offender, the treatment, or therapy, needs to focus on how the person can fulfil these goals in more acceptable ways, using a confluence of human controls and connections, structured routine activities and purposeful human agency, or choice, in a subjective reconstruction of the self (Cohler, 1982) into a more adaptive personal identity. Ward et al. (2007) argue that any treatment plan should explicitly be constructed to take into account an offender's strengths, primary goods, relevant environments, and what competencies and resources required to meet these goods. The aim of this is to provide the offender with the skills, values and attitudes necessary to live a meaningful and satisfying life that does not inflict harm on children or adults (Ward et al., 2007). This, it seems to me, has to be undertaken on an individual level. Maria Anslo (2022) agrees that it is time to use attachment theory in the probation service. Hitherto it has been a cognitive-behavioural approach that was confrontational, punishing, with any admission that the offender might have had a difficult life and might have been abused themselves being inadmissible. 'That was going soft, and did not fit with that era of the "punitive turn"' (p. 12). She contends that it is time to work in a humanising and respectful way.

Individuals who have grown up in toxic or chaotic environments may not know how to bring structure and stability into their lives, a feature of desistance, so homework tasks in building structure are immensely valuable. In therapy, identifying and working with toxic shame is key. Using time lines to find the salient trauma an individual experienced during their upbringing that took them on the trajectory of offending can provide the narrative the person needs in understanding their own behaviour. Life histories offer a narrative to break down the complex phenomena of offending, providing detailed information about traumatic events as they were experienced by the individual, and the significance for them (Laub & Sampson, 2003). Essentially, it's a cognitive understanding that what happened to them when they were a child was not their fault. Therefore, they are not a bad person. By breaking down the BAD-ME circuit, the self-sabotaging acting out can be arrested, and the cognition of guilt can be introduced. This leads to a distinction between being a bad person (so bad behaviour is inevitable) and having done bad things; the latter future being changeable. This can lead to the changing of states of mind, the process of human agency and personal responsibility, and ultimately, desistance.

Ward et al. (2007) also highlight the importance of language when working with offenders; to remove words from therapeutic vocabulary like 'deviant', 'distorted', 'predator' and 'risk prevention', all with negative evaluations and negative expectancies. That good outcomes mean treating the person with respect, which will add to their person agency. The treatment is a means to a rehabilitation end, but that cannot happen if the person is constantly receiving the negativity of the criminal justice system even post-conviction, for example in constantly trying to keep them away from children in society rather than helping them live with and around them. It is only by helping the individual live a more fulfilling life, will we reduce their risk of reoffending.

Bessell van der Kolk (2014) argues that the very first process in working with clients who have trauma in their history is to get them safe in the here and now; to get them grounded in the present. Unless they feel safe in the process, they will keep being pulled back into the subconscious memories of the past, the repetition compulsion. So bodily grounding exercises (feeling the feet on the floor, the bottom on the chair, identifying things in the room) helps to keep people in the present. Similarly, mindfulness exercises of deep breathing and bodily relaxation help the individual feel safe in the therapy room. This is not a verbal process. It's about using the body and the mind to deal with a damaged history (Rothschild, 2000). Daniel Siegel (2003) insists that healing can be achieved once the traumatic events and suboptimal developmental experiences trapped in a dysfunctional memory system can break free of the restrictive and chaotic behaviour patterns. By revisiting the early trauma in therapy, the client learns that remembering the trauma is not the same as experiencing it, as it now has a beginning, a middle, and an end, and can therefore assign it to personal history (van der Kolk, 2003). This therapeutic process also provides an attachment frame for the client, and for some, therapy may be the first real emotionally intimate relationship they have experienced, where they can be completely open and free to express their thoughts and feelings without fearing censure or criticism, but within the boundaries of a secure attachment frame. They can rehearse potential ways of being as they develop on their unique strengths in constructing a new perception of the self, while learning new ways of dealing with inner weakness. Andrew Smith (2018) highlights how important this therapeutic relationship is as a site of potential healing for attachment and trauma issues.

Gordon and Rachel's review

Irrespective of all the work Gordon had done to turn his life around with a StopSO therapist, and with letters of validation from his boss, his landlord and his therapist in his pre-sentence report, he had been sent to prison for 18 months and was placed on the sex offenders register for 10 years. Gordon had been labelled a paedophile and vilified by the press and by his fellow inmates, despite having no sexual preferences for children. Without undermining the fact that Gordon had committed a criminal offence, for which he should be punished, the media encouraged armchair psychiatry and elicited a vigilante process, based on a misunderstanding of what paedophilia actually is, assuming that all online offenders are perverts and 'pedos'. Of course, the media have no incentive to change this, as public outrage in the protection of children sells newspapers and encourages online readers.

Once the report of Gordon's offences hit the press, online trolls targeted Rachel, despite the fact that she had not seen Gordon for over a year, so she was forced to close down her social media accounts. Rachel was living in a small council flat with Connor, under the constant supervision of the child protection social workers, but needed to be rehoused following being targeted by neighbours, posting dog faeces through her letterbox and spraying graffiti on the external walls of her flat. This contributed to her mental breakdown, and her being sectioned under the Mental Health Act in a mental health facility, with her son being placed in foster care, as she was too medicated to care for him.

From prison, Gordon had written letters of contrition to Rachel, sent to her via his solicitor. When Rachel was rehoused into bed and breakfast accommodation, she visited Gordon in prison and their relationship was slowly reconciled. Rachel also went to visit Mrs Watkins at Gordon's request to check how Rex was doing. Soon, Rachel became a weekly visitor to Mrs Watkins, who started to teach her how to cook food from fresh ingredients rather than living on pre-cooked ready meals. Mrs Watkins also taught Rachel about other domestic activities, like household budgeting and shopping lists; the kind of thing Rachel's mother might have taught her had she not died when Rachel was so young. However, when the social worker found out about Rachel's visits to Gordon and to Mrs Watkins, she was adamant that as Gordon is a convicted sex offender, should Rachel and Gordon choose to live together on his release, Connor would not be released back into her care, and any subsequent children Gordon and Rachel may have, would be adopted. This is the rock and a hard place that prevents rehabilitation for people convicted of online sexual offences from living a normal life. It is loneliness and alienation that is a risk factor for recidivism, yet the system creates the environment for it to occur.

References

Abel, G.G., Becker, J.V. & Cunningham-Rathner, J. (1984). Complications, consent, and cognitions in sex between children and adults. *International Journal of Law and Psychiatry*, 7, 89–103. doi:10.1016/0160–2527(84)90008–90006.

Andrews, D. & Bonata, J. (1998). *The psychology of criminal conduct*. 2nd edition. Cincinnati, OH: Anderson Publishing.

Anslo, M. (2022). *Using attachment theory in probation practice*. HM Inspectorate of Probation.

Aslan, D. & Edelmann, R. (2014). Demographic and offence characteristics: a comparison of sex offenders convicted of possessing indecent images of children, committing contact sex offences or both offences. *The Journal of Forensic Psychiatry & Psychology*, 25 (2), 121–134. doi:10.1080/14789949.2014.884618.

Aslan, D., Endelmann, R., Bray, D. & Worrell, M. (2014). Entering the world of sex offenders: an exploration of offending behaviour patterns of those with both internet and contact sex offences against children. *Journal of Forensic Practice*, 16 (2), 110–126. doi:10.1108/JFP-02-2013-0015.

Baker, E. & Beech, A.R. (2004). Dissociation and variability of attachment dimensions and early maladaptive schema in sexual and violent offenders. *Journal of Interpersonal Violence*, 119, 1119–1135. doi:10.1177/0886260504269091.

Bates, A. & Metcalf, C. (2007). A psychometric comparison of internet and non-internet sex offenders from a community treatment sample. *Journal of Sexual Aggression*, 13 (1), 11–20. doi:10.1080/13552600701365654.

Cohler, B.J. (1982). Personal narrative and life course. In P.B. Baltes & O.G. Brim Jr (eds), *Life span development and behaviour*, vol. 4. New York: Academic Press.

Gannon, T.A., Olver, M.E., Mallion, J.S. & James, M. (2019). Does specialised psychological treatment for offending reduce recidivism? A meta-analysis examining staff and program variables as predictors of treatment effectiveness. *Clinical Psychology Review*, 73, 101752. doi:10.1016/j.cpr.2019.101752.

Göbbels, S., Ward, T. & Willis, G.M. (2012). An integrative theory of desistance from sexual offending. *Aggression and Violent Behaviour*, 17 (5), 453–462. doi:10.1016/j. avb.2012.06.003

Hillis, S.D., Anda, R.F., Dube, S.R., Felitti, V.J. *et al.* (2004). The association between adverse childhood experiences and adolescent pregnancy, long-term psychosocial consequences, and foetal death. *Pediatrics*, 113 (2), 320–327. doi:10.1542/peds.113.2.320.

Howard, P.D. & Barnett, G.D. (2015). The development and validation of the OASys Sexual Reoffending Predictor (OSP). In R.Moore (ed.), *A compendium of research and analysis on the Offender Assessment System (OASys) 2009–2013*. London: Ministry of Justice. Retrieved from www.gov.uk/government/uploads/system/uploa ds/attachment_data/file/449357/research-analysis-offender-assessment-system.pdf

Jamieson, S. & Marshall, W.L. (2000). Attachment styles and violence in child molesters. *Journal of Sexual Aggression*, 5, 88–98. doi:10.1080/13552600008413301

Jespersen, A.F., Lalumière, M.L. & Seto, M.C. (2009). Sexual abuse history among adult sex offenders and non-sex offenders: A meta-analysis. *Child Abuse and Neglect*, 33 (3), 179–192. doi:10.1016/j.chiabu.2008.07.004.

Jones, L. (2022). Risk assessment and intervention. In P. Willmott & L. Jones (eds), *Trauma-Informed Forensic Practice*. London: Routledge.

Kemshall, H. (2009). Working with sex offenders in a climate of public blame and anxiety: How to make defensible decisions for risk. *Journal of Sexual Aggression*, 15 (3), 331–343. doi:10.1080/13552600903031195

Kewley, S. & Blandford, M. (2017). The development of the active risk management system. *Journal of Criminal Psychology*, 7 (3) 155–167. doi:10.1108/JCP-10-2016-0034

Kewley, S., Osman, S. & McGuiness, A. (2020). How well do police specialists risk assess registered sex offenders? *Journal of Sexual Aggression*, 26 (3), 302–315. doi:10.1080/13552600.2019.1628315

Krone, T. & Smith, R. (2017). Trajectories in online child sexual exploitation offending in Australia. Trends & Issues in Crime & Criminal Justice, 524. Retrieved from www.aic.gov.au/publications/tandi/tandi524.

Laub, J.H. & Sampson, R.J. (2003). *Shared beginnings, divergent lives: Delinquent boys to age 70*. Cambridge, MA: Harvard University Press.

Laws, R.D. & Ward, T. (2011). *Desistance from sex offending: Alternatives to throwing away the keys*. London: Guildford Press.

Leibrich, J. (1996). The role of shame in going straight. A study of former offenders. In B. Galaway & J. Hudson (eds), *Restorative justice: International perspectives* (pp. 283–302). New York: Criminal Justice Press.

Levenson, J.S., Willis, G.M. & Prescott, D.S. (2016). Adverse childhood experiences in the lives of male sex offenders: Implications for trauma-informed care. *Sexual Abuse: A Journal of Research and Treatment*, 28 (4), 340–359. doi:10.1177/ 1079063214535819.

Levenson, J.S., Willis, G.M. & Prescott, D. (2018). Incorporating principles of trauma-informed care into evidence-based sex offending treatment. In E.L. Jeglic & C. Calkins (eds), *New Frontiers in Offender Treatment*. New York: Springer.

Mann, R.E., Hanson, R.K. & Thornton, D. (2010). Assessing risk for sexual recidivism: Some proposals on the nature of psychologically meaningful risk factors. *Sexual Abuse: A Journal of Research and Treatment*, 22, 172–190. doi:10.1177/1079063210366039.

Marshall, W.L. (1989). Intimacy, Loneliness and sexual offenders. *Behaviour Research and Therapy*, 27, 491–503. doi:10.1016/0005-7967(89)90083-1.

Marshall, W.L., Hudson, S.M., Jones, R. & Fernandez, Y.M. (1995). Empathy in sex offenders. *Clinical Psychology Review*, 15, 99–113. doi:10.1016/0272-7358(95)00002-7.

Marshall, W.L., Ward, T., Mann, R. E., Moulden, H., Fernandez, Y.M., Serran, G. & Marshall, L.E. (2005). Working positively with sexual offenders: Maximizing the effectiveness of treatment. *Journal of Interpersonal Violence*, 20 (9), 1096–1114.

Maruna, S. (2001). *Making good: How ex-convicts reform and rebuild their lives*. Washington, DC: American Psychological Association.

McNaughton Nicholls, C. & Webster, S. (2014). *Sex offender management and dynamic risk: Pilot evaluation of the Active Risk Management System (ARMS)*. Ministry of Justice Analytic Series. National Offender Management Service.

Mews, A., Di Bella, L. & Purver, M. (2017). *Impact evaluation of the prison-based core sex offender treatment programme*. London: Ministry of Justice.

Rothschild, B. (2000). *The body remembers. The psychophysiology of trauma and trauma treatment*. New York: Norton.

Seto, M.C., Hanson, R.K. & Babchishin, K.M. (2011). Contact sexual offending by men with online sexual offenses. *Sex Abuse*, 23 (1), 124–145. doi:10.1177/1079063210369013.

Siegel, D.J. (2003). An interpersonal neurobiology of psychotherapy. In D.J. Siegel & M.F. Solomon (eds), *Healing trauma. Attachment, mind, body & brain*. New York: Norton.

Smith, A. (2017). *Counselling male sexual offenders: A strengths-focused approach*. London: Routledge.

Smith, A. (2018). Sexual addiction and sexual offending. In T. Birchard & J. Benfield (eds), *The Routledge international handbook of sexual addiction*, Abingdon: Routledge.

Thornton, D., Mann, R., Webster, S., Blud, L., Travers, R., Friendship, C. & Erikson, M. (2003). Distinguishing between and combining risks for sexual and violent recidivism. *Annals of New York Academy of Sciences*, 989, 225–235. doi:10.1111/j.1749-6632.2003.tb07308..

Ungar, M. & Perry, B. D. (2012). Trauma and resilience. In R. Alaggia & C. Vine (eds). *Cruel but not unusual: Violence in Canadian families*. Waterloo, CA: WLU Press.

van der Kolk, B. (2003). Posttraumatic stress disorder and the nature of trauma. In D. J. Siegel & M.F. Solomon (eds), *Healing trauma. Attachment, mind, body & brain*. New York: Norton.

van der Kolk, B. (2014). *The body keeps the score: Mind, brain and body in the transformation of trauma*. London: Penguin.

Ward, T., Mann, R.E. & Gannon, T.A. (2005). The Good Lives model of offender rehabilitation: Clinical implications. *Aggression and Violent Behaviour*, 12, 87–107.

Ward, T., Hudson, S.M. & Marshall, W.L. (2007). Attachment style in sex offenders: a preliminary study. *Journal of Sex Research*, 33, 17–26. doi:10.1080/00224499609551811

Ward, T. & Stewart, C.A. (2003). Criminogenic needs and human needs: a theoretical model. *Psychological, Crime and Law*, 9, 125–143. doi:10.1080/1068316031000116247.

Webb, L., Craissati, J. & Keen, S. (2008). Characteristics of internet child pornography offenders: A comparison with child molesters. *Sexual Abuse. A Journal of research and Treatment*, 19 (4), 449–465. doi:10.1007/s11194-007-9063-2.

Williams, K., Papadopoulou, V. & Booth, N. (2012). *Prisoners' childhood and family backgrounds: Results from the Surveying Prisoner Crime Reduction (SPCR) longitudinal cohort of prisoners*. Research Series 4/12. Ministry of Justice.

Chapter 10

Do the forensic services meet the needs of their users?

Case study

Gordon was released from prison on licence after serving half his sentence for good behaviour. At first, he was required to live in one room in a hostel with other offenders, which made him very uncomfortable and withdraw into himself. He wanted to return to his work as a mechanic, but the probation officer overviewing his case refused, arguing that children could attend the garage with their parents when cars came and went for service. But his former boss contacted the probation officer on hearing this, pointing out that the reception and car sales area were in a separate building to the servicing area. The probation officer reluctantly conceded. Gordon was placed on a tight curfew, overseen by the hostel manager.

Following his release, Gordon adopted a new way of living by using what he had learned in his StopSO therapy, probation (iHorizon) and Lucy Faithfull courses. He used mindfulness exercises daily, visited Mrs Watkins to walk his little dog Rex, and helped her with her garden at weekends. He planned to work hard as a mechanic so he could save up to buy a small house of his own for him and Rachel, with a little garden for Rex. His was determined to be a better person. His therapy had taught him to acknowledge the victims in the online imagery, to face his shame, and to feel remorse for his behaviour to his wife and child. He and Rachel commenced couple counselling with a view to being reunited in the rented flat that Gordon moved into above the garage where he worked. However, our risk averse society created a situation that online offenders rarely can serve their time and get on with their lives like other offenders. In view of Gordon and Rachel's insistence on maintaining their relationship, Connor was removed from Rachel by the social workers and was placed in a care home while he waited for adoption.

Child sexual abuse material

Behind each and every one of the millions of images of CSAM on the World Wide Web is a real child suffering real abuse and torment at the hands of

DOI: 10.4324/9781003330899-10

adults, most of whom should be caring for them. In addition to the terrible physical trauma they suffer is the trauma in the knowledge of the perpetual imagery where viewers (predominantly men) are salivating and masturbating (or even directing in real time) over what was done to them. Many of these children are no longer children, but have grown up with the shame, humiliation and degradation of never being able to remove this imagery from the internet. Interpol keeps an international database of child abuse imagery (ICSE DB), and multi-jurisdictional access for law enforcement, which helps to improve the efficiency of identifying victims and offenders, and to prevent repeated investigations by differing international law enforcement agencies. The database helps identify young victims who may be experiencing harm in the present, so new presentations can be rapidly identified, and the children involved protected. However, this presents another dilemma for law enforcement and child protection agencies: should these children know when age-appropriate that their abusive experience is still circulating on imagery and video online, and that it can never be totally removed? Intellectually, people argue that they must be informed; that it is their right to know. Psychologically speaking, however, this knowledge is traumatic of itself, and can create deep mental health issues on top of the childhood experience.

The enormity of the damage that CSAM inflicts on these poor children cannot be overestimated, and as a humane society, we feel justified in feeling outrage at these terrible, publicly exposed crimes. Even if the imagery had been self-generated, particularly during adolescence, the knowledge that it is there can lead to long-term mental health issues as they move into adulthood. But equally, as a society, we fail to join up the dots to realise that these children may grow up into adolescents and adults who feel compelled to watch CSAM themselves; either looking for themselves online or watching experiences similar to what they had experienced as children (repetition compulsion). Why does our public outrage not turn to compassion for those traumatised, instead of abhorrence and vilification? This final chapter aims to address how this change to public condemnation comes about.

We underestimate the power of the internet

Pornography on the internet will take people, through their SEEKING system, into aspects of their sexuality that they would never have done, or even contemplated doing, had they not seen it graphically presented to them on their devices. Before the internet was available, individuals may have gone into sex shops to buy pornographic videos, or looked at live sex behind a carefully guarded cubicle, which would all have had to be paid and budgeted for, so there would be an element of careful selection of the material to fit a person's need and desires. Vanilla sex material was available through the television, but it was tainted with a smutty humorous connotation, as with Benny Hill, Carry On and St Trinian's films. It was considered a 'boys will be boys' culture as men leered at the buxom St Trinian girls in their school uniforms, which is now considered totally inappropriate. This kind of viewing can lead to the knock, when the algorithms of the internet sirens call – 'if you like those schoolgirls, what about these?' – leading the viewer down the rabbit hole of looking at 16–17-year-olds (or even younger) in school uniform, and as such illegal viewing.

Some material on the internet has to be paid for, especially in the dark web. But this accounts for less than 1% of the material to be found freely available online, and the diversity of this material is rich. Many porn addicts, after seeing and feeling aroused during watching, say, trans sex, or gay sex, or bestiality, will want to talk to others about what they have seen, without feeling judged or 'pervy', so they search for like-minded others on the internet. Conversations abound about the unusual material they have seen, and images may be passed between them. The thrill of new material encourages a desire to either want to view it for themselves, or go and pay a sex worker to see if that arousal happens in real life, as it is confusing, and they want to determine if it really is their sexual orientation. The assumption made in the criminal justice system and in some of the viewers themselves is that the arousal is a genuine desire and they like what they see, rather than an understanding of that is how the body works, indeed how it is supposed to work, when viewing any form of sexual material; it does not mean a change in sexual orientation.

As has been discussed in earlier chapters, this online imagery is particularly potent for people who are on the spectrum, or who may have ADHD, that is, the neurodivergent guys who struggle with making real relationships, so turn to their computer to learn about sex and relationships through pornography. Being obsessive is a co-occurring condition, as is being easily malleable and naive to the manipulative demands of others. 'I will be your friend', they persuasively suggest, 'but only if you get me pictures of …'. A person with Asperger's will be unable to see through the grooming process that is taking place. The need for friendships and connection becomes all-powerful as an attachment process, so they will do what is requested of them to keep that 'friendship' in place. They do not have the same motivation, or intent, to offend as maybe a neurotypical person may have, and the criminal justice system does not try to prove intent to harm; their default position is that possession implies intent.

Responses to online offences are not trauma-informed

Police, most probation officers, and certainly social workers, are not interested in the alleged offender's personal history nor in their psychological state. They are only interested in harm caused, and not harm experienced (Hocken, Taylor & Walton, 2022). An offence has been committed, and they must be caught and punished for it. Confusion and lack of understanding at the time of the alleged offender receiving the knock is interpreted as his denial and a lack of remorse. The alleged offender, on initial interview with the police, will be expected to have empathy for the victims in the imagery for the children he is viewing online, and many are indeed horrified as the shock breaks them out of their addictive fugue state to make them realise the import of what they have done. But victim empathy is harder for guys caught in chatrooms making sexual talk with what they presume is a teenager, and it proves to be an undercover police person or a vigilante. These bogus children/teenagers are very adept at saying the right thing to encourage their respondent to incriminate themselves, or to arrange to meet what they have believed was a willing participant. As Martellozzo (2012) argued, these bogus children/teenagers need to show enthusiasm, interest and commitment to the proposed communication to make themselves believable. But it is a fine line between being an enthusiastic surveillance officer and an *agent provocateur*, who is engaged in planning and encouraging the committing of a crime, as that will lead later to the court case failing if the defendant tried to end the encounter and was actively encouraged by the decoy.

New case law was introduced on 31 May 2022, which states, irrespective of whether the 'child' was bogus or did not actually exist, that the defendant should be sentenced 'as if' he intended to rape a child. As such, online communication sentences have been increased substantially, with life imprisonment if the rape of a child under 12 years old is being planned. For causing or inciting a child to engage in sexual activity and other similar offences, even where activity is incited but does not take place or no child victim exists, the maximum sentence is 14 years imprisonment. For the offence of sexual communication with a child, from 1 July 2022, offenders face a maximum penalty of two years in prison for sharing images, causing psychological harm, abuse of trust or the use of threats or bribes.

Our police forces have been driven by political targets, it is fair to say, so it is important they get as many arrests as possible as a tick-box exercise to keep the outcome statistics showing in a favourable light, to prevent the baying of the press or the police commissioner with his eye on his future election. This does not encourage a compassion-focussed arrest process. I am not saying that these men should not be punished for crossing the line, but I do feel that there might be a better way of doing it, that does not cost society so dear as it does now. It seems to me we need a subsidiary offence of, say, 'online offender', or using Outcome 21 and a caution rather than the label of 'sex offender' for people who have only looked at images online, as the offence of 'making indecent images of children' is based on the incorrect public assumption that the person intentionally looked and liked the image that they saw.

It has been known for a person to be prosecuted for images being accidently downloaded with legal pornography downloads, and the alleged offender merely looking at it for a matter of seconds to realise this is not the imagery wanted and thus deleted. Prosecutors argued that the deletion was a means of covering up the crime, rather than an unintentional viewing. Case law was brought to ascertain whether a person could be prosecuted for having deleted CSAM on their hard drive (*R. v. Porter (Ross Warwick)* (CLW/06/14/4), but produced more ambiguity depending on the IT skills of the viewer and their ability to access them from the hard drive. So the concept of *intent*, as previously discussed, has been lost in the prosecutions of these offenders, despite Section 1(1)(a) of the Protection of Children Act 1978 (PCA 1978) requiring that there must be a deliberate and intentional act, done with the knowledge that the image is, or is likely to be, an indecent photograph or pseudo-photograph of a child. Possession now implies intent, which is one of the fundamental problems here. At present, it is argued that if you have looked at illegal imagery, you must have intended to look, and if you have looked, you must have liked it, and must have been aroused by it. These arguments are fundamentally fallacious, as I have hopefully shown throughout this book.

But as the number of these online sexual offences coming through escalates, Seto (2017) argued that we cannot arrest our way out of this problem, as we are gridlocking the whole system. Simon Bailey, former chief constable and UK Child Protection lead, emphasised that they tried really hard to do just that: to arrest their way out of the problem (personal communication, 2022). A great deal of police time and attention is devoted to the proactive undercover investigations pretending to be a child online in anticipation of solicitation attempts (Briggs, Simon & Simonsen, 2011). The reality is that we cannot prosecute all these offences, and maybe we should consider prioritising cases, according to the actual risk to children, i.e. active risk, as opposed implied risk to children through viewing of CSAM, a passive risk. Triaging each case according to those who have prior sexual offences would be high risk, as would those who groom to meet what is presumed to be a child, or who actively encourage real-time online sexual activity, compared to the medium risk of those who engage in sexually explicit chat. High-level distribution of imagery would be high risk compared to the low risk of those who passively view images amongst a vast array of other sorts of pornography. Similarly, there needs to be a triage of determining those offenders who view indecent images of young children (potential paedophilia) compared to those who view teenagers online (potential hebephilia). Finally, Seto, Reeves and Jung (2010) argue that we need to discriminate between the explanations for viewing the imagery, i.e. looking at *intent*. We need to determine which potential offenders have indiscriminate sexual interests and have looked at whatever was available, compared to those who are experiencing repetition compulsion, or those who are addicted to online pornography *per se*, and those whose intent was a predatory act. The challenge for the Criminal Justice System is determining how this triage could be conducted, considering the length of time it is taking for each individual's devices to trundle through the high tech crime units.

The Sex Offenders Register

An offence listed under the Sexual Offences Act 2003 requires the offender to register on a Sex Offenders Register. This is designed for public protection, and thus when a conviction is made, the Court notifies the police, and the individual is required to inform them of the following for up to 10 years registration:

- Name and any aliases.
- Address and any other addresses where they regularly stay.
- Whether they live with a child or are staying in a household where a child lives for at least 12 hours a day.
- Details of conviction.
- Details of bank accounts to which they have access.
- Date of birth.
- National insurance number.
- Details of any passports they may hold.

As this is considered necessary for public protection, the police and probation officers are supposed to visit the person regularly to assess the situation. The offender will also have to notify if they are away from home for more than 7 days at a time, if they travel outside of the UK, if they move home, and this notification is expected in the new area within 3 days. Bizarrely, this registration can only be reviewed or challenged if they have been on the register for more than 15 years. However, many police officers give alleged offenders incorrect information on arrest, for example insisting that if the person wants to go on holiday, even for one night, they must give two weeks' notice. Similarly, some officers on initial arrest insist that the person has to disclose their arrest to their employer, potential employer, family, neighbours, children's school, etc. This bullying tactic takes advantage of a person who is in a scared and vulnerable position, and has no legality, as they are not yet convicted offenders. Similarly, some men have been 'advised' by the police that they should take a polygraph test without consultation with their solicitor before agreeing to take such a test. When one considers the massive amount of man hours involved on keeping a person on the sexual offender's register, and all the subsequent monitoring, it seems all the more inappropriate if the offender had never been considered at risk of a contact offence, and therefore it is not about public protection. And, as discussed in Chapter 7, the futility of putting children who may sexually harm on the Sexual Offenders Register is likely to become a self-fulfilling offending process.

In March 2022, the UK Government instigated an independent review into the police management of sex offenders in the community, with the aim of considering the risk posed by registered sex offenders and how it protects the general public. When one considers that the vast majority of the online offenders have never left their computers, again it shows a need to distinguish those who are a real physical risk to children, compared to those addicted to viewing internet imagery. Similarly, there is a campaign afoot to prevent registered sex offenders from changing their names, but my view is this should only apply to contact offenders. Considering the huge amount of vilification online offenders receive, changing their names may the only way they can protect their wives and children.

The delay in the criminal justice process

The criminal justice system, as it stands, can no longer keep pace with the speed and complexity of these relatively new online offences. At the time of writing when Barrister's have just balloted for strike action, it is estimated that the Crown Court has a backlog of 59,000 cases. It may be over a year before an alleged offender is even formally charged with an offence, but he has already been punished and vilified nevertheless by the community and the social workers. And I have worked with men, who for over a year after the knock, has been informed that no charges are being brought for lack of evidence. Yet they have still lost their employment, lost their home, their relationship has fallen apart, and the social services are still not letting him have free access to his children.

Duncan et al. (2020) discussed this delay in criminal processing as the family (as well as the alleged offender at this point) is being left in limbo, while they all wait for months and years for the police investigation to be completed, and the Crown Prosecution Service to make a decision on charges. The fear of the whole family being outed by the media, and the reprisals of the community exhausts their resilience and their coping strategies, as no aftercare or support is provided for them, or even to consider the families as innocent victims. They argue that the police need to seriously consider the necessity of sharing information about cases with the media, keeping in mind the backlash and stigmatisation that families face when their details are made public, especially if children reside at the published address. Similarly, is there any real reason why it needs six police officers barging into a house in a dawn raid, with up to three dogs in some cases (one wonders what one dog is supposed to be sniffing out, let alone three)? These are clearly shock tactics to make the alleged offender understand the enormity of what they propose to charge them with. But is it really necessary to terrorise the children in the household in this way, or to announce to the neighbours what is going on when they come and stand outside the house on seeing the number of police cars and the forensic teams searching the premises?

Damage to the families

The ripple-effect of the collateral damage of an alleged offender getting the knock, as discussed in Chapter 1, is substantial. The wives or partners of the arrestee often get tarred with the person's offence, and being accused of a 'you must have known' bias, especially from the social services. Their children get bullied at school as the rumour-mongers spread the word through Chinese whispers, or the arrest gets actively posted online in social media by the vigilantes, who have become investigators, judges, jurors, and punishers of what is yet to be a conviction of an offence. The children are accused by their peers: 'your dad's a pedo' or a 'perv', making the child consume the shame of their father. The family may find similar words sprayed on the outside of their home with red spray paint, or dog faeces shoved through their letter-box, punishing them for being 'guilty by association'. This does make me reflect on the witch-hunt trials of the 14th to 18th centuries, where the baying population enjoyed the public humiliation of women, whether or not they were innocent or guilty. Some families feel forced to change their names, change the children's schools; all of this can cause attachment injuries as the children wonder why they can no longer see their daddy. Such incidents, as well as the unwelcome visits from police and social workers, lead to the partners, and the children, fearing going outside into public places leading to isolation, feeling anxiety and depressed about the community rejection, and suffering the post-traumatic flashbacks from the knock that threw a landmine into their lives. Not only does the label of 'sexual offender' travel with the convicted person for the rest of their life, but it limits the life chances of their wife or partner and the children too, who perceive it as a joint punishment and life sentence for themselves (Bonnar-Kidd, 2010).

The most significant damage that occurs as a consequence of these events is the damage done to the children in the families, especially boys who are more at risk, as discussed in Chapter 3, particularly if they are around the ages of 8–10, and during adolescence, as that is such a significant time in their neural development. The trauma experienced as a consequence of their father getting the knock can vandalise their own sexual development. Kilmer and Leon (2017) argued that the registration policies and social service restrictions placed onto the family intending to protect children and families are in reality tearing these family members' lives apart. The children miss out on family bonding activities due to restrictions placed on their registrant parent, such as having their father attend school events, taking their children trick-or-treating or bomb-fire night, and going on family holidays where the father is not allowed to sleep in the same premises as his children.

In 2020, a strategic group was convened by the Marie Collins Foundation, the NWG Network and the Lucy Faithfull Foundation, called the IVIIC (Indirect Victims of Indecent Images of Children) Group, following concerns about the ripple effect that arrests for online offences has on the families and children of the offenders, leaving them traumatised by the experience of the current professional response and therefore becoming secondary victims. Yet this secondary victim status is not a position that the Ministry of Justice legally accept, so the status quo remains. The IVIIC group, however, goes from strength to strength as professionals argue for a reconsideration of the whole process. Duncan et al. (2020) recommended that an impartial family liaison officer be appointed to the families of alleged offenders to guide them through the process, being available to answer questions, provide updates of the case, and to check in with family's welfare and wellbeing. This would probably need to be independent of the police force, who are investigating and subsequently prosecuting the case, as it may be perceived as a conflict of interest.

Lack of consistency in social worker's responses

I am not intentionally being critical of child protection social workers as a profession, as I genuinely believe that they fall under the auspices of 'damned if they do, and damned if they don't'. In rare cases where children have been harmed, they receive so much high-profile press coverage, it can publicly out individual social workers as incompetent and ruin their professional and private lives. This is part of our societal blame culture, which I will discuss further in the chapter, which they do not deserve if they have been doing their best. But this has led them into defensive practice, and leads them, once informed of a police investigation, to remove children from their fathers even before charges are made. And because of the diversity of different responses made by different social workers to the same situation, it suggests that there is insufficient understanding of online offending and lack of training in this ever-increasing problem.

Draconian responses to non-offending partners have been reported, blackmailing them with the threat of removing children into care unless they separate and divorce their husbands or partners. They may infer to the non-offending partner that continuing to support their partner means that they approve of, or are colluding with, their partner's alleged offending behaviour. They may express their opinion, and the opinion of the police officer, that they know that these 'paedophiles' cannot change their behaviour. They demand, as do the police, information as to whether they have been having a sexual relationship with the alleged offender. These demands are made within days of the non-offending partner discovering there was a problem in their relationship at all. No time to process; no time to grieve. Risk management appears to be no longer conducted on a professional individual basis, and does not appear to be evidence-based. If it were, then there would be the understanding that the one consistent finding to emerge from research evidence is that marriage is a vital component of desistance. Laub and Sampson (2003) pointed out that marriage gives the alleged offender social support, and often provides an element of social control, which may range from zero tolerance to management and containment. From their research evidence they elaborated:

> Men who desisted from crime were embedded in structured routines, socially bonded to wives and children, and significant others, drew on resources and social support from their relationships, and were virtually and directly supervised and monitored. In other words, structures, situations, and persons offered nurturing and informal social control that facilitated the process of desistance from crime.
>
> (Laub & Sampson, 2003, pp. 279–280)

Yet both the police and social workers inform alleged offenders on arrest that they must leave the marital home and have nothing to do with their children or grandchildren. If spouses choose to support their partners, they are accused of being complicit in the offence. There is no evidence that a man who has viewed indecent images of, say, teenage girls online will commit contact offences with any child that comes into their vicinity, let alone their own children, especially when those children, may be young boys and girls, but this separation demand persists.

There seems to be a blanket response to any form of sexual offence, with no consistency across social workers about how to proceed with these cases. As discussed, some have become persecutory to the non-offending partners: 'you have anything to do with this person and I will take your children away' is a common response to partners who want to keep their relationships with an alleged offender. This is not only illegal, as there is a legal due process for that to occur, but it is also abusive to the partner and damaging to the child or children, who are forbidden any form of communication with their attachment figure. One example that came to my consulting room was when a non-offending partner was forced to sign 'a contract' to say she would not have anything more to do with her husband, else her children were to be removed. Subsequently, the non-offending partner was coerced to go to the police and complain of harassment because her husband had sent her an Easter card with £20 enclosed for his son to buy chocolate eggs. The police threatened the alleged offender with a restraining order. I am particularly emphasising the term 'alleged' in this dialogue, as the man in question had yet to be charged or convicted of an offence. So much for a person being presumed innocent until they are found guilty. Similarly, another partner was taken to court for removal of her children because she had rung a hospital to enquire after her husband, an alleged offender, after an unsuccessful suicide attempt. Fortunately, the judge threw this application out, but it indicates the abuse of power and the lack of knowledge and understanding that the social workers involved convey. I acknowledge that these are extreme cases, but it should not happen at all.

I do understand the subtext to this alienation process. Social service departments are underfunded and their cases are over-loaded. I previously discussed the massive backlog of the police investigations. This backlog gets transferred to the child protection social services team. They have more cases than they can practically handle, and social workers are leaving the profession in droves because of the difficulties they are facing, leaving the remainder inexperienced and untrained. It saves the department time and money in not having to undertake supervised access arrangements, and provide the facilities to do so, if the father is physically removed from his children. Risk is therefore reduced, even if there was little evidence of risk to the child in the first instance. Little thought is given to the damage done to the children, traumatised by their father receiving the knock, feeling scared and overlooked by an anxious and depressed now single parent, bullied at school as word has got out, or removed into a new school and new surroundings as a panicking carer tries to escape the fallout from the negative press, and feeling abandoned by the sudden disappearance and lack of contact with of a loving and caring father.

CAMHS overloaded and underfunded

Caroline Davies, writing for the *Guardian* in 2018, reported that CAMHS (Child and Mental Health Services) was facing a silent catastrophe (Davies, 2018), with the number of children and young people needing treatment falling through the cracks. Specialist services have disappeared, senior clinical roles have been disbanded to allow lower-banded staff to pick up the flack. Treatment is only offered to a youngster when their mental health or behaviour becomes significant, and even when they are accepted for treatment, may have to wait months or even years for it to commence, by which time more damage has been done. Layard et al. (2014) found from analysing data using the British Cohort Study that the most powerful predictor of adult life-satisfaction is the child's emotional health, followed by their conduct. The least powerful predictor was their intellectual development, followed by family income. Mental and physical health were the primary influences, yet this is the factor that gets repeatedly ignored.

Under different circumstances, CAMHS would have a lot to offer these childhood victims, offering help and support with the trauma experienced when their fathers disappear from their lives. At present, children may be given some treatment when they first start displaying distress symptoms, especially if they have experienced abuse, but it is a short-sighted cure process, that is not looking at the evidence base of trauma processes. These damaged children should be revisited for prevention of repetition compulsion at times when we know right-brain revisits the trauma the young person experienced: aged 8/9/10 and again in adolescence. Similarly, adopted, fostered and cared-for children should have psychological assessments at these critical stages, and stay under a monitoring system at least until they are 25 years old, when the brain finally matures, and not be left to their own devices to cope with the disturbance in their early to late teens. It is argued that such a prevention service would cost too much, and CAMHS simply isn't resourced enough to undertake this policy. But a true cost-benefit analysis would take account of preventing not only the mental distress of the young person, but also preventing them acting out and getting involved with the criminal justice system, and finally preventing transgenerational transmission. Stephanie Kewley et al. (2021) similarly contends that preventing child sexual abuse and victimisation requires a comprehensive change to criminal justice and public health services instead of the marginal attention given to prevention strategies so focused on 'at-risk' populations.

Over ten years ago, Elena Martellozzo (2012) highlighted how society has taken its eye off the boil, in understanding where the real risk to children is. It is not in cyberspace, public parks or playgrounds; the real risk to children is in the home. The popular media has focused on sex offenders as a risk to society, stranger danger, portraying them as deviant 'monsters', promoting public outrage, because this is what keeps their readers interested. Child protection laws are made on the back of a few high-profile individual cases, often driven by distraught parents and reinforced by the media, rather than appropriately considered evidence-base from research. Society has developed a blame culture with a lack of compassion for those who behave outside the norm. Whenever anything goes wrong in society, whenever anyone steps out of line, the press takes the moral high ground and demands to know who is to blame. Sexual abuse elicits huge media attention, stigmatising anyone within its focus (McGrath, 2019), including the victims. This demonstrates a lack of understanding of the ripple-effect damage caused to the families through community vilification of one person within it. The alienation of such an individual, if they were likely to offend again, would make it a reality. Sex is everywhere in our society. It is used to sell everything from cars to furniture, and society expects people to be able to keep it under control. No compassion is shown for people who get things wrong. Yet there is no moral panic about the most dangerous place for some children to be: within and surrounding the family. Martellozzo continues:

> There needs to be a greater recognition that the police officers, legal practitioners, social workers, therapists and psychiatrists etc who deal with abusers and their victims on a daily basis cannot be divorced from this cultural field. Rather the meaning and consequences of their activities need to be re-examined as part and parcel of the political and cultural discourses … on the one hand, practitioners' efforts to avert or minimise harm upon the victims of CSA and, on the other hand, the eminently problematic public discourses that have invented 'paedophiles' as demonic figures that provide the cultural fundament for practitioners' activities.
>
> (Martellozzo, 2012, p. 161)

This book started with trying to understand that childhood trauma, for whatever reason, left unresolved, can lead children, as a survival strategy and as a need to attach, to inappropriate viewing of pornography on the internet, and a naivety to the manipulative grooming that can occur. Thus, many damaged children from the age of 8 are already compulsively viewing adult pornography online, sharing sexual images of themselves via social media and chat rooms, and placing themselves at serious risk of stranger abuse. When these children become adolescent, their risky strategies and pumping sexual hormones place them at risk again. By this time, they may already have been using adult pornography for a decade. If they are neurotypical, they may form loving relationships (irrespective of gender), marry and have children, although the online pornography persists under the subtext 'this is what all guys do'. If they are neurodivergent, they are less likely (or lucky) to form long-term relationships, so again revert back to the internet for their sexual repertoire. It is this long-term use of online pornography, together with a history of unresolved trauma, that predisposes them to online addiction, and a preference to sex with the computer rather than sex with their partner. This leads them, subsequently, to keep searching for the next image and falling down the rabbit-hole of viewing illegal material.

Child sexual abuse material is an abhorrence and preferentially should not exist. However, the reality is that it does via the internet in magnitude. Persecuting and vilifying the exponentially rising population of people who view it as covert paedophiles is a fallacious assumption, and does nothing to alleviate this ubiquitous trend. A proportion of (predominantly) men who view CSAM are aroused by what they see, and may wish to put these fantasies into action by connecting with and potentially abusing children. They need to be stopped before that can take place. But I would argue that these potential contact offenders are in the minority of the population of CSAM online viewers. The majority are those who become addicted to viewing all forms of pornography online, and CSAM is part of their viewing repertoire. The visual stimulation of the internet *per se* activates the dopamine pathways of the viewer's brain. This is compounded by auto-erotic compulsive self-soothing, which the individual has indulged in since early teenage years. The habitual masturbation process leads to tolerance of the imagery viewed and an escalation into searching for more diverse material. A large proportion of these addicted viewers may view CSAM, and may not necessarily enjoy or like what they see, but still cannot stop themselves looking. Others may look and delete imagery as it is not to their preference, but the looking has still created an offence. The reason these men get trapped in their addictive cycle can be traced back to early years: insecure attachments, childhood instability at home and at school (ACEs), and sexual, physical and emotional trauma during critical times of their neural development. Persecuting these men promotes recidivism, as alienation from relationships will take them back to offending behaviour. In addition, the collateral traumatic damage done to their own children as a consequence of child-protection strategies will invite repetition compulsion in the next generation.

Trauma-informed therapy can provide the support and safety to guide an individual away from potential or actual offending behaviour. This therapy is never easy, and often the client may make three steps forward and two steps back. Yet every client who is motivated to do so has the ability to change. There is an evidence-based framework to make the client feel validated, safe and respected (Grady et al., 2022). It has four key assumptions, the four Rs: *Realisation* that trauma is widespread, *Recognising* the signs and symptoms of trauma in the client, *Responding* by integrating knowledge and procedures and *Resisting* re-traumatisation through confrontation (SAMSA, 2014). The framework has six guiding principles:

- Safety.
- Trustworthiness and transparency.
- Peer support.
- Collaboration and mutuality.
- Empowerment, voice and choice.
- Cultural, historical and gender responsiveness.

Its aim is to reduce post-traumatic stress symptomology in body, mind and spirit, giving the individual back a sense of worth that they may have never experienced before. As Grady et al. emphasised:

> If clinicians only focus on addressing client deficits or risks through the offending lens, they may miss opportunities to address the disruptive relational patterns, emotional and behavioural dysregulation, criminogenic needs, and maladaptive schemas as seen through the trauma lens.
>
> (Grady et al., 2022, p. 68)

We cannot prosecute our way out of this problem; internet CSAM has existed for two decades now, and the problem is getting worse, not better. Our society needs a complete rethink of how this issue is approached into a compassionate understanding of the offender's own victimhood that led them down their offending path. These men need to be supported within their family environment, not removed from it. Only a compassionate understanding, which is trauma-informed, is going to create the opportunity to for the offender to change, and this process is a child-protection issue.

Gordon and Rachel's review

The criminal justice processes, child protection services and therapeutic services have little crosstalk, and sometimes actively work against each other in the rehabilitation of offenders. Gordon's journey outlines the difficulties that many face, often as a consequence of what happened to them in their early years. The main problem is that the services are under-funded and compartmentalised, leading to a lack of understanding of the whole process. And whilst offenders do need to be punished, the time delay in making that happen is more likely than not to lead to recidivism. Gordon received his punishment just under three years after receiving the knock. During that time, he had placed himself in therapy, had undertaken courses from his own volition, had regained his employment and had turned his life around. In fact, the knock, *per se*, was the wake-up call he needed. And after he had done all this work, and was living a better life for the future, he was punished and sent to prison. Gordon is not unique. This a very common scenario with this form of offender, many of whom did not have the prior offence that Gordon had.

As already mentioned, the child protection social workers are in an invidious position. If they try to use some common sense with a case they are overseeing, and it goes wrong, public outrage and the mass media swoop in and publicly harangue them for making a mistake, leading to public humiliation and termination of employment. As a consequence, they act from a place of defensive practice, where no leniency for the client is allowed. If he has a conviction as a sex offender, he *must be* manipulative, devious, and not to be trusted. Similarly, if he has been violent in the past, he *always will be* in the future. Or even if, like Gordon, they engage in very extensive and targeted therapy and treatment, the way they are assessed thereafter remains the same as an offender who has done nothing to help himself. This does not seem to make sense in terms of what is supposed to be individualised risk assessment, treatment, rehabilitation and our understanding of what creates desistance. It is not in keeping with the ethos of the 'Good Lives' approach that is advocated so strongly, and similarly so strongly ignored.

Rachel felt bullied by her social worker, who was forcing her to choose between her husband and her son. She found the repetitive unannounced visits from the social services checking on her childcare difficult and intrusive, bearing in mind as a single parent she had a lot of stress, in addition to her vulnerable mental health status. She was struggling with Connor's behaviour anyway, as he acted out with her, punching and kicking her, grabbing her breasts, and constantly being sent home from school for vicious behaviour and stealing. When they finally took Connor away because Rachel refused to stop seeing Gordon, she sank into a deep depression, and was on the verge of being readmitted to a psychiatric unit, as her GP was really worried about her. But this time she had the loving care and support of Gordon, who called in daily before and after work to cook her meals, wash her clothes, and sit and watch TV in the evenings with Rex on her lap, before going back to his own home at bedtime. Their relationship was not yet sexual; there was plenty of time in the future for that.

To mix my metaphors, child protection social workers also suffer with 'the road to hell is paved with good intentions', as the children they desire to protect and remove from what is considered abusive parents by virtue of their criminal record, suffer attachment injuries and potential abuse when forced into alien environments, making them more likely in repetition compulsion to behave the same as their fathers. We therapists are just beginning to see this happen generationally; that the young clients coming through StopSO now have fathers who were also imprisoned for online offences when they were young, and removed from their care. Connor needed therapeutic support, not just immediately after his abuse occurred, but needed to be revisited and helped regularly during significant times in his neural development. An ounce of prevention is far better than a pound of cure.

Postscript

After a year of couple therapy, and six months after Connor was removed, Rachel and Gordon moved in together into a new one-bedroom house that Gordon had bought for them. After much soul-searching in the therapy, Gordon chose to have a vasectomy before they moved in together, so as 'to get the social services off their backs', in case Rachel conceived again. They both felt that Rachel's mental health probably could not sustain another pregnancy anyway. Gordon, under his Sexual Harm Prevention Order, had informed the police and probation of his new address. Before they were allowed the purchase, the police checked out that the intended home was not too close to a school or children's playground.

Connor is living in a children's home in a different county, to prevent any opportunity for the boy and his parents to bump into one another. He is still on the potential adoptee register, and is under the care of CAMHS for his undesirable sexual behaviour. Adoption is extremely unlikely now that he is over the age of 7 years and has challenging behaviour. He is probably condemned to spend the remaining years of his childhood in institutional care, as his foster placements never seem to work out. Gordon and Rachel have engaged a family law solicitor with the aim of trying to get Connor returned to them. The solicitor was not hopeful on their behalf, but they said it didn't matter how much it cost, they wanted to keep trying.

References

Bonnar-Kidd, K. K. (2010). Sexual offender laws and prevention of sexual violence or recidivism. *American Journal of Public Health*, 100 (3), 412–419. doi:10.2105/AJPH.2008.153254.

Briggs, P., Simon, W.T., & Simonsen, S. (2011). An exploratory study of internet-initiated sexual offenses and the chat room sex offender: Has the internet enabled a new typology of sex offender? *Sexual Abuse: A Journal of Research and Treatment*, 23, 72–91. doi:10.1177/1079063210384275

Davies, C. (2018). Mental health services for the young is the NHS's 'silent catastrophe'. *The Guardian*, 25 June 2018.

Duncan, K., Wakeham, A., Winder, B., Armitage, R., Roberts, L., & Blagden, N. (2020). The experiences of non-offending partners of individuals who have committed sexual offences: Recommendations for practitioners and stakeholders. Retrieved from hud dersfield.box.com/s/1sumdnyq9yjkgwhw0axzvgt7e2rfgcih

Grady, M., Levenson, J.S., Glover, J. & Kavanagh, S. (2022). Is sex-offending treatment trauma-informed? Exploring perspectives of clinicians and clients. *Journal of Sexual Aggression*, 28 (1), 60–75. doi:10.1080/13552600.2021.1942572

Hocken, K, Taylor, J & Walton, J (2022). Trauma and the experience of imprisonment. In P. Willmott & L. Jones (eds), *Trauma-informed forensic practice*. London: Routledge.

Kewley, S., Mhlanga-Gunda, R. & Van Hout M-C. (2021). Preventing child sexual abuse before it occurs: examining the scale and nature of secondary public health prevention approaches. *Journal of Sexual Aggression*, doi:10.1080/13552600.2021.200065

Kilmer, A., & Leon, C. S. (2017). 'Nobody worries about our children': Unseen impacts of sex offender registration on families with school-age children and implications for desistance. *Criminal Justice Studies*, 30 (2), 181–201. doi:10.1080/1478601X.2017.1299852.

Laub, J.H. & Sampson, R.J. (2003). *Shared beginnings, divergent lives: Delinquent boys to age 70*. Cambridge, MA: Harvard University Press.

Layard, R., Clark, A.E., Cornaglia, F., Powdthavee, N. & Vernoit, J. (2014). What predicts a successful Life? A life-course model of well-being. *The Economic Journal*, 124 (580), F720–F738. doi:10.1111/ecoj.12170

Martellozzo, E. (2012). *Online child sexual abuse: Grooming, policing and child protection in a multi-media world*. Abingdon: Routledge.

McGrath, K. (2019). *Understanding and managing sexualised behaviour in children and adolescents: Guidelines for parent and carers in the cyber age*. [Author] Retrieved from www.kieranmcgrath.com/understanding-managing-sexualised-behaviour-in-children-a dolescents/

SAMHSA. (2014). *SAMSA's concept of trauma and guidance for a trauma-informed approach*. Rockville, MD: SAMSA's Trauma and Justice Strategic Initiative.

Seto, M. (2017). Internet-facilitated sexual offending. In *Sex offender management assessment and planning initiative*. NCJ 247059 – T. Office of Sex Offender Sentencing, Monitoring, Apprehending, Registering, and Tracking, US Department of Justice. Retrieved from https://smart.ojp.gov/somapi/.

Seto, M.C., Reeves, L. & Jung, S. (2010). Explanations given by child pornography offenders for their crimes. *Journal of Sexual Aggression*, 16 (2), 169–180. doi:10.1080/13552600903572396

Author Index

Subject Index

POLIT (Paedophile Online Investigation Team) 6
pornography 3, 25, 71, 100, 107, 111, 121, 125, 128–9, 150, 162
addiction 19, 73, 76, 125, 128, 139, 156, 163
precipitating factors 83
predisposing factors 83, 113, 122
prefrontal cortex 33–4, 40
premature birth 20, 60
presenting factors 82–3
protective factors 84, 98–9
PTSD (post-traumatic stress disorder) 7, 113, 164
chronic 40

RAGE circuit 22, 30, 33, 36, 38, 56, 81, 93
recidivism 112, 129, 136–8, 140, 147, 163–4,
re-enactment
see repetition compulsion
relapse prevention 138, 140, 145
repetition compulsion 42, 44, 83, 108–9, 114, 125, 146, 152, 156, 161, 163
resilience 19, 32–3, 41, 73, 83, 125–6, 144, 157
risk assessment 44, 135–6, 140, 165

SAMHSA (Substance Abuse and Mental Health Services Administration) 163, 167
SEEKING circuit 21, 30, 34, 36, 38, 56, 72, 84, 100, 121, 125, 130, 152
self 33, 35, 38, 40–1, 43, 55, 146
esteem 58, 122, 125, 128, 141
harm 59–60, 75, 113
Sex Offenders' Register 143, 146, 156–7
sexual 2–3
abuse 19, 43, 62, 76, 94, 96–7, 107, 109–10, 115, 117, 129, 137, 139,140, 161, 162
addiction12, 19, 73, 76–8
compulsion 76–8
dimorphism 32

offending
aetiology 119–130
script 12, 108, 122, 124, 128
template 12, 36, 72, 76, 105, 110
vandalised 83, 97, 125, 128, 158
shame 34–5, 38, 40, 43, 63, 80, 105, 109, 114, 125, 138–9
external 35
internal 35, 99
toxic 35, 80, 92–3, 98, 145
SHPO (Sexual Harm Prevention Order) 166
SCT (sluggish cognitive tempo)
see CDD
social anxiety 25
SOTP (Sex Offender Treatment Programme) 137–9
stalking 84
Stop It! Now 14, 143
StopSO (Specialist Treatment Organisation for Perpetrators and Victims of Sexual Offending) 14, 143, 146, 151, 165
suicide 7–8, 10–11, 25–6, 40, 75, 83–4, 94, 120, 160
supervision 14, 17–8, 140
sympathy 35

temporal lobes 33
thalamus 34
testosterone 33, 110
trauma 39, 40–3, 77, 90, 96, 113, 123, 126, 128, 137, 140–2, 145, 152
-informed therapy 41, 135–7, 142–4, 163–4
transgenerational transmission 19, 59, 61, 81, 83, 90–102, 117, 126, 161
TOM (theory of mind) 34–5, 52, 55, 58, 80–1, 92, 108

vasopressin 37, 56
victim empathy 140–1, 154
victim-perpetrator cycle 90, 95–8, 139
violence 21, 36, 63, 94, 100, 141
virtuous paedophiles
see paedophile
voyeurism 71

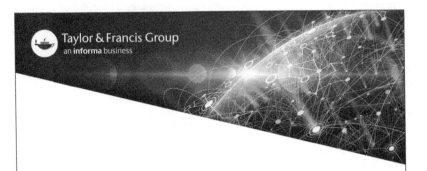

For Product Safety Concerns and Information please contact our EU
representative GPSR@taylorandfrancis.com Taylor & Francis Verlag GmbH,
Kaufingerstraße 24, 80331 München, Germany

Printed and bound by CPI Group (UK) Ltd, Croydon, CR0 4YY
08/06/2025
01897005-0011